IN THE NAME OF

CHILD LABOUR

IN THE NAME OF

CHILD LABOUR

(Eradication and Evaluation Programme)

Bupinder Zutshi
Mondira Dutta
Sudesh Nangia

SHIPRA

ISBN 81-7541-093-0

First published in India in 2002

In the Name of Child Labour

Published by
SHIPRA PUBLICATIONS
115-A, Vikas Marg, Shakarpur,
Delhi-110 092 (India)
Phs: 91-11-245 8662, 220 0954. Fax: 91-11-245 8662
Email: siprapub@satyam.net,in

Laser Typeset by:
Shivam Associates
Delhi-110 092

Printed at
Choudhary Offset Process
Delhi-110 052

Preface

The issue of child labour, especially bonded child labour and children working in hazardous industries got a focused attention from several Indian Non-governmental agencies around mid 1980's. Sensing the magnitude and momentum generated on the child labour issues, the Government of India, passed several legislative measures to prohibit or improve the working conditions of child labour. Child Labour Act-1986 (CLA-1986), National Policy on Child Labour-1987 (NPCL-1987), National Authority for Elimination of Child Labour-1994 (NAECL-1994) and Supreme Court directions-1996 were some significant steps in this direction. Several children were released from hazardous industries as raids and rescue operations were conducted by NGOs in collaboration with government officials. The government realised that mere legislation will not be sufficient, hence initiated action oriented programmes for the released children from hazardous industries. National Education Policy -1986 proposed opening of Non-formal education schools for the released children from hazardous industries. The Non-formal education schools arc to provide three years primary education along with vocational training, supplementary nutrition, regular medical check-up and stipend for the released children from prohibited employment. After the completion of non-formal education the children were to join formal education programme or to be provided vocational skills for employment.

To supplement the government initiatives, national and international donor agencies extended whole-hearted support to one such industry i.e., the carpet industry; campaign for the release of child workers from carpet industry. The basic need was to rehabilitate and provide education to the released children so as to stop their re-entry into the looms. Non-formal education schools were started by, Labour Ministry (Government of India) supported by International Programme for Eradication of Child Labour

(IPEC -ILO), Project Mala (United Kingdom), Carpet Export Promotion Council (CEPC), UNICEF, Child Relief and You (CRY) and REHA Consortium in the carpet weaving belt of Mirzapur and Bhadohi (Uttar Pradesh and Bihar). REHA Consortium, comprising of Terre Des Hommes, Bread for World, Misereor (Germany) and Christian Aid (United Kingdom) supported NGO's efforts to rehabilitate the released and rescued children from carpet weaving. A general rehabilitation fund was pooled together by these international donor agencies, to provide transitory rehabilitation to the released children from carpet weaving. Several local NGO's in the carpet weaving belt were identified by India REHA Committee to run these rehabilitation centres for this purpose.

The objective of the present research project is to evaluate and assess the functioning of these rehabilitation centres/Non-formal education schools funded by REHA Consortium and other funding agencies. Majority of the children enrolled in the rehabilitation centres funded by REHA Consortium are living with their families. These rehabilitation centres provide non-formal education, mid-day meals and health check-up. The government of India and other NGO's also provide same functions to the released children in the Non-formal education schools. In order to make the study comparable with the other non-formal education schools, funded by Government of India., IPEC (ILO), Project Mala, CEPC, UNICEF, & CRY, the rehabilitation centres funded by REHA Consortium will henceforth be referred to as Non- formal education schools in this research project report.

Contents

1 Introduction

1.1 CONTOURS OF THE PROBLEM

International approach to children needs has given way to the convention that children have rights, the same full spectrum of rights as adults: civil, political, social, cultural and economic. This convention, expressed as the convention of the Rights of the child, entered into international law on, 2 September 1990, nine months after the convention's adoption by the United Nations General Assembly. The convention has been ratified by majority of countries, including India.[1]

The country is obliged in law to undertake all appropriate measures to assist parents and other responsible parties in fulfilling their obligations to children under the conventions. Although the process of implementing the conventions still remains in its infancy, the issue of child labour took a pronounced tone in India during the last few decades as, International Labour Organisation (ILO) bracketed India along with other countries for the sheer magnitude of this problem. It necessitated certain fundamental changes in national laws, plans, policies and practices to bring them into line with the principles of the Right of the Child convention.

The issue has become more perplexing with the growing activism of the human right wings. The children of the loom-a film made by British Broadcasting Corporation (BBC), on children in Mirzapur, who were found to be bonded labourers has prompted many child welfare organisations in Europe to pressurise the carpet importers not to buy Indian carpets, unless the manufacturers took significant steps to humanise child labour.

Senator Harkin's proposed child labour Deterrence Bill, which was introduced in the United States (US) legislature on 5h August, 1992,[2] States "US ought not to import any item, from any country, that is made by child labour".

German carpet importer also threatened to boycott Indian hand knotted carpets, until they are satisfied, that no child labour has been employed in their manufacturing.

The issue of child labour has generated renewed interest, because of the new economic policy formulated in line with the structural adjustment programme, which hopes to put the country on the global market economy. These sweeping economic reforms aim to promote exports and offer incentives to foreign investors. The reforms would effect cuts in the expenditure on health, education, food subsides and on social services, all of these needed by poor. Thus the real cost of adjustment is paid by the poor and by their children. The logic of globalisation of the economy has now become a reality in the form of the World Trade Organisation (WTO), which is even vying to take over the social aspects in international cooperation through the proposed social clauses. Soaring inflation, massive retrenchment from the industrial sector, especially of women and unskilled labour, unprecedented displacement of the poor peasantry from land and traditional occupations have been the order of the day

In this background, strong sentiments are being evoked because of large scale, employment of child labour in general and their presence in hazardous industries in particular. There is, helplessness of the industrialists, legislative machinery and the social activists to reach a broad agreement for opposing this abominable practice. Completing the paradox is the virtual exclusion of parents and the working children from the whole debate, as well as divergent approaches of the intellectuals, while assessing this problem.[3]

Sensing the magnitude and momentum generated on the child labour issues, governmental of India, passed several legislative measures to prohibit or improve the working condition of child labour (Child Labour Act 1986 See Annexure–I) The government realised that mere legislation will not be sufficient, hence it initiated several action oriented programmes, to withdraw children from hazardous work and prevent them from entering into labour markets. Project based action plan in the areas of high concentration of child labour have been introduced and implemented under the action plan. Non-formal Education (NFE) schools have been opened to provide need-based education to the working children. National Policy of Education—1986 (NPE) proposed Non-Formal Education Programme for the released child labour from hazardous industries.

To supplement government initiatives, several national and international donor agencies got deeply involved in the elimination of child labour and protection of working children from exploitation and abuse. Non-formal Education schools were started in the Mirzapur-Bhadohi carpet belt of Uttar Pradesh and Bihar. The government sponsored NFE schools have been in operation since 1989. In 1992 Project Mala, a UK based NGO, got involved in the Non-formal education programme for the children working in carpet weaving. Other donor agencies like Terre Des Hommes (TDH), Misereor, Bread for world (Bfw) and Christian Aid together formed Rehabilitation Consortium to provide rehabilitation to the children released from carpet weaving. By1995-96 a large number of NFE schools were in operation in Mirzapur—Bhadohi carpet belt, providing Non-formal education to the released children from carpet weaving.

1.2 OBJECTIVE OF THE STUDY

The present study attempts to have an in-depth evaluation and assessment of the Non-formal Education schools run by local NGO's in Mirzapur-Bhadohi Carpet weaving area. The NFE schools are funded by Labour Ministry, Government of India, under IPEC Programme (ILO), REHA Consortium, Project Mala (UK), CEPC (India), UNICEF and CRY. The main objectives of the present study are;

- to examine issues of child labour and response to these issues from government, voluntary sector; manufacturers and social activists.
- to analyse, causes, consequences and magnitude of child labour in carpet weaving belt of Utter Pradesh and Bihar.
- to prepare a demographic, socio-cultural and economic profile of children and their families working in carpet weaving.
- to evaluate and assess the implementation of Non-formal Education schools, undertaken by local NGO's and funded by government, International and National donor agencies.
- to examine the coverage, scope, activities, curriculum and teaching aids and methods adopted by the NFE schools.
- to find out the performance levels in the field of inculcating education and general awareness by the NFE schools.
- to determine whether 'action programme'has been able to achieve any community participation for dissemination of information.
- to suggest recommendations for the effective implementation of Non-formal education Programmes.

1.3 METHODOLOGY

a) Theoretical and Conceptual frame Work

In view of the complexity of the issues of child labour, several approaches have been adopted to study the problem. Theoretical concepts regarding the definition of child labour, magnitude of child labour, issues of child labour as perceived by government, carpet manufacturers, social activists, parents of the children and the children themselves have been dealt in depth. The theoretical aspects examined provide broad framework to examine the issues in reality, based on the field survey conducted in the area. Vast data collected was sifted and analysed. Literature was reviewed and field survey conducted to examine and portray the issues systematically.

b) Data Collection and Field Work

In order to achieve the above stated objectives, information and data was collected from secondary sources viz., Labour Ministry, National Council of Educational Research & Training (NCERT) and other National and International Voluntary Organisation and NGO's associated with rehabilitation of child labour in general and carpet weaving in particular. The information was collected from ILO, UNICEF, IPEC, SACCS, CREDA, Project Mala, Rugmark Foundation (New Delhi), Bandwa Mukti Morcha (Mirzapur), Centre for Concern.for Child Labour (New Delhi), CRY (New Delhi), Children Welfare Society (Sonbhadra), CERT (Bhadohi), Samangra Gramin Vikas Sansthan (Sonbhadra), National Resource Centre on Child Labour (NOIDA).

Data was also collected from several REHA partners viz., Yuva Vikas Sansthan (Ghazipur), Swami Vivekanad Shiksha Samiti (Mirzapur), Bachpan Bachao Andolan (New Delhi), Ankur Foundation (Allahabad), Diocensan Development Welfare (Allahabad), Gramodaya Sansthan (Kanpur), Arpan Gramin Vikas (Patna), Kosi Seva Sadan (Saharasa), Kosi Lok Manch (Saharsa), Samuday (Samastipur), Manav Sansadhan Vikas Sansthan (Varanasi), J.P. Saraisa Sewa Ashram (Patna), Manavi (Patna), Sampurna Gram Vikas Kendra (Palamau), Chotanagpur Samaj Vikas Sansthan (Palamau) and Gramin Sewa (Madhubani).

The secondary data collected from the above stated NGO's and voluntary organisations were analysed to identify the schools providing NFE programme to the child labour released and rescued from the carpet industry. List of NFE schools in the study area was prepared (Table 1.1).

Table 1.1 Carpet Weaving Zone and Catchment Area Local NGOs & Non-formal Education Schools

Sr. No.	*NGO*	*Districts covered*	*Name of NFE Schools*	*Name of NFE Schools Selected for Survey*
1	2	3	4	5
1.	Swami Vivekanand Siksha Samiti (SVSS)	Mirzapur	1. Mujhera Khurd 2. Mujhera Kalan 3. Bhogan 4. Mavai Kalan 5. Bahuti	1. Mujhera Khurd 2. Mujhera Kalan 3. Bhogan 4. Bahuti
2.	Bachapan Bachao Andolan (BBA)	Mirzapur Sonbhadra	1. Purikatra 2. Ghabi Ghat 3. Jorukhad 4. Parsi Tola 5. Hinshinpur	1. Purikatra 2. Jorukhad
3	Manav Sansadan Mahila Vikas Sansthan (MS&MVS)	Bhadohi	1. Amva 2. Paniyara 3. Jegapur	1. Amva 2. Paniyara
4	Yuva Vikas Sansthan (YVS)	Ghazipur	1. Salempur 2. Narayanpur	1. Salempur 2. Narayanpur
5	Gramodaya Sansthan (GS)	Banda	1. Balapur 2. Matiyara 3. Media ka Dera 4. Biki ka Dera 5. Bhatla	1. Balapur 2. Matiyara 3. Media ka Dera
6	Ankur Foundation (AF)	Sonbhadra	1. Biluroa 2. Dhanavathan 3. Longa 4. Mithunia 5. Singha 6. Asan Bandh 7. Goura Singha 8. Barvahi Kholi 9. Jharia 10. Neemiyachee 11. Ghidia 12. Kaillul 13. Khempur	1. Biluroa 2. Dhanavathan 3. Longa 4. Mithunia 5. Neemiyachee 6. Ghidia 7. Gorasigha 8. Chekhwaheed 9. Kon 10. Ramgarh

(*Contd.*)

1	2	3	4	5
			14. Chekhwaheed 15. Kon 16. Ramgarh 17. Kachnarwa	
7	Arpan Gramin Vikas (AGV)	Patna	1. Bahpur 2. Patsi 3. Sikandarpur 4. Maner 5. Pandechak 6. Bahusi 7. Lodipur 8. Baank 9. Manergarh 10. Bihata 11. Bajitpur 12. Dyalchak	1. Bahpur 2. Maner 3. Baank 4. Manergarh 5. Bihata 6. Bajitpur
8	Kosi Sewa Sadan (KSS)	Saharsa	1. Kothia 2. Arapatti 3. Jhutiki 4. Moyalasthan 5. Mahishi	1. Jhutiki 2. Koyalasthan 3. Mahishi
9	Sampurna Gramin Vikas Kendra (SGVK)	Palamau	1. Chakka 2. Kala Phar 3. Kurin Patro 4. Duela	1. Chakka 2. Kala Pahar 3. Kurin Patro
10	SAMUDAYA	Samastipur Begusarai	1. Muradpur 2. Mathudumar 3. Modipur 4. Kander 5. Udaipur 6. Govindpur 7. Shankarbarsa 8. Rajwara 9. Milky 10. Samastipur city 11. Koksha 12. Sihama	1. Muradpur 2. Kanker 3. Shankarbarsa 4. Rajwara 5. Milky 6. Koksha 7. Sihama
11	SACCS/BBA	New Delhi	1. Mukti Ashram (Mohammadpur)	1. Mukti Ashram

(*Contd.*)

1	2	3	4	5
12	Project Mala (PM)	Mirzapur	1. Guria 2. Hasra 3. Amoi 4. Pathera	1. Guria 2. Hasra
13	CREDA*	Mirzapur Bhadohi Sonbhadra	1. Bikna 2. Lakhnia 3. Kaval 4. Dhuma	1. Bikna 2. Lakhnia 3. Kaval 4. Dhuma
14	RUGMARK Foundation	Bhadohi	1. Gopiganj	1. Gopiganj
15	Bandhu Mukti (Manch (BMM)	Sonbhadra	1. Jorukhurd 2. Mithunia	1. Jorukhurd
16	Child Eradication and welfare Society (CLE & WS)	Bhadohi	1. Newada Kalan	1. Newada Kalan
17	Child Welfare Society (CWS)	Mirzapur Bhadohi	1. Lalli 2. Parsona 3. Karsouta 4. Phoolwari 5. Browdhi 6. Sirsace 7. Majuhari 8. Noogdova 9. Madhka 10. Parsiya 11. Imliphokhar	1. Lalli 2. Parsona 3. Karsauta
18	Samangra Gramin Vikas Sansthan (SGVS)	Sonbhadra	1. Jorukhad 2. Gheevki 3. Keval 4. Dhuma 5. Madni Khurd	1. Jorukhad 2. Gheevki 3. Keval

• Other NFE centres of CREDA were stopped temporarily due to stoppage of funds from Ministry of Labour (India). Data from CREDA was not available.

The identified NFE schools run by local NGO's and sponsored by various funding agencies viz., National & International NGO's and voluntary organisations were mapped.

The methodology for selecting NFE schools for survey included, schools from various NGO's. Spatial distribution of the schools, Year of establishment of the schools and multiplicity of activities undertaken by the schools were considered for selecting sample NFE schools. Taking the above indicators into account, 58 NFE schools from various funding agencies, NGO's and spatial units were selected. The list of schools selected for survey was prepared. (Table 1.1).

Structured questionnaires were prepared for the survey. Eight sets of questionnaires were prepared to examine and assess the NFE programmes. Questionnaire testing and pilot surveys were also conducted in 4 selected schools to examine the coverage and response of the respondents. The field-testing of questionnaires was monitored by the expert committee, so as to prepare appropriate questions. Field test of questionnaires and pilot survey was conducted for 15 days in Mirzapur, Sonbhadra and Bhadohi. After an in-depth analysis of the pilot survey, final questionnaires were prepared for the survey. Separate set of questionnaires (see Appendix) were prepared for

1. Rehabilitation Agency
2. Rehabilitation Centre
3. Child Worker
4. Teacher/Technical Staff
5. Parents of the Child
6. Already Rehabilitated Child
7. Loom Owners
8. Village Survey

The criterion adopted for the selection of child /Parent of Child, teacher/ technical staff and respondents already completed rehabilitation includes, age, sex, caste and economic background of the family. The research team in the field did the selection after thorough discussions with NGO's. The other methods adopted for data collection was observations of the research team, audio recording of conversation. Collection of base line data from village head/ Panchayat/ NGO's and government officials.

Adequate steps were taken to create thorough understanding and rapport with the children and their families, so that correct data and information is ascertained. The field staff stayed in the villages so as to familiarise with the local people customs.

1.4 SAMPLE SIZE AND COVERAGE

The field survey conducted covers 18 NGO's, 58 NFE schools, 311 children, 73 teachers/ technical staff and 171 parents. (Refer Table 1.2).

The NFE schools selected for the field survey represent all major local NGO's engaged in child rehabilitation, in the carpet weaving area. The NGO's, NFE schools, children, teachers and parents surveyed cover all major spatial locations covering 12 districts and 22 blocks. These 22 blocks represent carpet-weaving core, peripheral zone, labour catchments zone and rehabilitation centre at New Delhi (Mukti Ashram. run by SACCS/ BBA which provides immediate rehabilitation to the released children from hazardous industries) Refer Table 1.3.

Table 1.2 Carpet Weaving Zone and Catchment Area

Serial No.	*NGOs Surveyed*	*NFE Schools Surveyed*	*No. of Children Surveyed*		*No. of Teacher Surveyed*		*No. of Parents Surveyed*
			M	**F**	**M**	**F**	**M**
1.	Project Mala	2	3	3	-	4	7
2.	CREDA*	4	14	1	2	2	10
3.	MS & MVS	2	9	4	1	1	4
4.	CLE & WS	1	2	2	2	-	2
5.	B.B.A	2	4	1	1	2	4
6.	C.W.S	3	14	3	3	-	11
7.	Ankur Foundation	10	36	8	6	4	35
8.	Yuva Vikas Sansthan	2	12	6	1	3	6
9.	Gramodaya Sansthan	3	21	8	4	–	13
10.	SVSS	4	25	7	5	1	15
11.	RUGMARK	1	5	–	2	–	2
12.	Arpan Gramin Vikas	6	18	19	5	2	22
13.	Kosi Sewa Sadan	3	5	8	3	–	6
14.	SAMUDAYA	7	14	21	3	4	22
15.	Sampurna Gramin Vikas	3	6	6	3	–	6
16.	Samangra Gramin Vikas	3	1	3	3	–	4
17.	BMM	1	6	1	2	–	2
18.	SACCS/BBA	1	15	–	4	–	–
	Total	**58**	**210**	**101**	**50**	**23**	**171**

The respondents surveyed represented males and females as well as, all social groups including Scheduled caste/Scheduled Tribe/other Backward castes and higher castes (Refer Table 1.4).

Table 1.3 Carpet Weaving Zone and Catchment Area Administrative Areas

Sr. No	*Districts*	*No. of Block Covered*	*No. of NFE Schools Surveyed*	*No. of Children Surveyed*		*No. of Teachers Surveyed*		*No. of Parent Surveyed*
				M	**F**	**M**	**F**	**M**
1	Badohi	2	4	11	5	4	1	8
2	Mirzapur	5	5	45	14	6	7	32
3	Sonbhadra	3	21	58	13	16	4	54
4	Varanasi	1	–	5	1	1	2	2
5	Ghazipur	1	2	12	6	1	3	6
6	Banda	1	3	21	8	4	–	13
7	Patna	3	6	18	19	5	2	22
8	Saharsa	2	3	5	8	3	–	6
9	Samastipur	2	10	12	18	3	4	19
10	Palamau	1	3	6	6	3	–	6
11	Delhi	–	1	15	–	4	–	–
12	Begusarai	1	1	2	3	–	–	3
	Total	22	58	210	101	50	23	171

Table 1.4 Surveyed Respondents Profile

Respon-dents	*Sex*		*Mean Age*	*Caste*					
	M	*F*		*Brahmin Thakur*	*Vaisya/ Kayastha*	*SC*	*ST*	*OBC*	*Others*
NGOs	17		37	5 (29)	3 (18)	2 (12)	–	4 (24)	3 (18)
School Centre	42	16	30	6 (10.0)	6 (10.0)	19 (33.0)	4 (7.0)	18 (31)	5 (9.0)
Teachers	50	23	28	7 (10.0)	1 (10.0)	29 (40.0)	3 (4.0)	27 (37.0)	6 (8.0)
Child	210	101	11	6 (2.0)	10 (3.0)	138 (44.0)	38 (12.0)	111 (36.0)	8 (3.0)
Parents	171	–	–	3 (2.0)	4 (2.0)	76 (44.0)	21 (44.0)	59 (34.0)	8 (6.0)

(Figures in brackets indicate percentages)

25 respondents, who had already completed NFE programme, were also surveyed. These respondents represent several NFE schools, run by 11 NGO's (Refer Table 1.5).

Loom owners survey was also conducted, covering 5 blocks having high magnitude of child labour in carpet weaving. These blocks include Kon, Dudhi, Chopen, Ghorawal and Mau, 177 loom owners were surveyed. (Refer Table 1.6).

Table 1.5 Sample Size of Respondents completed Non formal Education

S. No.	*NGO's Surveyed*	*NFE Schools*	*No. of Respondents Surveyed*		*Present Age*			*Caste*			
			M	*F*	*<15*	*15-18*	*19& more*	*SC*	*ST*	*OBC*	*Others*
1.	Project Mala	2	2	–	1	1	–	1	–	1	–
2.	CREDA	2	1	1	2	–	–	–	1	–	1
3.	MS & MVS	–	–	–	–	–	–	–	–	–	–
4.	CLE & WS	1	1	–	1	–	–	–	–	–	1
5.	B.B.A	–	–	–	–	–	–	–	–	–	–
6.	CWS	2	2	–	2	–	–	1	1	--	–
7.	Ankur Foundation	7	7	–	1	1	2	4	–	–	–
8.	Koshi Sewa Sadan	2	2	–	–	2	–	2	–	3	–
9.	YVS	4	2	2	4	–	–	–	–	4	–
10.	Gramodyog Sansthan	4	4	–	3	1	–	–	–	4	–
11.	SACCS/BBB	1	1	–	–	1	1	–	1	–	–
	Total	25	22	3	14	8	3	6	3	13	3

Table 1.6 Sample Size of Surveyed Carpet Weaving Loom Owners

S No.	*Block Name*	*District*	*No. of Looms Surveyed*		*Present Age of Respondents*			*Caste of Respondents*			
			M	*F*	*Up to 25*	*26 -45*	*45 & Above*	*SC*	*ST*	*OBC*	*Others*
1.	Kon	Mirzapur	85	–	–	79 (93.0)	6 (7.0)	67 (79.0)	–	18 (21.0)	–
2.	Dudhi	Son-Bhadra	10	–	–	9 (90.0)	1 (10.0)	8 (80.0)	–	2 (20.0)	–
3.	Chopen	Son-Bhadra	24	–	–	16 (67.0)	8 (23.0)	16 67.0	5 21.0	1 (4.0)	2 (8.0)
4.	Ghorawal	Son-Bhadra	1	–	–	1 (100)	–	–	–	1 (100)	–
5.	Mau	Banda	57	–	30 (53.0)	25 (44.0)	2 (3.0)	–	–	53 (93.0)	4 (7.0)

(Figures in parenthesis represant percentages)

The criterion for selecting Child/Teachers/Parent and child already completed NFE, include respondcnts from different age, sex, caste and economic status of the family. This was done in order to represent all groups in the survey. The selection was done in the field by the research team.

The survey commenced from 15th August and lasted till 15th, November 1997.

1.5 STATISTICAL METHODS USED

In order to workout levels of performance for the selected NFE schools based on field data, several major indicators and sub indicators were chosen. Composite score for each major indicator was worked out, after assigning weights to each sub indicator. Weights were assigned based on subjective understanding of the research group. Principal Component Analysis was worked out to examine the nature of correlation and association between various indicators. Stepwise regression analysis was also attempted to examine the extent of explanation of dependent variables selected. The results obtained were examined and analysed. Based on the results broad recommendations have been suggested.

REFERENCES

[1] The Government of India acceded to this convention on 11th. December 1992. The convention of the Rights of the child enshrines as interdependent and indivisible the full range of the civil, political, economic, social and cultural rights of all children that are vital to their survival, development, protection and participation in the lives of their societies. One of the tenets of the convention is that all actions concurring children, their best interests should be taken fully into account. Article 32 recognises children's right to be protected from work that threatens their health, education or development and enjoins states, to set minimum ages for employment and to regulate working conditions.

[2] As of March 1998, the Bill had yet to find its way into the Statute book. But the mere threat of such a measure panicked the garment industry of Bangladesh. Child workers, most of them girls were summarily dismissed from the garment factories.

[3] Weiner, Myron; (1990):The Child and the state in India, Oxford University Press, New Delhi,

2 Child Labour — Concepts, Magnitude and Issues

2.1 CONCEPTS AND DEFINITIONS

According to Haks, the chairman of the US National Child Labour Committee, the term 'child labour' is generally used to refer, "any work by children that interfere with their full physical and mental development, the opportunities for a desirable minimum of education and of their needed recreation". It also is seen as, children prone to accidents, often fatal, at work sites, and children chained to looms in dark mills. Currently the term is used in a pejorative sense, suggesting hateful and exploitative.

In reality, children do a variety of work in widely divergent conditions. At one end of the continuum, the work is beneficial, providing or enhancing a child's physical, mental, spiritual, moral or social development without interfering with schooling, recreation and rest. At the other end, it is palpably, destructive or exploitative. There are vast areas of activity between these two poles, including work that need not impact negatively on the child's development.

Fyfe[1] (1989) attempts to provide a distinction by differentiating between "Child Work"and "Child Labour". The former being seen as permissible and the latter as exploitative.

> "Clearly, not all work is bad for children..... there is little doubt that many children welcome the opportunity to work, seeing in it the site of passage to adulthood..... work which does not detract from other essential activities for children, namely leisure, play and education is not child labour. Child labour is work which impairs the health and development of children"(Fyfe 1989:p4).

According to the convention of the Rights of the Child (Article 32).

"State parties recognise the right of the child to be protected from economic exploitation and from performing any work that is likely to be hazardous or harmful to the child's education, or to be harmful to the child's health or physical, mental, spiritual, moral and social development" (Article 32).

Child labour therefore is the work, which involves some degree of exploitation i.e. physical, mental, economic. It denies the joy to children and access to social opportunities (like education), which eventually impairs the personality and creativity, the evolution and growth of full being and the health, and mental development of a child. The problem of child labour therefore, does not constitute the age of child, but its exploitation and abuse. The perception of what constitutes exploitation/abuse can be very subjective, as it is not easy to differentiate between the socialisation aspects of a child's activity and its exploitative aspects.

The problem of defining exploitation would depend on every researcher or reformers approach. (Nieuwenhuys 1994)[2]. Exploitation will always be in the eyes of the beholder.[3] Child work in some form has existed from historical times. Children were employed to supplement the family income and to help family in their traditional crafts, by acquiring necessary skills at a very early stage. The situation became bad, with the advent of industrialisation, when factory owner found it more profitable to employ children.

At the most destructive end the clear cases of child labour are super-exploitation i.e.; Children used as prostitutes,[4] 'bonded child labour'[5] (the term widely used for the virtual enslavement of children to repay debts incurred by their parents or family members) and children working in the industries or activities notorious for the dire health and safety hazards.[6] But to treat all work by children as equally unacceptable is to confuse and trivialise the issue and to make it more difficult to end the abuses. It is therefore important to distinguish between beneficial and intolerable work. Much child labour falls into a grey area between these two extremes.

B.N. Juyal[7] has categorised child labour in two broad groups.

2.2 PRODUCTIVE CHILD LABOUR

The productive use of child worker in the family could provide process of learning, the skills for a particular trade or craft. This could help the child to turn into a reasonably proficient craftsman or a skilled worker, not all might make the grade, but most of them do. Thus the childhood labour, paid or unpaid, might become an investment for at least a modest future. Nearly all the child workers in this category live with their families.

This category of child worker, without interfering with schooling (formal or non formal), recreation and rest can not be viewed as exploitative.

2.3 CONSUMPTIVE CHILD LABOUR

The consumptive use of child labour denotes use of children, purely for profit motive, either by the family or by the society. Child labour is used in various kinds of manual work or menial services. It exploits the children coming from land-less or marginal peasants families. Such children are picked up by the unorganised sectors in the cities. Majority of children suffer from distress and helplessness. Such children are torn off from their family, community life and natural environment.

UNICEF determined that child labour is exploitative if it involves:

i) Full time work at too early an age;
ii) Very large and arduous working hours;
iii) Work that exerts undue physical, social or psychological stress;
iv) Inadequate wages;
v) Work that hampers access to education;
vi) Work that undermines child's dignity and self-esteem such as slavery, bonded labour and sexual exploitation.

The children under consumptive category could be further classified under following type/nature of work.[8]

2.3.1 Domestic Work

This includes the job undertaken by children, which is unpaid work for the maintenance of the household, thus allowing their parents to go out and work as wage labourers. Caring for younger sibling, cooking, cleaning, washing, fetching water etc. are source of the tasks performed usually by girls (Kishwar and Harowitz 1984:)[9] The denial of education to the girls reinforces their lower status in the eyes of parents; due to largely non-productive character of work. Although domestic service need not be hazardous, but children in domestic servitude may well be the most vulnerable and exploited children, as they are most difficult to protect.

2.3.2 Non-domestic, Non-monetary Work

Boys, in the rural areas from the age 6 onwards are usually engaged in family tasks like looking after the cattle, grazing goats, collecting fodder and scaring away birds. They are gradually involved with full-time agriculture work. Naturally such children are deprived of schooling, play and social activity, which hampers their mental development and creativity, children under this category, whether in agriculture, plantation or cottage industry are engaged either independently or as part of family labour.

2.3.3 Bonded Child Labour

Children are bonded both in the rural agriculture and in the unorganised sector. The principal feature is the pledging of children against a loan (small or large) or an agreement between the child's parents and the employer, where by the child would work throughout its life in exchange for money or food. There life long servitude never succeeds in even reducing the debt. Children are "kidnapped or lured away or pledged by their parents for paltry sums of money. Most of them are kept in captivity, tortured and made to work 18 to 20 hours a days"[10]. The reasons for bondage could be immediate need for money. (for several purposes like; medical treatment, repayment of earlier loan) or agreement to replace the bonded worker with a healthier sibling child worker (Murla 1977). Even the child in a 'womb'is pledged to the factory. Loans for consumption and maternity expenditures are obtained on the undertaking that the child born, girl or boy, would work (Kulkarni, 1983)".

2.3.4 Commercial Sexual Exploitation

Commercial sexual exploitation of children especially girls is common world wide. Girls are lured or forced into this form of hazardous labour, which can verge on slavery. Agents often act as procurers for city brothels. Reuse and rehabilitation for such workers is complicated. The physical and psychological damage inflicted by commercial sexual exploitation makes it one of the most hazardous child labour.

2.3.5 Wage Labour (Industrial, Plantation and Street Work)

Children also work as wage labourers. They are often preferred to adults, because of low wages, docile nature, pliability and for non-compliance of labour laws. Wages are paid at piece rate basis, putting tremendous pressure to work faster. The children are exploited both by parents and by the employers. Thus child is deprived of education, joy of childhood, which eventually impairs his personality, creativity and development of health. The work nature in industries is highly hazardous like carrying molten matter, working in furnaces with temperature between 1500 to 1800°c, etc.

Child work in rural areas of India is not considered as exploitative, by the society, since it is carried out under the protective guidance of parent/ family members in the family. Work is not viewed as being antithetical to children, although there is usually a notion of appropriate work for particular age groups and also a appropriate time for learning particular skills (Dube, 1981)[11]

All cultures share the view that the younger the children, the more vulnerable they are physically and psychologically and less they are able to fend for themselves. Age limits are formal reflection of society's Judgement about the evolution of children's capacities and responsibility. ILO, establishes a general minimum age of 15 years-provided 15 is not less than the age of completion of compulsory education. The age criterion for fixing child labour had been accepted by the frames of the Indian constitution and by the law makers. According to Article 24, which is a fundamental Right, "NO child below the age of 14 years shall be employed to work in any factory or mine or engaged in any other hazardous employment".

2.4 MAGNITUDE OF CHILD LABOUR: BROAD TRENDS AT THE NATIONAL LEVEL

The statistics on magnitude of child labour is vastly inadequate. The process of data collection is fraught with complications. The information on children working in informal sectors, or attending school, who might also be working is difficult to procure. The collection of reliable data regarding child labour is limited also by the fact that, officially the work undertaken by children in domestic and informal sectors are excluded from worker's category, as it is difficult to assess the productive value of such labour. Thus official child labour figures are always at such variance with statistics quoted by non-governmental agencies. The magnitude of child labour is estimated by government agencies like. Census of India, National Sample Survey Organisation (NSS), Government Departments and Non Governmental Organisations like Operation Research Group (ORG). The current estimates of child labour vary from 13.5 million reported by NSS reports to 44 million estimated by ORG (Baroda).

The Census of India reported 9.08 million full time child workers and 2.20 million marginal child workers in 1991. The proportion of child workers to child population (Aged 5–14 Years) has shown constant decrease from 12.7% in 1961, 7.1% in 1971, 6.1% in 1981 and 4.32% in 1991. The proportion of marginal child workers has also decreased during

1981-91 from 1.3% to 1.04%. Thus the over all proportion of child workers (full-time and marginal) has decreased during 1981-91 from 7.4% to 5.37%. Although proportion of students has increased regularly from 30.4% in 1961 to 49.65% in 1991, yet a significant size of child population 44.98% were neither reported as workers or marginal workers, nor students in 1991 Census Reports. This "Nowhere"category of children is really a cause of worry, as it is generally assumed that children not attending schools end up usually as child workers. Thus 94 million children in 1991, constituting 50.34% child population in the age group (5-14 years) were "Nowhere Children", along with children working as full-time or marginal workers. Majority of these children contribute to family income by caring for cattle, working in fields or engaged in household industries, and still others work at home collecting water, fuel and taking care of young siblings. However "Nowhere Children"has shown declining trends from 57% to 45% during 1961–91, which is no doubt a positive sign, but the magnitude of decline is slow which needs to be accelerated (Refer Table 2.1).

Table 2.1 Child Labour Estimates—India 1961–91

Year	*Child Population (5–14 Yrs) (Millions)*	*Child Population (5–14 Years) %*				
		1 Workers	*2 Marginal Workers*	*3 Students*	*4 Nowhere*	*Total (1, 2 & 4)*
1961	113.9	12.7	–	30.4	57.0	69.6
1971	150.7	7.1	–	33.6	59.3	66.4
1981	179.5	6.1	1.3	43.3	49.3	56.7
1991	209.9	4.32	1.04	49.65	44.98	50.35

NSS report of 1983 (43rd round) indicated 17.4 million children in the labour force which decreased to 13.5 million in 1993-94 according to 52nd NSS report. A study sponsored by labour Ministry reports 44 million child labourer in the age group of 5–14 year[12]. Planning commission estimated 20 million child workers by 2000 AD (UNICEF 1994).[13] Several non-government organisations have given their own figures on child labour. Operation Research Group (ORG) Baroda, placed 44 million working children in 1983.

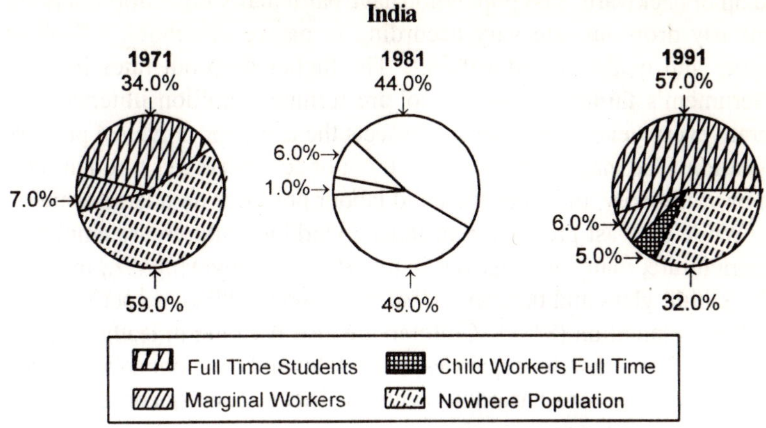

Fig. 2.1 Child Labour Estimates/Nowhere Child

Even children enrolled in school need not necessarily be attending schools, as *drop-out rate/push out rates*[14] are extremely high. (enrolment means registration irrespective of dropouts). Institute of socio-economic change[15] has reported 35% dropout rates in first two years, at the end of 4 years it was 68.3% for boys and 78.5% for girls. Thus actual enrolment after 4 years was only 33%.[16] Several estimation of drop-out rates have been reported (Table No. 2.2). Muslims, scheduled caste, scheduled tribe

Table 2. 2 Drop-out Rate Estimates
% Drop-out Rate of Students

	Class I-V			*I-VIII*			*I-X*		
Source	*Boys*	*Girls*	*Total*	*Boys*	*Girls*	*Total*	*Boys*	*Girls*	*Total*
Ministry of Human Resource Development (1990–91)	40.10	45.97	42.60	59.12	65.13	60.91	67.50	76.96	71.34
Institute of Socioeconomic charge Bangalore	68.3	78.5	–	–	–	–	–	–	–
Giri Institute Uttar Pradesh	–	–	65.0	–	–	80.0	–	–	–
J.P. Naik	–	–	60.0	–	–	75.0	–	–	–

Source: National Council of Educational Research & Training (NCERT) Weiner, Myron (1992): Child & the State in India Uttar Pradesh Education Department.

and other backward class population have particularly high drop-out rates. Similarly drop-out rate vary according to nature of school, efforts of teacher and quality of education.[17] The higher drop-out rates indicate government's failure, as our school are turning 2 million illiterates not literate every year. This adversely effects the drive for universal primary education. The magnitude of children out of schools either through push out or voluntarily, indicates the child labour presence on a large scale.

While the vast proportion of India's working children are employed in agriculture, many are engaged in industrial employment Viz., matches (42%), bidi, glass and bangles (33%), brass-ware (25%), carpet weaving (9%) and plantation (8%).[18] Children are also working in leather works, polishing, fireworks, stone quarries, brick- kilns and handlooms. A majority of these activities are hazardous with significant consequences on their future health and work capacities.

2.5 CHILD LABOUR ISSUES

Child labour issues have generated considerable attention during last one decade from government, non-governmental agencies and social workers. Each of them have elucidated, their own views and subsequently formulated action programmes. However the main actors; parents and working children have been excluded from the whole debate. Unless the parents and working children are involved, the success of the programme for elimination of child labour may not yield the desired results.

In essence, the government's approach continues to be oriented, focusing on ameliorating the working conditions, of the employed. At the best government's approach appears to eliminate child labour is the hazardous industries, which incidentally do not include family or household enterprises. The enactment of the child labour (Prohibition and Regulation) Act, 1986 (Refer Annexture I), has at best emphasised on regulation rather than prohibition of child labour. Similarly the National Policy on Education 1986, announced non-formal education for working boys and girls as a major thrust area. This constituted an expression of helplessness in the matter of confronting the issue of child labour and additionally gave legitimacy to the employment of children. It also force-closed any further discussion on the issue of abolition of child labour and the provisions of compulsory education for some time to come. The only apology offered with respect to child labour was to accept its existence as a "harsh reality". The exploitation of child labour was thus not addressed and instead more ambiguous policies of Non formal Education (NFE) were designed to reach working children.

Officials and employers argue that children serve as apprentices, acquiring needed skills for adult employment. They contribute to the income of their families. They agree the small contribution of child's income or assistance at home, allows the parents to work and this makes the difference between hunger and a bare sufficiency. Children's work is considered essential to maintaining economic levels of the household. They further argue that the employment of children sustains India's traditional craft industries and makes exports competitive.

The manufacturers consider enactment of the child labour Act-1986 as "conspiracy against poor"and further elaborate "Government enacted the child labour Act, which does not want the children of poor and down trodden to come up and whole-heatedly devote themselves to the learning of technical and vocational crafts for bright future.[19]

All India Carpet Manufactures Association (AICMA) has in fact agreed that "Carpet industry, should be treated under cottage industry as a *Khadi and Village* industry and should not only be exempted from the operation of labour laws, but also of fiscal laws, like; sales tax, excise duty and the like".[20]

The government officials and manufacturers argue that expansion in exports especially gems, brass-ware and carpets is made possible through the employment of children. Competition (or rivalry ?) from neighbouring countries in these exports are used as a major nationalists argument. Export becomes a matter of patriotism, the human and social cost do not matter. The 'Myth of nimble fingers' is also put forward for the continuation of children in handicraft activities. 'Captains' of industry argue that children can produce a greater number of Knots in the weaving of carpets. They can carry molten near furnaces, under conditions that adults would find intolerable. They can work better in polishing gems, tasks that need diligence, dexterity and speed. Without child labour, it is agreed, carpets and hand loom textiles might be replaced by machine made products. This would lead to more poverty. With these arguments government has accepted the continuation of child labour on economic compulsions and accepted it as a "harsh reality".

This tendency to regard the issue as a matter of social justice, i.e., the children of the poor be allowed to work or declaring the problem as a "harsh reality"and a 'necessary evil in any under-developed economy"are pointers to the lack of concerted efforts to eradicate the menace of child labour. As a result the issue of eradication of child labour got clouded in an omnibus category of labour laws. It is essential to have a comprehensive change in mind-set, when viewing the problem associated with child labour. The basic approach of the government does not deal with the root of the problem i.e. compulsory primary education and exploitation of poverty. Hopefully the 83rd Amendment of the constitution declaring education as a fundamental right will be adopted soon to approach the problem of child labour effectively. As long as child is seen as an economic problem, there will be arguments supporting it and as a result, a lack of conviction on the part of policy makers and society to eradicate it. Child labour must be seen as less of a phenomena of poverty and more of social attitudes, exploitation, compulsions and sensibilities. This is evident from the experiences of developed countries as well as some developing countries, who tackled this problem much before the economic advancement.[21] Research conducted by the social scientists did not support the arguments put forward by officials and manufactures.

If employers were not prepared to exploit children, there would be no child labour. The parents of child labourers are often unemployed or under employed, desperate to secure employment and income. Yet it is not they but their children, who are offered the job. Why ? Because children can be paid less and they are more malleable: they will do what they are told without questioning, its authority. They are less likely to organise against oppression and can be physically abused without striking back.

The studies of Burra,[22] Bhatty[23] and weiner[24] point, that skills acquired by children in young age could be easily learned by older children and younger adults like; buffing machines, electroplating, spray painting, filing components, assembly and packaging. In-fact early entrance into the labour force has often shortened the working lives of young people, who, now adults, are too ill to remain in the labour market (Burra, 1987). In many cases the hazardous conditions result in accidents (some fatal) or health problems that make them unfit to continue working. As a result, they earn much less than what they could have earned, had they not been forced into working during their childhood.

Besides, the so called skills learnt do not in any way augment their learning capacities, as most of the jobs done by them are highly monotonous, low skilled, tedious jobs, that condemns them for ever in low paying jobs. Clearly the earnings forgone in the adult life, due to disability, lack of training and education, that could have been attained in childhood, are for greater than what is earned as a child. Hence a closer and sterner look at the so called 'economies'are not justified. (Weiner 1990)[25] observed that 'it remains unclear how much worse off the family will be, if the children were in schools. Financial contributions by children to household income are often small.[26] In majority of the cases the money earned by children are used for conspicuous consumption (alcohol, family prestige like giving gifts, marriage ceremonies etc.;). Child labour has also kept girls out of schools, as they are paid less than boys and are employed at younger ages. In the Sivakasi match industry, most of child workers are girls and their wages are well below the agricultural wages in the region.[27]

Moreover the so called advantages to the employers in wage front, in the long run would cost them heavily in terms of efficiency and quality. True competitiveness can only be achieved through improvements in efficiency. Quality could be improved through modern technology and not by using child labour. Neera Burra (1986)[28] has indicated low wage child labour as the major cause for less production in Ferozabad Glass factory, compared to Thailand glass factory. With increasing globalisation and integration with the world economy, India can not afford to persist with low grade technologies more so, with a predominantly illiterate, low skill labour force.

The social workers like, Swami Agnivesh [29]and Kailash Satyarthi[30] have in-fact argued that child labour perpetuates poverty, rather that reduces it (See Fig. 2.2). They argue that child servitude is equally, if not solely,

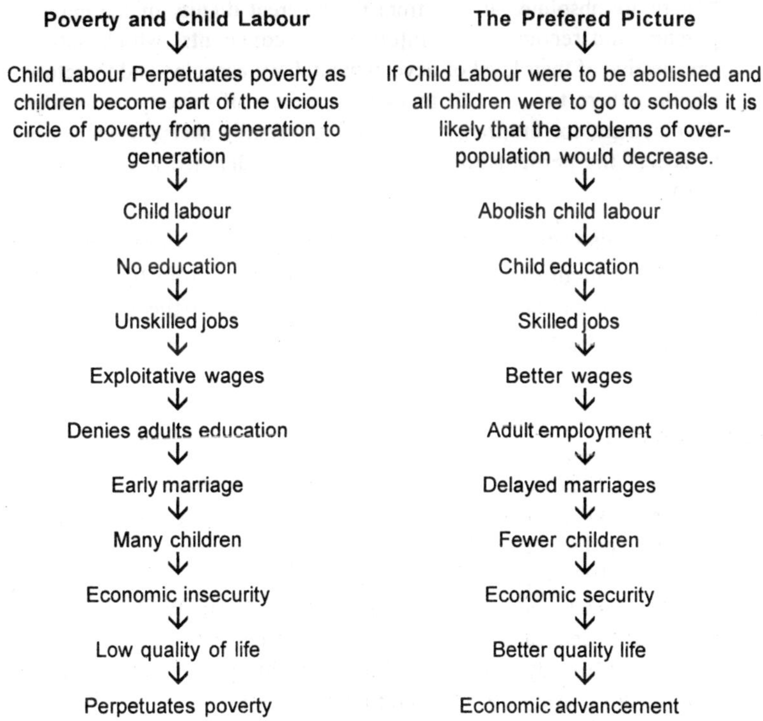

Fig. 2.2

responsible for causing and perpetuating adult unemployment, poverty, population growth and mass illiteracy. They argue that socio-cultural factors, including abominable caste system, ethnic and gender discrimination, nexus between politician and manufacturers, absence of compulsory primary education and profit motivating concerns are responsible for the perpetuation of the scourge of child labour.

Experiences from several countries show that merely belonging to a low income country is not reason enough to condone the use of child labour. Historical comparisons with Sri Lanka, Vietnam, Tanzania, Uganda, Zaire, Burma, Kenya, and China shows that even in developing countries, the principal of compulsory education (whether sponsored by state or a religious or social group), can be successfully adopted, with corresponding decrease in child labour.[31] Thus, the notion of economic well-being acting as pre-cursor to the abolition of child labour may not be necessary. Instead the political will and strong commitment of the society to abolish the child labour can initiate the process of eradicating child labour. ILO has observed;

> "There are absolutes arising from the inherent dignity of the human persons and recognised in international covenants, which nation irrespective of their level of development, have accepted and therefore should adhere to ——. To invoke the pretext of poverty and under development for the transgression of universally accepted values is to accept the perpetuation of universally condemned abuses"(ILO, 1983: 20).[32]

UNICEF also acknowledges the need to seriously address child labour as a key component of the organisation's policy in order to advocate the implementation of the convention on the Rights of the child, and the achievements of goals for improving the conditions and well being of children.

REFERENCES

[1] Fyfe, Alec, (1989): Child Labour, Cambridge Polity Press.

[2] Nieuwehuys, Olga (1994): Children's Life Worlds, Gender, Welfare and labour in the developing world. London, Routledge

[3] Fyfe, Alec, (1989): op. Cit; p.4

[4] Rodgers, G & G. Standing, (eds.), (1981): Child Work, Poverty and Employment, Geneva, International Labour Office, p.V.

[5] Anti-Slavery Society, (1988): A Pattern of Slavery-India's Carpet Boys, London, Anti Slavery Society Child Labour, Series.

[6] Child Labour Act-1986.

[7] Juyal, B.N.: Child Labour and Exploitation in the Carpet Industry, Indian Social Institute, Monograph Series (29).

[8] UNICEF, (1986); Exploitation of Working Children and Street Children, Executive, Board Document; pp 3–4.

[9] Bequele, A ; and W.E. Myers, (1985): First Things First, in Child Labour; Eliminating Work Detrimental to Children, UNICEF/ILO, Geneva, pp.6-7.

[10] Bequele, A; and W.E., Myers, (1995): First Things First in Child Labour; Eliminating Work Detrimental to Children, UNICEF / ILO, Geneva, pp. 6-7

[11] Dube, Leela; (1981): "The Economic role of children in India: Methodological Issues", in Rodgers, G & G. Standing, Child Work, Poverty and Underdevelopment, Geneva, International Office; p. 193.

[12] Fernandes, Walter; (1987); "Current Comments, New laws and Human Rights", Social Action, 73.

[13] UNICEF; (1994): "The Right To Be a Child"UNICEF, India Background Paper.

[14] Weiner, Myron; ((1991): The Child and the State In India, Child Labour and the Education Policy in Comparative Perspective. Princeton University Press, Princeton.

[15] Seetharamu, A and Usha Devi; Education in Rural Areas; Constraints and Prospects; New Delhi, Ashish Publication House, p. 3-25.

[16] *Ibid.*

[17] National Council Of Educational Research & Training (N.C.E.R.T):; (!978): Fourth All India Educational Survey, pp. 838-839.

[18] Weiner, Myron; (1994): Op.Cit; p.10.

[19] Carpet-e-World, Annual, 1991.

[20] AICMA; (1989): Proceedings of Annual General Meeting.

[21] Myron, Weiner; (1991): Op. Cit; p .109

[22] Burra, N; (1995): "*Born to Work: Child Labour in India*," Oxford University Press, New Delhi. (1986):

________ "Child Labour in India: Poverty, Exploitation and Vested Interest", *Social Action*, July-September

________ (!986): "Glass Factories in Ferozabad" *Economic and Political Weekly*, Number 2033-2036.

________ (1987): "Report on Child Labour-A Case Study of Pottery industry of Khurja" Uttar Pradesh, (mimeo), *DANIDA, New Delhi.*

[23] Bhatty, Kiran; (1996): "Child Labour: Breaking the Vicious Circle", Economic and Political weekly, February, 17, .

[24] Weiner Myron; (!990): *The Child and the State in India*, Oxford University Press, New Delhi.

[25] Weiner, Myron; (1990); Op. Cit; p. 50.

[26] *Ibid.* p.50.

[27] *Ibid.* P. 56.

[28] Burra, N; (1986): Op. Cit;

[29] Swami Agnivesh; (1994): "Child Slavery in India", *The Child and the Law*, UNICEF . p.40
[30] Satyarthi, Kailash; (1996): *Break the Chains Save the Childhood, SACCS.*
[31] Weiner, Myron; (1990): Op.Cit;;
[32] International Labour Organisation; (1983): Report of the Director General of ILO Geneva.

3 Child Labour Eradication

3.1 GOVERNMENT INITIATIVES

The Government of India is greatly concerned about the magnitude and plight of child labour in various sectors of employment. India has stood for constitutional, statutory and development measures that are required to eliminate child labour.

Six ILO conventions related to child labour have been ratified.[1] The framers of the Indian constitutions consciously incorporated relevant provisions in the constitution to secure labour protection for children (Article 24 and 39 (e) and (f)) and compulsory universal elementary education (Article 45).[2] Several legislation have been passed from time to time to prohibit or improve the working conditions of child labour (Annexture-II-IV). Legislation relating to the regulation of child labour concentrates mainly on four basic issues;

a) Minimum age for employment of children,
b) Maximum period of work per day and forbidding work at night,
c) Prohibition of certain types of work for children, and
d) Medical examination of all working children.

A number of constitutional, statutory and development measures to eliminate child labour have been undertaken (Refer Annexture-II). The Government realised that mere legislation will not be sufficient. It adopted, National policy for children the (NPC) in August, 1974. The policy stated "It shall be the policy of the state to provide adequate service to children both before and after birth and through the period of their growth, to ensure their full physical, mental and social development"(NPC, 1979).[3] In 1975, a National Children's Board was established to create greater awareness and promote the welfare of children, including working children.

The laudable objective projected by NPC, did not find equally vigorous endorsement by the Gurupadaswamy committee on child labour 1979.[4] The committee appeared to be impressed more by the "harsh reality"theory of child labour. The committee did not suggest the total abolition of employment of children in Industrial establishments, but emphasised, all round development of the child including his education, health and employment in industries. The committee made a distinction between "child labour"and the "exploitation of child labour".[5] It suggested an establishment of a special Central Advisory Board on Child Labour (March 4, 1981) to review existing legislation, suggest welfare and legislative measures for working children and identify industries, where there must be progressive elimination of child labour.

The child labour (prohibition and Regulation) Act, 1986, was the culmination of Gurupadaswamy committee and Central Advisory Board on Child Labour group's recommendations. The Act was enacted with a view to rationalise earlier legislations on child labour, progressive elimination of child labour in hazardous employments, and regulating condition of child labour in non-hazardous industries.

The major loophole of the Act is that it only covers the child in the organised sector and not, the 90% working in the unorganised urban, rural sector and family units. Moreover, many occupations, which are hazardous are not included. However Technical Advisory Committee (TAC) has been empowered to add other occupations and processes to the existing schedule. The Act does not specify the minimum age of employment of children in processes and occupations where the child labour is not prohibited.

It is well known that legislation alone cannot bring an end to child labour. The government initiated several action oriented programmes to withdraw children from hazardous work and prevent them from entering into labour markets again. The most significant step in this direction was the adoption of National Policy on child labour (1987).[6]

The policy was formulated is conjunction with the legal measures to address the social-economic issues, having a bearing on child labour and to provide a framework for a concrete programme of action. The policy encompasses action in the fields of education, health, nutrition, integrated child development and employment. The future action programme is set out under the following three heads;

i) The legislative action plan
ii) The focus of general development programmes, for benefiting child labour, where ever possible, and
iii) Project-based plan of action in areas of high concentration of child labour engaged in wage/quasi wage employment.

3.1.1 Legislative Action Plan

Under this head, a Child Labour Technical Advisory Committee has been set-up to advise the Central Government on addition of occupations and processes to the schedule contained in the child labour (Prohibition and Regulation) Act, 1986 (CLA, 86). The committee was empowered to undertake reviews and frame rules as necessary to ensure that the work is regulated in accordance with part III of the CLA, 86. Government will also bring forward legislation to delete the provision contained in the *Minimum Wage Act,* allowing different wages to be fixed for children, adolescents and adults. This will remove the economic incentives to employ child labour on lower wages.[7]

3.1.2 General Development Programmes

While focusing on the general development action programme, the NPCL envisaged utilisation of Non-formal education (NFE) centres proposed under the National Policy of Education 1986 (NPE). With this goal in view, 490,00 non-formal education schools are to be opened nationally to supplement the formal education scheme.[8] These NFE centres for child labour will be set up with the involvement of voluntary agencies and Panchayati Raj institution (self-governing organisations with the participation of people's clected representatives. 73rd and 74th Amendments of the constitution, provides a statutory framework for a decentralised democratic policy).[9]

It empowers village Panchayats and Municipalities to spear-head the process of development. Thirty per cent reservation for women in these local bodies would advance the interest of women and children. Funds from the National Rural Employment Programme (NREP) and the Rural Land-less Employment Guarantee Programme (RLEGP) will be used on priority basis to create the infrastructure for these centres. For continuing education of child labour, who have successfully completed NFE, efforts would be made to link the NFE institutions with the open schools, or with the forward education system. Along with NFE, the NPCL also recommended to the state Governments, to intensify medical inspection of children in the child labour prone areas, especially in the NFE centres. Programmes, utilising funds under Integrated Rural Development Programme (IRDP), NREP and RELGP etc. meant for poverty-alleviation, would be undertaken to generate employment among poorest families, who often are forced to send their children to work for wage/quasi-wage employment.[10]

3.1.3 Project Based Plan of Action Under National Child Labour Projects (NCLP)

The project based plan of action identified 10 areas with high incidence of child labour in hazardous industries. The areas identified were;[11]

i) The match industry in Sivakasi, Tamilnadu
ii) The diamond polishing industry in Surat, Gujrat
iii) the precious stone polishing industry in Jaipur (Rajasthan)
iv) The glass industry in Ferozabad (U.P)
v) The brassware industry in Moradabad (U.P)
vi) The handmade carpet industry in Mirzapur-Bhadohi (U.P)
vii) The Lock-making industry in Aligarh (U.P)
viii) The handmade Carpet industry in Jammu and Kashmir
ix) The Slate industry in Mandsaur (M.P)
x) The Slate industry in Markapur (M.P)

The strategy in these industrial areas will be to evolve a package comprising the following elements:

a) Stepping up the enforcement of Factories Act 1948, the Mines Act, 1952, and CLA, 1986. If necessary special enforcement staff will be created for this purpose.
b) Coverage of families with child labour to be covered under/employment generating programs.
c) Scheduled Caste (SC)/ Scheduled Tribe (ST) families with child labour to be covered under special component and tribal sub-plans.
d) Provision of formal and non-formal education to all children engaged in hazardous employment, the setting up of special schools providing vocational training and supplementary nutrition for child workers, and a programme of adult education for the parents of working children. The policy also anticipates a stipend for children withdrawn

from prohibited employment. Health care for all children attending special school.

e) Co-ordination of different departments, ministeries of the central and state Governments to benefit child labour.

Existing infrastructure from, the departments of education and health will be suitably modified and incorporated into these schemes. Special funds will be collected for special schools, stipends, anti-poverty programs, and health and nutrition programmes. These additional funds will be channelled through the Ministry of labour, which will be responsible for planing and co-ordinating the projects.[12]

The NCLP project emphasized the coordination and convergence of the existing infrastructure from different departments of state and central government for effective support to the children and their families. Special fund were made available for providing NFE, stipends, anti-poverty programmes, health and nutrition programmes for the identified children and their families. These fund have been channelled through the Ministry of labour which is responsible for planning and co-ordinating the projects.[13] The Ministry of Labour, Government of India in addition to its own funds received financial support, under the International Labour Organisation – International Programme for Elimination of Child Labour (ILO-IPEC), and under the Child Labour Action Support Programme (CLASP) aided by Government of Germany, for the operation of NCLP scheme in the identified areas. A sum of US $ 6.9 million or 270 million rupees under ILO-IPEC scheme was provided to central employees' organizations, central trade union organizations and NGOs between 1992-1999 for opening NFE schools under the NCLP.[14] This amount has been utilized under 160 projects benefiting about 100,000 children.[15] The scheme is extended till 21.12.2001 and is extendable by a further period of one year.

As against the ten project areas selected initially, nine projects have been sanctioned for the benefit of child labour. (Handmade carpet industry in Jammu and Kashmir and Diamond polishing in Surat (Gujarat) could not be started. Instead tile industry in Jaggempet, (A.P) was included). In 1994-95, a total of 12 projects in 8 states were under implementation covering 13,668 working children. Subsequently, 76 projects were started in 11 states, covering 1,55,250 child labour in 2571 special schools with an allocation of Rs. 65.43 cores.[16] Government of India is implementing NCLP in 93 districts of the country as on June 2000 (see table 3.1).

The principal agencies for implementation of these projects were societies, which were formed and regulated under the Registration of

Societies Act, 1860. A part time/full-time project Director, who is an officer of the state government is entrusted with the execution of the projects. The actual implementation of various schemes under the projects are carried out by local NGOs. Project society/NGO, receive funds directly from Ministry of labour, Government of India.[17]

Table 3.1 Coverage Under National Child Labour Project (1996–97)

State	*Districts covered*	*Sanctioncd schools*	*No. of children sanctioned*	*Actual schools functioning*	*Actual children covered*
Andhra Pradesh	20	807	43,550	610	36,249
Bihar	08	174	12,200	173	10,094
Gujarat	02	040	2,000	023	1,254
Karnataka	03	100	5,000	024	1,200
Madhya Pradesh	05	138	9,800	087	6,524
Maharastra	02	074	3,700	024	1,200
Orissa	16	430	33,000	239	14,972
Rajasthan	02	060	3,000	054	2,700
Tamil Nadu	08	379	19,500	307	14,684
Uttar Pradesh	04	150	11,500	105	7,488
West Bengal	06	219	12,000	164	8,250
Total	76	2571	1,55,250	1810	1,04,615

Source: Annual Report, 1996-97, Ministry of Labour, and Government of India.

3.1.4 National Authority for Elimination of Child Labour (1994)

The government constituted a National Authority for Elimination of Child Labour (NAECL) in September, 1994. The function of the NAECL are,

i) to lay down the policies and programmes for elimination of child labour, particularly in hazardous employments;
ii) to monitor the progress of implementation of programmes, projects and schemes for elimination of child labour; and,
iii) to co-ordinate implementation of child labour elimination related projects of the various ministeries of the Government of India.

The NAECL adopted a scheme on "Identification, Release and Rehabilitation of child labour"(Refer Annexture-V). Two recommendations made by NAECL in this regard were:[18]

- Launch publicity blitz through electronic and print media to sensitise society against child labour
- All 133 child labour endemic districts of India, identified on the basis of Census, 1981 were asked to submit project proposals based an the NCLP scheme to the Ministry of Labour, for sanction

A two-day workshop on the issue of child labour in hazardous employment was held during September 13-14, 1995 in New Delhi. The workshop was attended by District collectors/District Magistrates from 62 districts and other officials from 13 states of the country.[19]

The conduct of the workshop coincided with the sanctioning of about Rs. 46 crores for child labour elimination projects in 70 districts, benefiting over 1.2 lakh children. Out of this, in the initial phase, over Rs 5 crore was released. This is in addition to the 16,000 children who were already being covered under NCLP programme.[20]

3.2 The Voluntary Sector

In pre-independence days, voluntary actions were related to social reforms or undertaking constructive activities complementary to the freedom struggle itself. After independence, this sector got involved with the task of nation building by undertaking programmes and activities to complement the official policies of Independent India. Voluntary groups from Gandhian and even from the church and religious background entered into critical programmes in pursuit of the 'aspired 'swarajya'(self reliance). With the 7th five year plan, the voluntary sector got new official status as the Non Government organisations (NGO's) sector. The financial allocation made by the five year plan and the official status granted, attracted a lot more professionals to the voluntary sector. Thus, highly professional and qualified cadres entered the voluntary sector and transformed the entire sector into an independent force. This sector even occasionally claimed and tried to becomc an alternative to corrupt government sector.

The official recognition and the national status of NGOs has also been the result of the prominence the NGO sector received internationally. The NGO sector has been propped up by the international finance and social organisers. The United Nations, World Bank, bilateral agencies of the Western Governments and other voluntary international funding agencies have highly favoured the NGO sector in the developing and under-developed countries. They view NGO sector as an alternative to the highly inefficient and corrupt Governments in the less developed countries. Massive funding and the influence vested on this sector, has also contributed to the proliferation of such organisations in India.

The voluntary sector/NGO sector has a self-image of being socially radical, politically wise, organisationally non-hierarchical, gender sensitive, secular, sensitive to under privileged sections and programically open (non sectarian). Closeness to grassroots reality, strong and real involvement in participatory democracy are traits often attributed to this sector.[21] But the main drawback of this sector is its non-homogeneous character and sensitising several issues which can be harmful to the national integration and countries interests internationally. The NGO sector has largely become a representative of World bank sponsored Social Sector solutions. Though paradoxical, many of them are in the fore-front of opposition to liberalisation of the economy. The issue of poverty, unemployment, starvation and disease have been largely absent from the national debate.[22]

These NGOs purely think in term of return on the investment theory. The Social Sector issues are also treated as exchangeable commodities and each donor/NGO is free to sell his package.

In general, the voluntary organisation can be categorised into 3 types:[23]

a) Organisations implementing Government programmes or, are duplicating such/similar programmes.
b) Organisations critical of the system, to a certain extent but believe, system can be changed through critical collaboration. These organisations, while working with the Government, also keep their independence, criticise the system and also indulge in dissident activities.
c) Organisations, who believe that only structural changes can improve the situation of people.

However the rationale behind the voluntary action is purposive social action for a better society. The community should not abdicate responsibility. The voluntary organisations must equip the community to resist mechanism of appropriation and exploitation. It must act as an instrument to actuate people's involvement and participation in decision process.

To supplement and pressurise the government initiatives at the national level, several NGO's have shown tremendous courage and enthusiasm to highlight the bondage servitude conditions of working children. The formation of South Asian Coalition on Child Servitude (SACCS) in 1989 and Campaign Against Child Labour (CACL, Tamil Nadu), were attempts to protect the neglected childhood under conditions of bondage and servitude and to restore all the children the right to primary education.

3.3 SOUTH ASIAN COALITION ON CHILD SERVITUDE

SACCS a conglomerate of over 410 NGOs, Human Rights Organisations Trade Unions and Child Rights Groups, from South Asia, is one of the largest, joint NGO initiative against bonded child labour and child servitude.[24] Two pronged strategy i.e. Direct Action (raids, rescue operation, consumers awareness programmes, rehabilitation etc.), and Indirect Action (campaigns, marches, demonstration and seminar and workshop) are being adopted for the crusade against bonded child labour and child servitude. The NGO has liberated over 40,000 children languishing in servitude. The SACCS works with police, government officials and judiciary in raiding sites, where children are known to be working in intolerable circumstances, in various hazardous and non hazardous industries.[25] A transitory, rehabilitation cum vocational training centre for the liberated children (Mukti Ashram) was set-up by Bachpan Baccho Aandolan (save childhood) a sister concern of SACCS in 1991 at New Delhi.[26]

SACCS launched a big Consumer Awareness campaign in European Countries and United Stated about the inhuman malpractices in the carpet industry. The impact was terrific and the carpet exports to these countries dropped considerably, sending waves of panic among the manufactures and exporters. SACCS efforts, with the help of United Nations Human Rights Commission (Sub Group an Contemporary Form of Slavery), UNICEF, Indo-German Export Promotion programme (IGEP), and other carpet manufacturers, resulted in the creation of independent, monitoring and labelling system-RUGMARK.[27] The label RUGMARK, certifies carpets made without the use of child labour, there by providing a positive alternative to the consumers.[28] Domestic consumer boycott campaign has been launched against industries employing child labour, especially in fireworks, bangles etc.[29]

The indirect actions of SACCS are to raise the awareness of the masses on the issue of child labour and enlist their support for the cause. Several marches have been organised from 1993 onwards to achieve this objective. SACCS also organised several school campaigns, to motivate the young minds against the evil of child labour.[30]

Campaign for Universal primary education has been the hall mark of SACCS. Several pressures were applied on the political parties, to incorporate the compulsory education is their election manifesto. SACCS played a catalyst role in expanding the rehabilitation programme to the released child labour form hazardous industries and non hazardous industries. The rehabilitation programmes (NFE Centres) is oprationalized by local NGO's having significant footage and influence in the areas. Funds for these NFE Centres were mobilised with the effort of SACCS from several international donor agencies, especially Bread for World(BFW), Terra Des Hommes (TDH), Miserior, and Christian Aid (REHA GERMANY).

3.4 INTERNATIONAL DONOR AGENCIES

Several international donor agencies have provided monetary and technical support to national and local level NGO's for various welfare programmes for child, Women and marginalised social groups. The help provided has created mass awareness among these under-privileged groups, especially in the field of child education. Some of the international donor agencies are

i) Terra Des Hommes, Bread for the World, Rugmark Foundation, Care and fair, Misesior (Germany).
ii) Christian Aid, Anti Salavery-International and Project Mala (United Kingdom)
iii) Asian American Free Labour Institute, Child Labour Coalition and International Labour Rights Education and Research Fund, National Consumer League (United States)
iv) Radda Barmer BLLF (Sweden)

3.5 TERRA DES HOMMES (GERMANY) INDIA PROGRAMME (TDH)

TDH (Germany) has been involved in supporting development action in 26 developing countries, covering 3 continents. Helping Child Welfare is the major focus of TDH project support, with special emphasis on children from the marginalised communities.[31] It tries to support an integrated and sustainable development process, focusing on children's situation along with focusing the entire community. The following programmes are listed as priority for TDH support in India.

- Programmes for promotion of elementary education, along with nutritional status, health care, eradication of child labour, and simultaneous rehabilitation of abandoned and orphaned children, development and promotion of the status of the girl child through information dissemination (both in terms of informing people about available schemes and motivating them to demand acceptability from public institution).

- Programmes of advocacy through campaigns, lobbying, for the continuation of welfare measures affected by structural adjustment programmes, undertaken from the pressure of global financial institutions.

TDH(G) India programme started in October, 1975 and has its co-ordination office in Pune, and regional offices in Delhi, Pune and Bangalore. Several action oriented projects have been funded by TDH. The projects are operationalised through local NGOs.

TDH (G), along with BFW, Miserior and Christian Aid have framed Rehabilitation Consortium (REHA). REHA, funds several NGO's in the carpet weaving zone of Uttar Pradesh and Bihar, for the released children. The funds are provided to local NGOs through REHA (India) committee and SACCS secretariat. The overall monitoring of these NFE Centres is done by TDH (G) India.

3.6 INTERNATIONAL LABOUR ORGANISATION (ILO)

International Support for the Elimination of child got significant boost from ILO and UNICEF in 1992. Two parallel programmes intended to build financial and human capacity of government and non-government agencies were started.[32]

i) Child Labour Action Support Programme (CLASP)
ii) International Programme on the Elimination of Child Labour (IPEC).

The ILO implements these programmes under the overall guidance and supervision of national level steering committees, headed by Union Labour Secretary. The Steering Committees has representatives of government and non-government organisations.[33]

CLASP was aided by the government of Germany. Assistance taken under this programme has been used for the purpose of supporting on-going activities under National policy on Child Labour.

IPEC-a global initiative of the ILO was launched in 1992, to support participating member countries in their national efforts to combat and eliminate child labour progressively, based on ILO Conventions, in particular, convention No. 138.[34] The Programmes would be implemented through Various Action Programmes, selected by National Steering Committee of the Ministry of Labour. The Action Programme was characterised by:

- Setting up of non-formal education centres for working children in these NFE centres, teaching low-level vocational skills along with the basic curriculum.
- Supplementing Nutritional and health care.
- Carry-out awareness-raising project for the children, their parents and community and employers.
- Elicit community support and involvement for sustainability and continuation of welfare programmes.
- Training programmes for labour inspectors for effective enforcement of child labour legislation.

A total of 99 action programme were initiated, out of which 57 were funded using the US $ 2.25 million in 1992-93 and 42 have been funded from the US $ 1.4 million in 1994-95 biennial budget. The action programmes were implemented through local NGOs covered in these action programmes.[35]

3.7 UNICEF

UNICEF acknowledges the need to advocate the implementation of the convention on the Rights of the Child. The objective of UNICEF are;

- promote compulsory primary education;
- advocate revision and enforcement of legislation to prohibit child labour, particularly in hazardous industries;
- assist central and state government for an action plan for the withdrawal and rehabilitation of child labour.
- Strengthen alliance between NGOs, media, industry and legal set-up for social mobilisation in support of elimination of child labour.

3.8 SUPREME COURT DIRECTIONS

In a landmark judgement, on 10th, December, 96 the Hon'ble Supreme Court of India has given same directions, regarding the manner in which the children working in hazardous occupations as defined in CLA, 86 are to be withdrawn from work and to be simultaneously rehabilitated. The direction was also given to regulate and improve the working conditions in the non-hazardous occupations. Several measures were proposed by the supreme court to solve the problem of child labour. The measures include, free and compulsory education for children below 14 years of age, payment of compensation of Rs. 20000 per child from the offending employer of a child in contravention of CLA, 1986A. and a matching contributes of Rs. 5000/- by the state to compensate the family of the child against loss of income. This amount to be deposited in a fund called "Child Labour Rehabilitation-cum-welfare fund". The fund generated should form a corpus, where income shall be used only for the concerned child. (for details, Refer Annexture-VI).

The initiatives and support for the Eradication of Child Labour in India, through government sector, non-government sector, judiciary, social workers and public at large has raised hopes for creating mass movement against the menace of child labour and provide universal compulsory education for children.

REFERENCES

[1] V. V. Giri National Labour Institute: (1996): *Towards Eliminating Child Labour*, NOIDA

[2] *Ibid.*.

[3] V.V.Giri, National Labour Institute . (1996): *Child Labour Challenge and Response*; NOIDA.

[4] Gupta, Manju; (1987): " Government Programme for the rehabilitation of Working Children", (Eds); *Young Hands At Work*; Atma Ram.

[5] *Ibid.*

[6] V.V.Giri, National Labour Institute; (1996): *Towards Eliminating Child Labour*; NOIDA.

[7] *Ibid.*

[8] Gupta, Manju; (1987): Op.Cit;

[9] Terra Des Hommes; (1996): *Project Policy Meeting*;

[10] Narayan, Ashok; (1988): " Child Labour Policies and Programmes: The Indian Experience" in (eds) Assefa Bequele, Jo Boden, *Combating Child Labour*, Geneva, ILO

[11] V.V. Giri, National Labour Institute: (1996): Op. Cit;

[12] *Ibid.*.

[13] *Ibid.*.

[14] Dr. L. Mishra, (2000) 'Child Labour in India, Problems Constraints and Challenges,' paper presented in Trade Union Workshop, July 14-16.

[15] *Ibid.*.

[16] Mohsin, Nadeem: (1997): *Social Clause and Child Labour*, NRCCL, NOIDA.

[17] V.V. Giri National Labour Institute, (1996): Op.Cit;

[18] V. V. Giri, National Labour Institute; (1996): *Child Labour, A Report of Workshop for District Collectors and Project Directors*. NOIDA.

[19] *Ibid.*.

[20] *Ibid.*.

[21] Terra Des Hommes; (1996): *Project Policy Meetings*,

[22] Gramodaya Sansthan: (1997): ***Rehabilitation and Prevention of Child Labour Project.***
[23] Terra Des Hommes: (1996): Op. Cit;
[24] South Asian Coalition On Child Servitude: (!997): *India Core Group At A Glance*.
[25] *Ibid.*.
[26] SACCS: (1996): *MUKTI ASHRAM*
[27] RUGMARK FOUNDATION: (1996 & 1997): *Special News letter.*
[28] *Ibid.*.
[29] SACCS; (1996): Op. Cit;
[30] *Ibid.*.
[31] Terra Des Hommes: (1996): *Project Policy Meeting.* ——————: *In Support of Children In Distress.*
[32] Joseph, M.P.; (1996); *IPEC In India:1992 -1995: Looking Back*
[33] V.V.Giri, National Labour Institute: (1996): ***Child Labour Challenge and Response***, NOIDA.
[34] IPEC (1996): Op.Cit;
[35] IPEC, (1996): *Looking Back ILO, IPEC*, New Delhi, p.5.

4 Carpet Weaving Area — Demographic, Economic and Social Profile

4.1 THE AREAL EXTENT

Hand knotted carpet manufacturing in India is concentrated in Uttar Pradesh, Jammu and Kashmir and Rajasthan. The Mirzapur-Bhadohi belt in Uttar Pradesh holds the pre-eminent position in carpet weaving. According to AICMA survey in 1974,[1] 62% looms were concentrated in Bhadohi, 18% in Mirzapur, 15% in Jaunpur and 4% in Allahabad district, out of the total looms in Bhadohi-Mirzapur carpet belt.. The distribution of weavers recorded are 62% in Bhadohi, 21% in Mirzapur, 12% in Jaunpur and 7% in Allahabad. These areas accounts for about 85 to 90%, of total value exported and 75% of total loomage in India.[2] The traditional carpet belt has far outgrown in terms of geographical spread.. Both the growth in loomage and child weavers has been witnessed, in the area due to sudden demand of carpets for exports.

Three carpet weaving zones, have been identified taking into account, density of looms, nature of looms, type of labour and magnitude of child labour. The areal expansion and areas covered by these three zones are presented in table 4.1.

4.1.1 The Core Zone

The core zone is the traditional carpet belt, a zone of 30 kms with heavy concentration of looms, operated by company branches as well as, by private loom holders. The core zone is characterised by intensive production. The incidence of hired and migrant child labour was higher.[3] The 'core'carpet weaving zone covers Bhadohi district and parts of Mirzapur, Allahabad and Jaunpur district.

Table 4.1 Carpet weaving Zone and Catchment Area Areal Extent

Area/Zone	*District*	*Carpet Weaving Block/Areas*
1	2	3
Core Zone	1. Varanasi/Bhadohi	(i) Bhadohi (ii) Gyanpur (iii) Sewapuri (iv) Araziline (v) Suriyawan (vi) Anrai (vii) Khamaria (viii) Maharajganj (ix) Ghosia (x) Gopiganj
	2. Mirzapur	(i) Kon (ii) City Block (iii) Lalganj (iv) Chunar
	3. Allahabad	(i) Handia (ii) Phulpur (iii) Pipari (iv) Saidabad (v) Phaphamau (vi) Hanumanganj
	4. Jaunpur	(i) Rampur (ii) Badshahpur (iii) Machhilishahr
Peripheral Zone	1. Mirzapur	(i) Hallia (ii) Marihan
	2. Son-Bhadra	(i) Dhorawal (ii) Dudhi
	3. Palamau	(i) Garhwa (ii) Lesliganj (iii) Daltanganj
	4. Banda	(i) Mau
	5. Allahabad	(i) Chail
	6. Jaunpur	(i) Kerakat
	7. Ghazipur	(i) Mohamadabad
Labour Catchment Zone	1. Saharsa (Bihar)	(i) Kosi Embankment Area (ii) Meheshi
	2. Samastipur	(i) Rosera (ii) Bihata
	3. Patna	(i) Maner (ii) Bibhutipur
	4. Palamau	(i) Garhwa (ii) Daltenganj

Source: Field Work and Researchers' Analysis done by research team.

4.1.2 The Peripheral Zone

The peripheral zone includes the district of Son-Bhadra, Palamau, Ghazipur, Banda, Allahabad and Jaunpur. Carpet weaving was extended by implanting carpet looms in the new areas through appointing agents, weaving contractors and loom holders. In fact looms were constructed by the contractors in the households. The loom owner was obliged to take orders only from the contractor, irrespective of the wages offered. The main purpose was to avoid strict vigil imposed by Government and NGO's and to reach out for the cheap labour.[4] The expansion had been towards the South and South eastern part, coinciding with the vast drought prone, flood prone, mono cropped and relatively backward Vindhyan-Kaimur plateau region. Most of the workers, are either from family members of loom holders, or other workers from the same village. Thus, this arrangement helps in transferring the onus of employing child labour to the families, to avoid legal prosecutions.

4.1.3 The Labour Catchment Zone

The area for drawing in child labour in the core and peripheral zone has expanded as far as, Saharsa and Purnea districts in north east Bihar, Sidhi, Shahdol in Madhya Pradesh and Manipur-Karwi area of Banda (U.P.). The child labour is brought through well organised net work of labour procurers and suppliers by dubious means (false promises, inducements, advance given to parents, pledging the children for ever against the advances and even kidnapping. Large scale induction of labour from Nepal has also been witnessed. (Refer Table 4.1).

4.2 LAND UTILIZATION PATTERN

The surface area of core zone is mostly concentrated in the North Ganga plain, where the average elevation is below 300 feet from sea level. It is traversed by small streams drawing into the Ganga river. The South Ganga plain is higher than the northern one. The elevation generally ranges between 250 feet and 300 feet. The eastern position of the southern plain in low lying and some of it is affected by floods. The peripheral areas are lying mostly in the Vindhyan upland and Pent lands. The area is mostly composed of sand stones. The area is deficient in water.[5] Catchment area for child labour is concentrated is north Bihar, south Son-Bhadra & Palamau. The north Bihar area lies in the Kosi embankment area. The zone is flooded leading to vast devastation, forcing the people to migrate for means of livelihood.

The land use pattern among the three identified zones indicate significant variations. (Table 4.2 and Fig. 4.1). Main results of the land use pattern depict:

i) Very high proportion of un-irrigated areas in peripheral and catchment zone area, reflecting primitive subsistence economic activities, prevailing in these two region.
ii) Proportion of cultivable waste area and area not available for cultivation is exceptionally high in the peripheral and catchment zone. The area has vast stretches of drought prone, flood prone and mono cropped area,

which is of highly primitive level of agriculture. Vast tracts of inaccessible forest lands are concentrated in these region.

Table 4.2 Carpet weaving zone and Catchment Area Land use Pattern 1991

Area	*Area under forests %*	*Area available for cultivation %*	*Irrigated area %*	*Unirrigated area %*	*Cultivable waste %*	*Area not available for cultivation*
Core Zone	0.53	75.0	52	23	7	18
Peripheral Zone	34.0	42.0	12	30	18	40
Catchment Zone	–	65.0	32	33	12	23

Source: Primary census-1991. The data has been compiled for the blocks identified in the core/peripheral and Catchment Zone (Refer Table 1 for Blocks identified for the three zones).

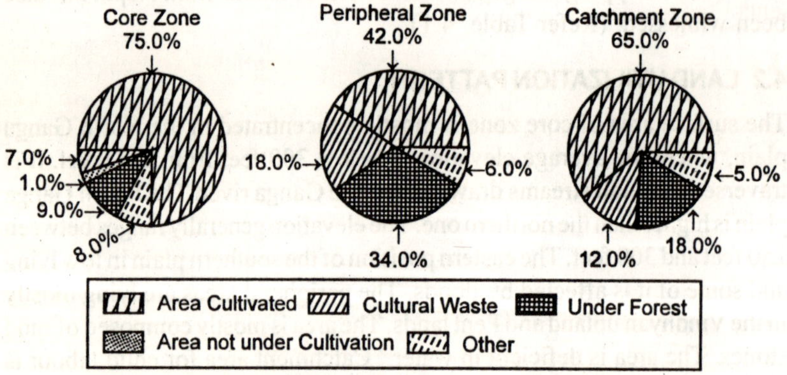

Fig 4.1 Mirzapur-Bhadohi Carpet Weaving Belt Landuse, 1991

iii) The core zone adjacent to Ganga river is also unsuitable for cultivation due to regular flooding. New alluvium soil brought down by river, adds to the cultivable waste and non cultivable area, due to recurrent floods and non availability of irrigation facilities during winter months.

iv) Thus the agricultural activity of the area, is not sufficient enough to provide the means of livelihood to the population.

v) General land use pattern also indicates fairly vast tracts of areas either under forest cover (in South Son-Bhadra) or Non-cultivable and cultivable waste.

4.3 COMMUNICATION AND TRANSPORT

Communication and transport linkages in the core zones of carpet weaving area are comparatively better than that of the peripheral and Catchment areas. Several rivers in peripheral and catchment zone areas, remain flooded during rainy season, inundating large areas These areas have limited accessibility with rest of the areas during this period. The high level of inaccessibility in the interior areas have contributed significantly for the mushroom growth of looms in households especially in the peripheral zone. The child labour is inducted in the looms, so as to avoid regular raids from Government officials and NGO's. Transport and communication linkages are extremely poor in North Bihar and Palamau. Kosi embankment remains cut off for nearly four to five months from rest of the areas during rainy season. The inaccessibility and area not suitable for agricultural activity, compel the inhabitants to look for economic activities elsewhere. Labour scouts engaged by carpet manufacturers roam in these areas and induce child's parents with some advance money, thus encouraging bonded child labour from these areas.

4.4 SOCIAL AND CULTURAL ENVIRONMENT

The demographic and social profile of the carpet weaving and catchment zone, as indicated by Fig. 4.2 and table 4.3 reflects.

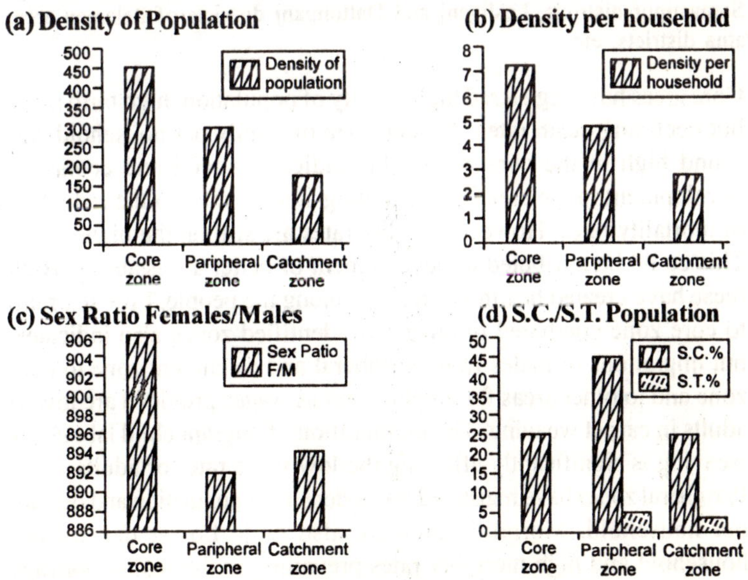

Fig. 4.2

Table 4.3 Carpet Weaving Zone and Child Labour Catchment Area Demographic and Social Profile 1991

Area	*Total Population*	*Density of Population*	*Density per Household*	*Sex Ratio F/M*	*Percentage scheduled caste Population*	*Percentage scheduled tribe Population*
*Core Zone	e3792062	474	7.19	906e	23.75	–
**Peripheral Zone	1838415	285	5.97	893	45.75	2.76
***Catchment Zone	2643710	197	5.67	895	19.74	1.73

Source: Primary Census Abstracts (Uttar Pradesh & Bihar District-1991)

* Core areas include tehsil Handia and Meja in Allahabad, tehsil Machhilishahr in Jaunpur, tehsil Bhadohi and Gyanpur in Varanasi and tehsil Mirzapur and Lalganj in Mirzapur.

** Peripheral Zone include tehsil Marihan and Chunar of Mirzapur, Block Dhorawal, Chopan, Dudhi and Chatra of Son-Bhadra, Block Garhwa of Palamau and Block Mau of Banda, Block Chail of Allahabad and tehsil Kerakat of Jaunpur and Block Mohamadabad of Ghazipur.

*** Catchment zone includes Kosi embankment regions of Saharsa, Dharbanga and Samastipur districts, Lesliganj and Daltonganj districts of Palamau areas of Patna districts, etc.

i) Core areas have registered high density of population, high birth rates, but declining death rates. Average size of family per household was found high in the core zone. This indicates social and economic development in the area is contributing significantly to the reduction of mortality rates. However fertility rates are still on the higher side. This could be attributed to development of better accessibility. Both these have created health awareness among the people. Low sex ratio to core zone compared to other two identified zones also indicates, out migrations of males from peripheral and catchment zone to core zone and to other areas for employment as wages provided are low to adults in carpet weaving. The immigration of migrant child labour for weaving is significantly affecting the low wage rate for adults..

ii) Peripheral zones have registered lower density of population and density per household. Mortality rates are also high. Lower density per household and high mortality rates prevailing in the region portrays poor social and economic development of the area. The area is inaccessible. Proportion of marginalised groups of population like scheduled caste and backward classes are dominant is this area. These marginalised groups are susceptible to exploitation as means of livelihood are few and most of them are agricultural labours.

iii) The catchment area also recorded low density per household, and high mortality rate, due to poor social and economic development. Sex ratio is also low inspite of male out migration from the area. Twentyone per cent of the total population belong to scheduled caste and scheduled tribe population. Most of the out migrants are from these marginalised groups.

4.5 WORK PARTICIPATION AND INDUSTRIAL CLASSIFICATION

Work participation rate and industrial classification of workers also indicate dominance of primary sector and prevalence of high participation rate in the area, thereby indicating large scale induction of child labour in the area. (Refer Table 4. 4 and Fig. 4.3).

i) Peripheral zone has recorded high proportion of workers (38.75%) compared to core (31.75%) and catchment zone (33.71%), reflecting induction of child population into work.

ii) Participation of workers among the three sectors of economy, indicates prevalence of agriculture sector in periphery and catchment zone. But the agricultural activities are of primitive subsistence nature due to absence of irrigation facilities and complete dominance of natural factors.

Table 4.4 Carpet Weaving and Catchment Zone
Work Participation and Industrial Classification of Workers 1991

Area	*Percent Workers 1991*	*Proportion Workers*				
		Primary	*Secondary*	*Tertiary*	*Agri. Lab.**	*Household** Industry*
Core	31.75	65.73	22.76	11.51	25.67	13.67
Periphery	38.75	85.74	7.96	6.3	36.74	5.34
Catchment	33.71	92.75	3.20	4.05	48.71	0.76

Source: Census 1991, Uttar Pradesh & Bihar District Census Abstracts.
*Agri labour is part of primary activities.
**Houschold Induslry workers a part of secondary activities

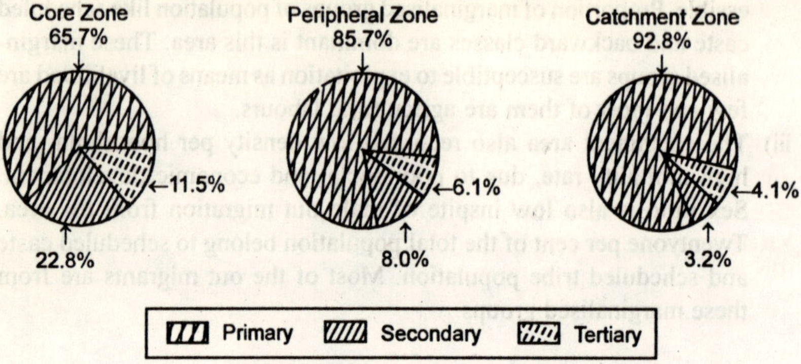

Fig. 4.3 Participation Rate and Industrial Classification

iii) High proportion of agricultural labourers in the area, also reflects poor economic base of the people and dependence on other source of incomes during lean agricultural season.

4.6 LEVELS OF EDUCATION

A comprehensive strategy to combat child labour must begin with quality schools and relevant educational programmes to which families will want to send their children. Work can keep children away from school. At the same time, poor quality of education often causes children to drop out of school and start working at an early age.

Literacy rate[6] (Table 4.5 and Fig. 4.4), in the carpet weaving belt and catchment area was extremely low compared to overall India's figure (57.34%). The districts of Varanasi/Bhadohi and Mirzapur in the core carpet belt recorded 43% and 37% literate respectively while the rest of the districts recorded even lesser. Significant variation in the literacy rate was found between boys and girls in all the districts. Not only is the literacy rate low, the education level among the literates also reflect high drop-outs, as majority of literate are only educated below the primary level. This reflects very poor quality of education in the carpet weaving and Catchment zone.

Table 4.5 Carpet Weaving and Catchment Zone
Literacy Rate and Education Levels 1991.

District	*Literate Population* %*			*Children 7–14 Years*				
	Males	*Females*	*Total*	*% Literates*	*Below primary*	*% primary*	*Middle*	*Above middle*
Varanasi/ Bhadohi	61.07	20.99	42.83	55.9	31.65	17.5	6.1	0.59
Mirzapur	52.22	18.55	36.54	48.9	27.70	15.44	5.3	0.42
Son-Bhadra	41.11	12.49	27.92	41.34	22.35	14.02	4.5	0.42
Ghazipur (Mau)	50.58	13.48	33.48	55.0	30.86	16.72	6.4	1.0
Banda	48.27	12.21	32.01	44.0	23.10	14.44	5.4	0.95
Samastipur	48.98	19.56	34.83	45.2	21.14	15.32	8.1	0.62
Saharsa	39.49	12.82	26.91	35.15	12.66	14.09	7.72	0.68
Palamau	42.98	13.91	29.03	40.0	19.29	13.34	6.66	0.81
India	63.86	39.91						

Source: Census of India, Uttar Pradesh C-Series, 1991
*(Percent) Literate population to total population above 6 years.
**Literate Population among children aged (7-14 years) to total child population aged (7–14 years).
1. Literate Population includes those who can read, write and understand.

Percent Literate Population

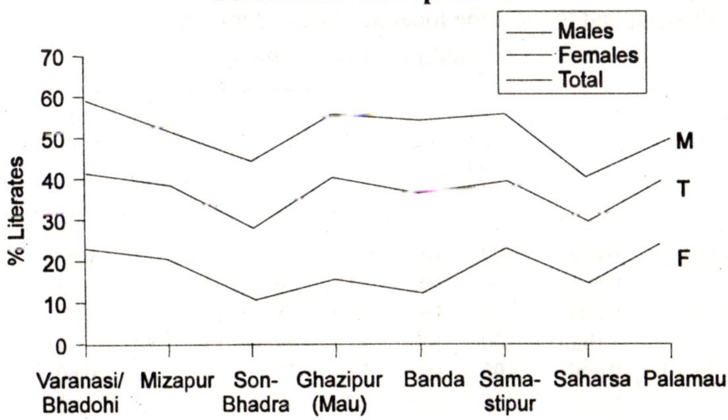

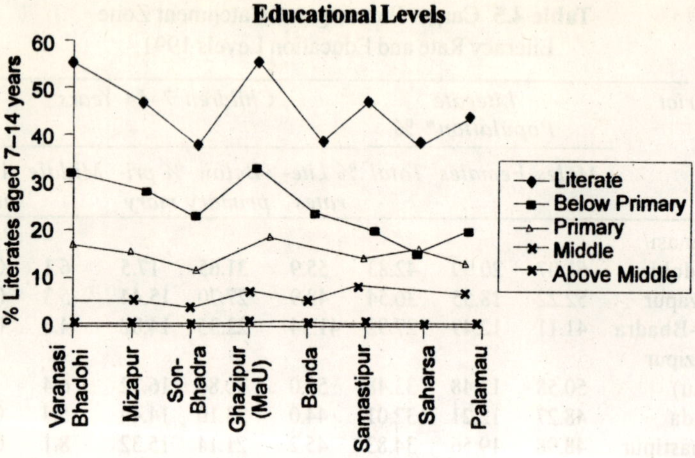

Fig. 4.4

The drop-out rates for school going children were much higher compared to National average (Table 4.6 and Fig. 4.5). Of every 100 children enrolled in schools, only 33 reach up to class V, 10 reach up to class VIII and only 1 child reached up to class X. All the districts recorded insignificant variation in the drop-out rates, between boys and girls indicating higher drop-out rates for boys in this region, compared to rest of India. It reflects induction of male child labour in the work force. The high demand for male child labour in Carpet Weaving can be seen as a cause for low education demand and high drop-out rates. The existing educational infrastructure is inefficient and ill-equipped to meet the local needs and demands.

Table 4.6 Drop-out Rates

District		*Total Attending School*		*Attending Class V*		*Attending Class VIII*		*Attending Class X*	
		M	*F*	*M*	*F*	*M*	*F*	*M*	*F*
Varanasi	Rural	100	100	30	25	10	7	0.69	0.45
	Urban	100	100	31	30	12	13	1	2
Mirzapur	Rural	100	100	30	18	10	9	0.72	0.60
	Urban	100	100	31	29	10	10	1	1
Son Bhadra	Rural	100	100	31	27	9	7	0.60	0.68
	Urban	100	100	32	30	14	12	1	1
Ghazipur	Rural	100	100	31	27	11	9	1	0.91
	Urban	100	100	29	28	15	16	1	1
Banda	Rural	100	100	31	25	11	6	0.70	0.41
	Urban	100	100	30	30	17	14	2	2

Patna	Rural	100	100	34	34	22	19	2	2
	Urban	100	100	30	29	23	23	2	3
Samastipur	Rural	100	100	32	30	17	15	0.97	0.98
	Urban	100	100	29	27	21	22	2	3
Saharsa	Rural	100	100	40	37	20	18	1	1
	Urban	100	100	32	33	28	30	3	3
Palamau	Rural	100	100	33	29	15	13	0.69	0.50
	Urban	100	100	26	27	26	23	2	2

Source: Census 1991, C-Series Uttar Pradesh and Bihar.

Enrolled School Children Classwise

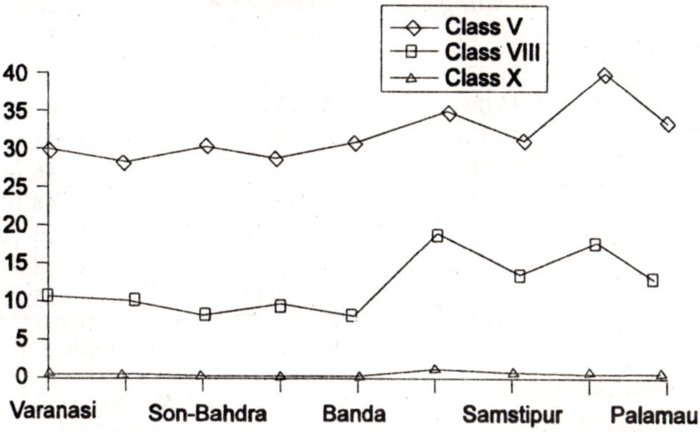

Rural Male

Enrolled School Children Classwise

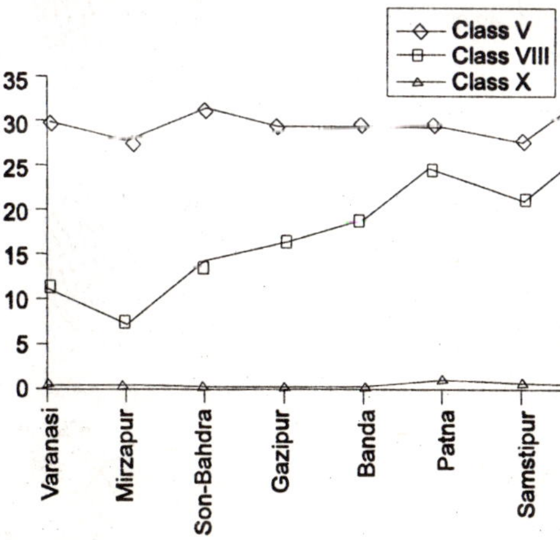

Urban Male

Fig. 4.5

Carpet Weaving belt and catchment area have also recorded very high proportion of children (7-14 years) as 'No where'population.[7] 'No where'population was higher for peripheral zone and catchment area, as more than 50% children, were neither attending school nor were recorded as workers. This high magnitude of 'Nowhere population'indicates a high presence of child labour in the study area (Table 4.7 and Fig. 4.6).

Table 4.7 Carpet Weaving and Catchment Zone
Children (7–14 year) in School, Labour force and Nowhere 1991

District	*Percent Children Attending School*	*Percent Child Workers & Marginal workers*	*Percent Children Nowhere*
Varanasi/Bhadohi	51.77	5.63	42.60
Mirzapur	45.09	7.06	47.85
Son-Bhadra	39.33	9.49	51.18
Ghazīpur	50.38	3.41	46.21
Banda	40.71	11.19	48.10
Samastipur	43.50	3.39	53.11
Saharsa	33.06	8.25	58.69
Palamau	37.38	7.40	55.22

Source: Census 1991, Uttar Pradesh C Series. (based on 5 % sample population).

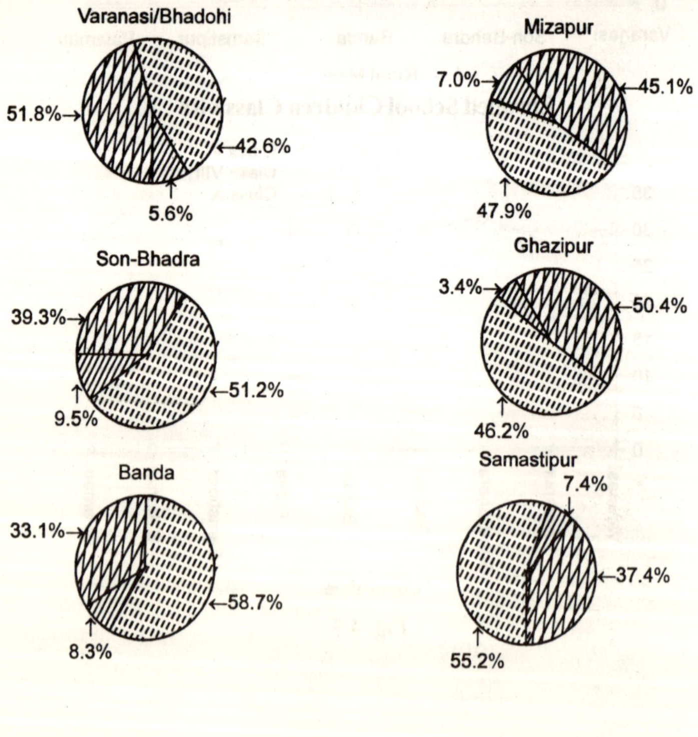

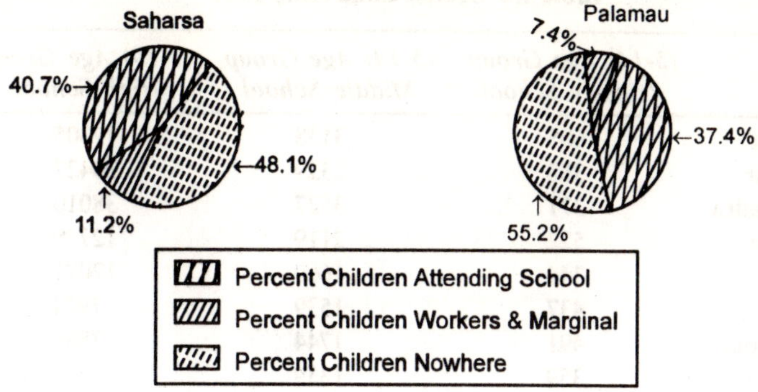

Fig. 4.6 Carpet Weaving and Catchment Zone, 1991 Children (7–14 year) in School, Labour force and Nowhere Children

4.7 EDUCATIONAL INFRASTRUCTURE

The distribution of educational infrastructure (Primary, Middle and High Schools) in the study area, shows highly uneven distribution, as several villages are not served with schools. Children have to travel long distances for the basic primary school facility.

The presence of schools (Primary, Middle and High) for children aged 5 to 14 years (Table 4.8) depicts that the number of children per primary school varies from 236 children to 605 children among the selected district. In the case of Middle school it varies from 1014 children to 3138 children, while for High school the school/child ratio was from 6612 children to 17305 children aged 5–19 years. Although the result show a low child population/school enrolment ratio, yet the proportion of children enrolled in schools was extremely low. This indicated that a majority of schools are non-functional because of poor quality and thus the children feel uninterested to enrol themselves in these schools. People do not see this type of education as suitable for children because it only leads to unrealistic aspirations as the curriculum taught is unproductive. Wiener's[8] unshakeable assumption that provision of compulsory primary education will solve the child labour problem, irrespective of the quality of education needs further testing. Majority of government primary schools are not really appropriate to the needs of many rural children. If the schools are to attract and retain children, their courses have to be seen as relevant by both parents and children. The lessons taught should link to the community life. Schools have to adapt to children's requirements. The annual calendar and daily time table of a school must be adjusted to seasonal farming calendar in the area.[9]

Table 4.8 School/Child Ratio 1991

District	*(5-14) Age Group Primary School*	*(5-14) Age Group Middle School*	*(5-19) Age Group High School*
Varanasi	605	3138	17305
Mirzapur	388	2329	20427
Son-Bhadra	371	3527	38010
Ghazipur	522	2119	12739
Banda	344	1669	17071
Patna	437	1539	7974
Samastipur	491	1744	7865
Saharsa	359	1339	6757
Palamau	236	1014	6612

Source: Census 1991, C-series Table Uttar Pradesh & Bihar (based on 5 % Sample Population)

The proportion of children enrolled in schools in the rural and urban areas of the carpet weaving belt reflects wide variations among males and females (Table 4.9 & Fig. 4.7) Percentage of children enrolled in schools among boys and girls did not record significant variations in the urban areas. On the other hand significant variations were found among the boys and girls in the rural areas. The proportion of school enrolled girl children were extremely low in the districts of catchment zone.

Table 4.9 Percentage of Enrolled Children (Rural/Urban Areas) (7-14 years) 1991

District	Rural		Urban	
	Male	Female	Male	Female
Varanasi/Bhadhoi	64.37	33.95	60.81	50.20
Mirzapur	54.61	27.51	67.60	54.99
Son-Bhadra	42.03	19.66	85.25	79.07
Ghazipur	61.77	34.18	78.53	65.31
Banda	50.65	20.19	71.66	56.51
Patna	62.58	40.92	78.98	71.42
Samastipur	51.61	30.73	74.58	64.71
Saharsa	41.35	18.45	64.63	49.09
Palamau	47.57	23.11	68.70	57.23

Source: Census-1991 C-Series Uttar Pradesh & Bihar (Based on 5% Sample Population.)

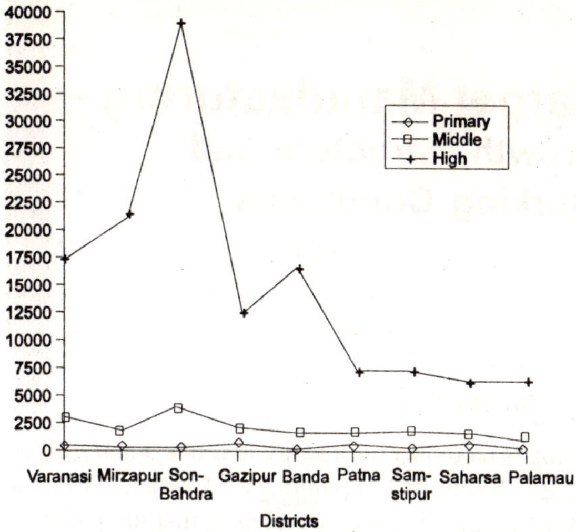

Fig. 4.7 Children Population per School (5–14 & 5–19 years)

REFERENCES

[1] A ICMA: (1974): *Census of Hand knotted Carpets*; Mirzapur

[2] Juyal, B.N.; (1993): *Child Labour is the Carpet Industry in Mirzapur-Bhadohi*, ILO. N.Delhi

[3] Juyal, B.N.; *Ibid.*

[4] Juyal, B.N.; *Ibid.*

[5] Singh, R.L. (1981): *Regional Geography of India*

[6] Literacy Rate is defined as population who can read, write and understand a language.

[7] Chaudhri, D.P, (1996): *Statistical Profile of Child Labour in India*, 1961-91 ILO, New Delhi

[8] Weiner, Myron (1994): "Indias case against compulsory education," *SEMINAR*, January.

[9] In Himachal Pradesh and Kerala the school time table is adjusted to the agricultural calendar of the area. Both these states have very low drop-out rates.

5 Carpet Manufacturing — Growth, Structure and Working Conditions

5.1 HISTORICAL PERSPECTIVES

Carpet Weaving is an old Craft industry in India. This Craft was practised as long back, as 1300 BC[1]. The painting of Ajanta and Elora also confirm that carpet weaving industry was prevalent at that time. The king of Persia gifted a piece of carpet to the Mughal Emperor, Akbar, in 16th century. Reference occurs to the carpet making industry in northern India[2]. The artisans initially started carpet weaving industry at Delhi, Lahore and Agra, but later it spread to other parts of India. Some artisans, on the way to Calcutta via G.T. Road, stayed at the village Modhosing & Ghosia, a place 20 kms. away from Bhadohi. With the permission of king of Benaras, they started carpet weaving. The twin village settlements have all along continued to enjoy reputation of excellence in carpet making. Gradually the local people also learnt this art, which currently has spread to other districts, and is now world famous as Mirzapur carpet belt.

During the 18th Century, the British traders sent some carpets to England for exhibition. These carpets gained international distinction. It seems to have been a lucrative trade. References occur to the supply of carpets in the trade agreements made by the East India company, with the rulers of certain carpet producing territories. Many British traders turned their attention to this industry, following the decline of indigo plantation and manufacturing of salt petre. Subsequently some foreign companies like H. Tetley & Sons, E. Hell & Co. and Obettee (PVT) Ltd, Mitchel & Co. and Hadow & Co. set up their shops. The intrusion of foreign companies and opening up of foreign markets revived the industry. But, in the process of commercial production, the industrial structure also changed. The artisans became subservient to the Companies/Merchant traders. Indian carpets also lost its artistic quality.

The industry went through a series of crises, the worst was during second world war, owing to shortage of basic raw material and shipping facilities.

Before World War II, (1920–1940), the bulk of exports were to USA. This market was lost mainly to Iran, which brought about drastic changes in both pattern and design.

The changes in the method of Knotting, patterns, and design and the mix of materials were made to suit the new demand. Carpets of more than 250 Knots were started. Bhadohi carpets acquired a distinct name in the international market for their excellence in texture, design, pile and finish. The Bhadohi-Mirzapur belt in now world famous for the production of quality carpets with a turn over of over 90% to the country's total carpet production.

5.2 GROWTH PROFILE

At the time of independence, the value of carpets, exported from India stood at a mere Rs. 32 Million (1947–48) and rose to Rs. 58 million during (1951–52) and was hovering around Rs. 55 million until 1960s. Nearly 90% of the Indian carpets are exported to US and European Countries.[3]

In its foreign trade the first major break came in 1966–67, with the value rising to Rs 78 million. However it is generally acknowledged even by official circles that this boost was mostly due to devaluation of Indian rupees (by a hefty 50%). The exports rose to Rs. 360 million in 1974–75.

The major boost for the carpet industry was in 1985–86, due to the economic 'boom' in Iran, in the wake of rising oil prices. Consequently, the rising wage levels severely affected the production of carpets in Iran. The large displacement of child and women labour in carpet weaving in Iran helped the carpet prices to rise sharply in Iran. Consequently, western importers turned to India, Pakistan, Nepal and China for the alternative source of supply. As a result, the exports rose to Rs. 2450 million in 1987-88. Currently the exports in 1996-97 are around 580 million (US $). The proportion of world carpet exports from India is around 17 to 20%, showing a declining trend during the last one decade. This is probably due to strict measures adopted by importers for humanizing the child labour and also the proactive role adopted by major international NGOs to ensure consumer consensus. The other producers are Iran (26%) China (18%), Nepal (10%), Pakistan (8%) and Turkey (7%). Majur importers, of carpet from India are Germany (54%), USA (29%) and EEC Countries (14%) (Table 5.1 & Fig. 5.1).

Table 5.1 Carpet Exports From India

S. No.	Year	Exports (Rs. Million)
1	1947–48	32
2	1951–52	58
3	1960–61	55
4	1970–71	81
5	1975–76	359
6	1980–81	1712
7	1985–86	2447
8	1990–91	5699
9	1992-93	9167

Source: The export figures significantly vary from source to source. The above table is based on.

1. Census of India 1981 Bhadohi woollen carpet Industry
2. Juyal, B.N. Child Labour in the Carpet Industry in Mirzapur Bhadohi, ILO, New Delhi.
3. Handicraft Department. Govt. of India.

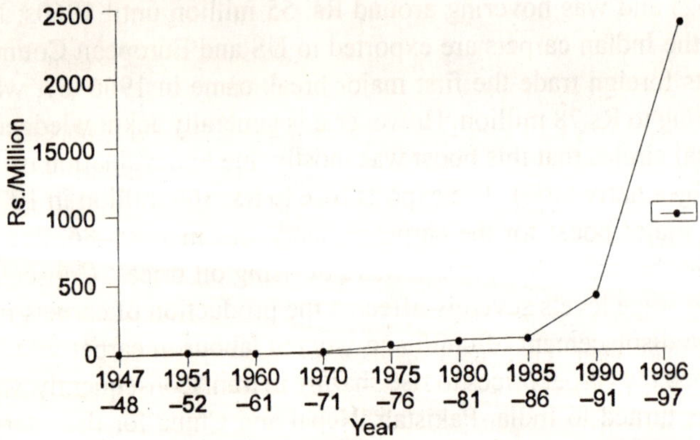

Fig. 5.1 Carpet Exports from India

Govt. of India has taken great interest in the carpet manufacturing, as it provides employment in rural areas. The Capital labour force ratio is very low, a limited investment generates employment. Estimates are that an investment of Rs. 100,000 generates 40 Jobs.[4] State initiatives taken for the enhancement of production include several concessions like income tax concessions, sales tax exemption, cash incentives and availability of institutional credit.[5] In addition massive training programme for carpet weaving was started. There are now 200 state training centres and each centre is training 50 children. Each child is paid Rs. 100 per month as stipend in Uttar Pradesh.[6] However they drop out inbetween as factories offer Rs. 100 to 150 per month. The training given was responsible for high drop-out rates from the schools and encouraging the child into carpet weaving. The parents of the children felt attracted by the stipend scheme. This encouraged child entry into carpet weaving at the cost of schooling.

5.3 STRUCTURE

The structure of the Carpet industry is described as a simple three tier arrangement, by the carpet business.

a) Manufacture/Exporter
b) Master weaver/Loom holder
c) Weavers (adult, children) family: members and hired.

> Manlindra Yadav, aged 27 years, whom I met at Kon (Duddhi) during my visit. He narrates that he was taken to village Madhopur, near Gopiganj in 1980 as a child labour to work on the Carpet looms. He worked there for 5 to 6 years (he isn't sure) but was asked to return home, when he was 17 years or so. Meanwhile a Carpet Company from the same area opened a weaving loom at Kon (Duddhi). Manlidra Yadav attached himself with the company. He operated two looms which were deemed to be against a loan, to be adjusted against wages earned over a period of time. Besides his own family children, he engages other children from the village and thus from a Child Labour he became a child 'employer'. But he feels the profit from this work is meagre and hardly keeps away starvation, at bay. He blamed the middle man and agents for this state of affair. He says "Katouti Bahut hoti hai" (there are too many deductions) He feels this craft will die as many loom owners are forced to shut their looms due to the intermediates pocketing maximum benefit. He attributes this as the main cause of Child Labour. Too many deductions are made on flimsy grounds by agents. Manlindra is unable to manage the looms any more and would prefer to do some other job. Now he is supporter of Child Labour eradication programme and feels education is a must for children till 15 years.

However in reality, the advocacy of a simple, 'decentralised', three tier arrangement is fallacious and misleading. Contractors (commission agents of various categories) constitute, a separate category with a long line of "intermediaries" between the loom holder and the exporter/ manufacturer. Recently a class of elite loom-holders (Non-artisans-dominant caste loom holder) has emerged as a separate category and a sizeable one. Thus, far from being an industry of self employed weavers, there has been increasing concentration of Ownership of power in the non-artisan class.

Several studies indicate that, there has been emergence and proliferation of a series of middlemen, under the agency system and creation and enlarging of the category of loom holders and loom owners in the non-artisan sector. Emergence of this non artisan owner class is, in fact, a major contributory factor to the exacerbation of the problem of Child Labour, more so the migrant captive type drafted from outside the village or locality. These children are employed in the night or odd hours of the day. The enforcement machinery rarely comes to know this practice of employing children in hazardous work. This phenomena is widely prevalent in the interior isolated areas in peripheral belt.

At present the industry field is a kind of 'Jungle' infested virtually with all sorts of middle order operations, on behalf of both exporters and the foreign importers on the production side, frequently one could count 5 or 6 intermediaries, operating between the exporters at the top and the weavers at the bottom. This line gets longer, as we move from core to periphery. (Fig. 5.2)

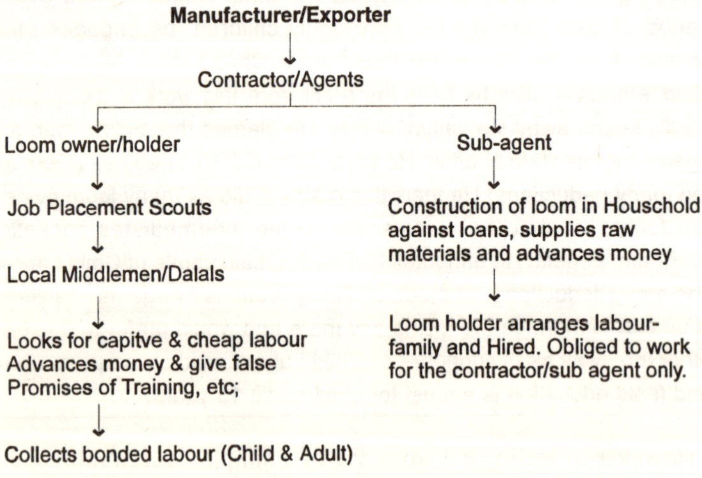

Fig. 5.2 Carpet Manufacturing Structure

Manufacturers operating directly or through a contractor, assigns job to a loom holder/owner, who gets 25% commission on weaver's wages. The commission agents, operating between loom owner and the manufacturer in the 'peripheral areas' charge further commission of 10 to 15%, thus wages paid in peripheral areas are 30-35% less.[7]

The loom holder/owner, need not be master weaver.[8] They pay 5% commission to the master weavers, who in addition gets 25% wages computed for work done by the child worker. Thus the elite loom holder/owner, could straight away make a commission of 20%, practically doing nothing.[9]

In order to earn maximum commission, general tendency has been to capture captive labour. These people are generally the traditional authoritarian feudal leaders of the rural areas.

The deeper involvement of political, influential and power holders further strengthen the hold of commission agents, branch holders. Quite a few of these people are operating through political connections. Carpet companies that dominated the industry in pre 1970 period, have lost their hold, except for few, who may control 20%. Between themselves new manufacturers like Mishras, Dubes and Rajputs have sprung up. They are all from the dominant caste in the agricultural sector, with no background of trade, commerce, industry or artisanship. They have used their political influence to come to top and in return they control the economic power to "tighten their grip over the community structure".[10]

Only 5% carpet production takes place in registered units and the rest 95% is not registered under any law be it factory law or even the shops and Establishment Act.

A study conducted by (Nand Lal Ji 1985) in 1982-83 reveals, that ownership pattern of carpet manufacturing was.[11]

i) Private proprietor ship (81.25%)
ii) Private Ltd. company (18%)
iii) Partnerships (0.75%)
iv) Co-operative (Nil)

Similarly, the study also reflected majority of units, had less than 10 workers, signifying the cottage Industry pattern of the carpet weaving. The study also indicated 'Jobber System' prevailing in the labour recruitment. Employers Universally follow the practice of *Badli Shramk* (Substitute Labour). No worker is employed for more than 240 days.

5.4 MANUFACTURING-PROCESSES

The quality of a carpet is judged in terms of density of knots and pile, besides the specifications of the yarn, design and colour used. Bhadohi-Mirzapur used to produce inferior quality of carpets as compared to other centres like, Srinagar, Jaipur and Agra. The qualities produced until then were of 49 to 155 Knots per square inch. Now, 125 Knots quality is extensively woven in the region and weaving of superior quality up to 500 Knots per sq. inch is common in core zones. In fact, one of the reason for the expansion of the market is that this region can produce a very large variety and range of carpets in widely different designs.

The technique of carpet making has remained same, as the same set of hand tools have been used for hundreds of years. However the cotton yarn and woollen yarn, used for warp and weft are all spun in the modern mills, rather than being spun by hand.

Carpets are woven on vertical (upright) looms. The weft strings are tightly strung on the upper beam and the weaver separates alternate warp strings. In carpets of higher knottage, the weft strings are drawn very closely and the weaver has to pierce his fingers through them in order to draw the woollen thread. Depending upon the size, knottage, design and pile, completing a carpet can take one month to one year. The higher the quality, the more the labour input. There is an obvious relation with labour-cost factor.

Hand knotted carpet passes through various stages before final shape is given to it. Spinning of woollen yarn from processed and carded wool, dying of woollen yarn with chemicals, drying, winding of woollen yarn, stretching of warp and framing it to looms are some of the major preliminary stages of weaving operation. The dyeing of woollen yarn is now mostly done through chemicals as traditional natural vegetable colours used to fade away soon. Using of chemicals is harmful to children, as they inhale the fluff of woollen yarn. The preparatory work is done by weaver with the help of children/women, and other adult weavers, before actual weaving operation commences. This preparatory work consumes on an average one week to 10 days. No remuneration is paid for the preparatory work.

Besides preparatory work, the main stages arc weaving, inspection, clipping, brushing, washing, drying, embossing and finishing. Weaving and pre-final clipping at weavers level and beating of Knots are the main operations at the weaving stage. The post weaving stage operations include inspection, final clipping, brushing, washing, dying, embossing and finishing. Child Labour is used during preparatory work and weaving stage (Refer Table 5.2).

Table 5.2 Carpet Weaving-Nature of Work
(Children Eugesged)

Age Group	*Preparatory Work*			*Weaving*		*Post Weaving*
	Winding of Yarn	*Warp & weft. weft. framing Mixing*	*Dyeing Yarn*	*Weaving*	*Clipping*	
8–10	98%	–	5	20%	–	–
11–12	100%	10	30	100%	20%	–
12–14	100%	30	40	100%	40%	–
15–20	–	80	20	100%	100%	100%
21 & Above	–	100	15	30	100%	100%

Source: Field Survey Conducted in the Study Area.

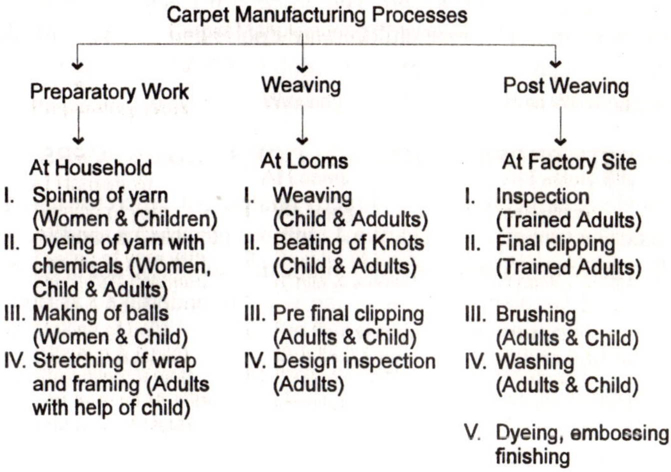

Fig. 5.3 Carpet Manufacturing Processes

The important tools and implements used hy weavers are:

i) **Looms (locally called as *Kath*):** It is made of wood. Looms are of different sizes, depending upon size of carpets to be woven. However, on bigger looms smaller size of carpets can be woven, it has different accessories *Kath* (upper and lower beams), *Satun* (Pillers) *dam, tang, Jeri, Kera Chhar, ankura, Joti,* Kamara *and guly.*

ii) **Knife:** Locally known as *Chhura*, it has wooden handle, curved iron blade and is used cutting woollen yarn after knotting. Major accidents in case of children are reported due to negligence in using knife.

iii) **Scissors:** Locally called as *Kainchi*, made of iron. Normal size in about 16 inches (sometime difficult to handle by small children)

iv) **Comb:** It is called as *Punja*, made of iron and is about 10 inches in length. It is used time and again, so that weft are driven home perfectly. Scars of Panja are usually seen on the body of children, as it is weighty.

v) **Charkhi:** It is made of iron and is used for making coil of the woollen as well as cotton yarn.

vi) **Plank:** Locally called *Pata.* It is wooden board meant for sitting of the weavers, at the time of weaving. It matches with the horizontal size (length) of the loom and is installed near and parallel to it. The weavers are supposed to sit on patta, in one posture for hours together and weave the woollen and cotton warps as per the design kept hanging. On an average 4 to 5 weavers sit on Pata (length 6-8 feet). The *Pata* is closed to *Weaving Khatti*. The process of weaving is cumbersome and monotonous. Since children are docile and can be controlled by pressure, hence on an average Adult/Child Weaver ratio is 1:3 per loom.

5.5 GROWTH PROFILE-WEAVING LOOMS AND WEAVERS

The growth of carpet industry is directly related to the increase in loomage, (the basic instrument of production), number of weavers, and workers in the allied activities. There is no systematic data available about the number of looms and weavers, as most of the work is undertaken as household industry in the unorganised sector.

There have been numerous estimates of the number of workers and child labourers in the carpet industry. The estimates show a wide variation ranging from 100,000 to 500,000 child workers. Many of these estimates appear to have no factual basis and are suspected to be purposely exaggerated in order to make some preconceived point.[12]

As a part of government initiative in 1975, all India Carpet Manufacturers Association (AICMA) undertook a census of carpet looms in this region. This census simply counted the number of looms and weavers, size of looms operated and qualities woven. In the head count of weavers, there is no mention, whatsoever of child labour or child weaver. According to this census there were 26,731 looms and 73,420 weavers.[13] A 1985 survey found that out of 230,000 carpet workers in Mirzapur-Bhadhoi, the number of child workers was estimated to be around 75,000 (Kanbargi).[14] AICMA estimated 1,20000 looms[15] in this region during 1986. A study done by Juyal estimated the number of child workers to be around 1,50,000 in 1987. Gupta confirms this figure of 150,000.[16]

Table 5.3 Child labour Estimates—Mirzapur-Bhadhoi (Carpet Weaving Belt)

Name of source	*Year*	*Number of looms*	*Number of weavers*	*Number of child weavers*	*% Child weavers to total weavers*
AICMA	1975	26,31	73,420	N.A.	N.A.
Kanbargi	1985		2,30,000	75,000	33
AICMA	1986	1,20,000			
Juyal	1987			1,50,000	
Manju Gupta	1987			1,50,000	
NCAER	1992				8
Juyal	1993		6,50,000	4,50,000	70
CORT	1993		6,00,000**	1,20,000	22
Neera Burra	1995			1,500,00	
Zutshi, B*	1998				8

* The study was conducted in looms located near the vicinity of Non-Formal Education schools operated by NGOs for the children working in carpet weaving. Hence impact of NGOs for eradicating child labour was found. This study may not be construed as depicting actual child labour in carpet weaving, for the entire carpet-weaving belt as the purpose of the study was to find out the impact of NFE in the areas.

** The survey assumed 6,00,000 weavers in the carpet weaving.

A survey conducted by National Council of Applied Economic Research (NCAER) in 1992, placed the total child labour component in carpet weaving at approximately 8% of the total workforce, out of which 4.4% was family child labour. Hired child labour, including local as well as migratory child labour, was found to be 3.6%. Another survey conducted by NCAER in 1994 shows that there has been a decline in the percentage of hired child labour which has come down to 2.4%.[17]

Juyal estimated that carpet weavers in the region range between 5,00,000 and 7,50,000[18] in 1993. AICMA and other industry sources put it at about 5,00,000 carpet weavers (Both adults and children). A study conducted by Juyal[19] in 5 selected rural/urban clusters, returned, 3456 adult and 7792 child workers in selected 2666 looms, depicting nearly 70% child labour component in the carpet weaving. Carpet manufacturers point out the fault with these surveys. "The samples taken are microscopic as compared to total carpt industry and secondly most of these surveys were conducted in areas outside the main carpet weaving areas of the hub centre of the Bhadhoi-Mirzapur carpet belt, which is in the north of the River Ganga, in the districts of Bhadhoi and its surrounding. The consequences have been that the samples taken for these surveys are not representative of the main carpet weaving area with the largest concentration of looms".[20]

A study initiated by ILO and conducted by Centre for Operations Research and Training, Baroda in 1993 indicated 22% child weavers in the industry. The estimates worked were based on the sample study conducted in 362 carpet weaving enterprises covering 14 villages. The study assumed 6,50,000 weavers in the areas based on Juyal's estimates and concluded an estimated "1,20,000 child weavers and perhaps 1,30,000 children in the carpet industry" in Mirzapur-Bhadhoi belt.[21]

Neera Burra (1995) has estimated 1,50,000 child weavers in the Mirzapur-Bhadhoi carpet weaving belt.[22] This figure was quoted by the Hon'ble Supreme Court of India while delivering historic directions in 1996 for the eradication of Child Labour in India.

5.6 LOOM HOLDERS' SOCIAL COMPOSITION

The social composition of loom holders indicates that land-less households had obvious limitation, as loom requires minimum of 6.25 sq. yard on the ground. Thus manufactures/Exporters and their agents generally promote 'Loom Owner'[22*] from backward class. These loom owners apparently own the looms, but are dictated by the financers. Thus manufacturers/contractors have captive looms, even though these are not in their premises or schools. Prem Bhai says "The loom owners are tied to specific manufacturer and they generally work only for them in lieu of advance taken from them". However it is also true that some master weavers became loom holders by installing additional looms and employing wage labour to man them. The present study also indicated higher proportion of loom owners from Backward Classes followed by scheduled castes and others (Table 5.4).

5.6.1 Loom Weavers' Social Composition

Traditionally, most of the weavers come from the low peasant groups, who were simultaneously small or marginal owner cultivators. They combined weaving with cultivation, more so because the looms remained idle for long intervals and did not provide regular employment. Land less peasants were tied to agriculture labour. Weaving is still a "Supplementary" occupation for the small cultivating class. Even now a large majority of weavers comes from the small/marginal cultivating class, now being identified as a 'backward class' or from traditional occupational category of weavers, mostly Muslims.

Table 5.4 Bhadohi-Mirzapur Carpet Belt
(Magnitude of Weavers)

S. No.	*Block*	*Number of Looms*	*Total weavers*	*Below 14 years*	*Above 14 years*
1	Kon (Mirzapur)	85	361	42 (12)	319 (88)
2	Dudhi (Son-Bhadra)	10	42	7 (17)	35 (83)
3	Chopen (Mirzapur)	24	87	6 (7)	81 (93)
4	Ghorawal (Mirzapur)	1	5	–	5 (100)
5	Mau (Banda)	57	282	12 (4)	270 (96)
	Total	177	777	67 (9)	710 (91)

Source: Survey conducted in October '1997- November' 1997.
Figures in brackets represent percentages.

- The survey is not reflective of actual child labour magnitude in carpet weaving zone, as the looms selected for survey, were only from those villages where NGO's have opened NFE special schools for children, especially for those children who have been withdrawn from weaving.

Nandlal Ji's,[23] study indicated that 48.75% of weavers were from Hindu backward caste, 16.50% from Muslims and 18.30% from scheduled caste. The scheduled caste had large proportion in the relatively younger groups, pointing their recent induction. The present study, reveals that land less and agricultural labours belonging to backward classes and scheduled caste like; Chamar, Pasi, Slipkar, Jamsari, Bind, Kol, Giri, Kumhar, Lohar, Ahir, Kahar, Dhobi, Kurmi, Bhuj and Teli are generally associated with carpet weaving (Refer Table 5.5, 5.6) This probably could be attributed to our selection of villages as only those village with NFE special schools were selected)

Table 5.5 Bhadohi-Mirzapur Carpet Belt Carpet
Loom Holders (Social Composition)

S. No.	*Block*	*Number of Loom Holders*	*Percent Loom Owners*			
			Backward Owners	*Scheduled Caste*	*Scheduled Tribe*	*Other*
1	Kon	67	58	29	–	13
2	Dudhi	7	70	20	–	10
3	Chopan	18	67	29	–	4
4	Ghorawal	1	100	–	–	–
5	Mau	42	67	25	–	8
	Total	135	63	27	–	10

Table 5.6 Bhadohi-Mirzapur Carpet Belt
Weavers Social Composition

S. No.	*Block*	*Number of looms surveyed*	*Total workers*	*Percent Workers*			
				Backward Caste	*Scheduled Caste*	*Scheduled Tribe*	*Others*
1	Kon	85	361	45	52	–	3
2	Dudhi	10	42	37	59	2	2
3	Chopan	24	87	39	56	–	5
4	Ghorawal	1	5	100	–	–	–
5	Mau	57	282	36	57	–	7
	Total	177	777	38	54	3	5

5.7 CARPET WEAVERS-CLASSIFICATION

The carpet weaving is a cottage industry. Carpet looms are spread all over the villages in small huts, as a single or double row units. The master weaver generally installs looms in his house and works with family members and hires labour generally from the local villages, coming daily from their houses (Prem Bhai, 1985).[24]

The present study also confirms the above results, 34% of the labour was from family, while 56% were from local families and 10% were migrants. However the peripheral carpet zone areas (Comprising of Dudhi, Chopen and Ghorawal blocks) had higher proportion of workers from own family, compared to Kon block which is in Core Carpet belt. This indicates that, peripheral zone are basically 'reach act zone's to induct family labour to avoid legal prosecutions. The magnitude of migrant labour in these sample looms was found much less compared to Juyal's survey[25] and a study conducted by U.P. Government official (1986), in 10 villages from 5 blocks of Varanasi.[26] (However the sample chosen in the present study was mostly form peripheral zone, where migrant labour is generally less). (Refer Table 5.7).

5.8 EDUCATION LEVELS OF WEAVERS

The child who is working full-time to support its family is likely to be out of schools. This is corroborated with several studies conducted in Sivakasi (Tamil Nadu) and Mirzapur carpet belt. The literacy status and school going record of the sample weavers indicate large proportion of weavers were illiterate or literate without formal schooling. Even drop-out rates

Table 5.7 Bhadohi-Mirzapur Carpet Belt
Type of Labour

Block	*Number of Loom Holdens*	*Number of Looms*	*Number of Worker*		*Type of Labour (Percentages)*		
			Child	*Adult*	*Own Family*	*Local Family*	*Migrant*
Kon	67	85	42	319	26	60	14
Dudhi	7	10	7	35	69	24	7
Chopan	18	24	6	81	43	48	9
Ghorawal	1	1	–	5	60	40	–
Mau	42	57	12	270	35	60	5
Total	135	177	67	710	34	56	10

were extremely high. However in case of child workers, due to pressure of NGO's 18% are attending schools which are operative at evening hours. This indicates that given the proper schooling, children would be interested to join NFE special schools. The overall education levels for the workers is very poor, proving the fact that illiteracy is the out come of child labour as well as lack of access to education. Some studies indicate that the employer has a vested interest in keeping the children illiterate, to ensure their continued existence of a captive cheap labour.[27] The support of NGO's to provide NFE to working children is therefore essential to reduce the low level of illiteracy. (Table 5.8)

Table 5.8 Bhadohi-Mirzapur Carpet Belt
Educational Levels

S. No.	*Educational Level*	*Total Wevers*	*Percent*	*Child*	*Percent*	*Adult*	*Percent*
1	Illiterate	610	76	22	33	588	81
2	Literate without formal schooling	102	13	15	23	75	11
3	Literate with formal schooling	26	3.5	4	6	22	3
4	Literate up to primary level	27	3.5	9	13	18	3
5	Literate up to Middle Level	4	1.0	1	1	3	1
6	Literate Above Middle level	8	1.0	4	6	4	1
7	Workers continuing school	12	2.0	12	18	-	-
	Total	**777**	**100**	**67**	**100**	**710**	**100**

5.9 CHILD WEAVER-WORKING CONDITIONS — HOUSING

Several surveys conducted, shows that existing working conditions in the work places (looms) are highly unsuitable for long hours of arduous work of weaving. The plinth area is too small to provide comfortable sitting place to the weavers. Pits, where the weavers, sit, does not have proper ventilation. Working space, seating capacity and lighting are insufficient. In addition the primitive technology, old and often dilapidated premises, improper and inadequate ventilation, over-crowding, air laden with wool fluff, haphazard and inconvenient layout are obvious limitation, under which weaving is carried out.

Many high caste loom owners, follow the social status principal and do not want low caste worker to enter their residential places. They have put up separate work-sheds, frequently using asbestos or iron sheets as roofing material. These sheds have better natural light, but have no protection against heat and humidity.

Other basic amenities like; safe drinking water, toilets, cooling facility (fans) are absent. (Refer Table 5.9)

5.9.1 Working Hours

An officer of the concerned department admitted, the daily working hours average up to one and half time to those prescribed under law, the weekly off day is rare, nor are there arrangement of paid leave. Moreover there are no fixed hours of work. Working day usually consists of 8 to 10 hours.[28] If there is an urgent order to be delivered, the working hours are extended. Even if the workers are let-off late in the evening, they have to spend at least an hour on setting up things for the next morning e.g.; wool sorting, ball making etc., (Refer Table 5.10).

U.P. Govt. has recognised that working hours should be regularised "Children shall not take work before 8 A.M. and after 5 P.M. and they must be given[29] one hour's recess in the afternoon" (Anon)[30]

5.9.2 Food

The food given to the child weavers is usually inadequate and are usually nights left-overs (*Roti* or Rice with Salt).[31] UP Govt. report says "the quality and quantity of food taken leaves a lot to be desired, and that the kitchen hygiene is extremely poor and food quality inadequate.

Table 5.9 Physical Set up and Working Conditions at Looms

	Size	*Percentage of Respondents*
i)	**Loom Size**	
	Large (9"-12")	23.3
	Medium (8"-10"), (7"-12")	60.9
	Small (4"-6")	15.8
ii)	**Space to Work**	
	Congested	78.8
	Satisfactory	19.2
	Good	2.0
iii)	**Windows**	
	Yes	94.0
	No	6.0
iv)	**Sunlight**	
	Enough	15.7
	Inadequate	74.8
	No, do not get any	9.3
v)	**Room location**	
	Basement	1.0
	Ground floor	98.0
	1st floor	1.0
vi)	**Electricity**	
	Yes	29.3
	No	70.7
vii)	**Room Type**	
	Kutcha	48.1
	Pucca	42.8
	Semi Pucca	9.1
viii)	**Water facility**	
	Yes	80.3
	No	18.4
	Yes, but not safe water	0.7
xi)	**Toilet & Bathroom**	
	Yes	5.3
	No	94.1
	Bathroom at some place	0.7
x)	**Cooling facility**	
	Yes	4.7
	No	95.3

Source: Based on Field Survey.

Table 5.10 Work Place-Working Hours

i)	**Time taken to reach your work place from your home**	**Percentage Respondent**
	Up to 10 minutes	38.3
	11-20 minutes	34.8
	21-30 minutes	23.5
	31-60 minutes	2.6
	60 + minutes	0.9
ii)	**Working Days in a Weak**	
	6 days	23.7
	7 days	76.3
iii)	**Holidays**	
	All festival days	53.6
	No holiday	45.7
	No idea of holidays	0.7
iv)	**Working Hours**	
	8 Hours with a recess of 30 minutes	35
	8 Hours with a recess of 60 minutes	20
	10 Hours with a recess of 30 minutes	40
	10 Hours with a recess of 60 minutes	5
v)	**Do you have any paid leave**	
	Yes	0
	No	100
vi)	**Do you feel tired**	
	Yes	95
	No	5
vii)	**Accident**	
	Yes	65
	No	35
viii)	**Tired after Hours of Work**	
	up to 2 hours	22.3
	2-4 hours	22.3
	4-6 hours	51.5
	6 + hours	3.9

Source: Field survey conducted in October '97' to December '97'. Total respondents 109.

5.9.3 Wages

Child Labour involved into carpet weaving for wage purposes can be put into 4 broad categories.

i) Children working on own family looms, without any direct remuneration

ii) Children assisting, adult family members, who actually work for a wage, again without direct remuneration.

iii) Children treated (formally or informally) as "Chela" or (unpaid apprentices). The practice of chela is institutionalised, only variable aspect is that of time span of the chela status. Although every child picks up the skill of knotting/weaving in six month, but they are treated as '*Chela*' for 4 or 5 years; during which they are not paid any wages except for food. The chela is usually engaged in preparatory jobs, assisting the weaver, as well as doing menial jobs. The transition between Chela and formal wage labour, is very indefinite and arbitrary.

iv) Children treated as wage earner, are usually paid at piece-rate basis.

The wage rate fixed varies in term of age, length of experience and skill attained. Wage is fixed on the basis of '*dihary*' (Day work) i.e. 6000 Knots per square yard, according to the quality of the carpet. The general impression given is that, a weaver can weave 1 to 2 '*dihary*' a day (which can fetch Rs. 15 to 25). But the weaver can at best do only ½ to 1 *dihary* in a day after all kinds of wage cuts. Any slight defect in the weaving, the wages are cut, and if they fail to sell the goods, they hold back the weavers wages and make drastic cuts.[32] The seven to ten days for the preparatory work for a carpet like; setting the looms, preparing of yarn balls; dyeing of yarn etc. do not fetch any wages. The wage rates decreases from core zone to peripheral zone (Due to high rate of commission for agents/ middlemen).[33] The work is discontinous, not due to absenteeism, slackness on part of the weavers, but due to lag between work orders and supply of raw material etc. It is estimated that 15% looms are idle and 50% under utilised at any given time.[34]

The wages earned by children are usually paid to their parents or guardians. The system involves calculation of the job-rate wages (for a job frequently done with other) along with adjustments made on account of damaged or alleged wastage of material, food, clothing, etc. Parents have no option but to accept, in good faith, whatever the employer may place in their hands. Payment is also adjusted against the advance given to them at the beginning.

The wages received by the children vary from age to age. Prem Bhai[35] found that 45.5% of children received between Rs. 3 and Rs. 5 per day, 24% between Rs. 6 and Rs. 8, 18.6% received between Rs. 8 to more than Rs. 10 per day. The present study, however indicates slight increase in the daily wages, but the job work is not continuous through out the month, hence average monthly wage vary from Rs. 100 to Rs 200 depending upon age and work experience (Refer Table 5.11).

Table 5.11 Average Wages of Child Worker in Carpet Weaving

Age Groups (in years)	*Average hours of work per day (hrs.)*	*Work Experience*	*Worked As*		*Remuneration Received*		
			Chela %	*Wage Earner %*	*Only Food*	*Food & wages*	*Only wages (Rs per Month)*
Below 8	4 to 6	6 Month	100	Nil	100	Nil	Nil
8-10	6-8	6 Months to 2 year	35	65	35	Rs. 95-110	100-120
10-12	8-9	2-4 year	15	85	15	125-175	140-190
12-14	8-10	4-5 years	2	98	2	150-200	190-250

Source: Survey conducted in October '1997 to December' 1998. Total children surveyed 109.
Chela: is unpaid apprentices.

5.10 INCIDENCE OF BONDED CHILD LABOUR

The existence of bonded Child labour in the carpet belt came into light following *Bilwaria* case, where 114 children were rescued from loom holder in the Chilh Police Station (Mirzapur). A fact finding committee appointed by the Supreme Court of India (writ petition civil No. 12125) visited villages Tilth, Josowar, Harsinghpur and Balwabilwari. They found large number of bonded children working in the looms.[36]

Bachpan Bachhoo Andolan (BBA) and SACCS a South Asian, NGO, have been working for the release of the bonded children. They have released several children from bondage (Refer Table 5.12) with the help of government. Majority of the released children were from Katihar, Garhwa Saharsa, Palamau, Dharbangha, Aria, Khagharia and Madhubani districts and blocks of Bihar. Most of the rescued children were below 11 years age. The organisation has also given list of various newspaper cuttings indicating release of children in the carpet belt region, who are released from time to time from the year 1988 onwards. They have list of bonded children with complete details and are in constant touch with Govt. officials for their release.

Commissioner appointed by the Supreme Court, received several complaints from parents in Palamau district stating that "their children are taken away by the loom owner/Job placement workers of Mirzapur, Varanasi and Allahabad or are missing, sold or dead". The commissioner submitted a list identifying 4 children who had died in loom sheds and 22 children, who were missing."[37*]

Malina Choudhary aged 54 is a Casual Labour with Seven Children (3 boys and 4 girls). He belongs to Pasi caste near Bahuti Gaon (Mirzapur). Four years back his two sons Malan and Kurnil aged 9 and 10 years, went to play and they did not return home. When their father searched for them, he got the information that Govind, a loom owner's agent had lured them away.

They were promised jobs worth Rs 250/- each so that they would help their father financially Choudhary managed to get the loom owner's address and left for Bhadohi to fetch his sons back. There the loom owner promised that he will teach them carpet weaving and will send them back after 6 months. Choudhary was given Rs 100 by loom owner for the return journey. Even after one year the children did not return. He managed to go again but did not find his children, as they were taken away by some other loom owner/Agent. He finally approached BBA activists. After 2 years of searching, a raid was conducted in the village Naidini. His son, Malan was rescued. Malan is now aged 11 to 12 years. Malan's story was pathetic and worth reproducing. "If we moved slowly we were beaten on our backs with a stick. We wanted to run away but the doors were always locked. The top of the boundary wall had glass pieces fixed on them. We were never allowed to go alone. Even when we wanted to ease ourselves, we were always accompanied by a Chowkidar. The food given was often stale. It being left overs of the previous day. During excessive orders in order to meet the deadline, we were made to work the whole night so that we could complete our tasks. Any slight mistake in weaving would entail punishment. One day Malan was hurt during weaving. He was given some local treatment. A kind of match stick powder was put on the wound and then the wound part was burnt. He continued, "I Yelled in pain, but was asked to start working again after half an hour". "In case we requested permission to meet our parents, there used to be a standard answer." "Your parents have taken heavy amounts of money, once you repay by working for us then you will be sent back home."

Choudhary has not been able to trace the other child. Milan is now studying in BBA/School at Ghabi Ghat. He has learnt the basic skills of reading and writing. He wants to pursue his education in formal school after completing NFE programe from this school. Choudhary continues his search for Kurnal even today. He is hopeful that, one day with the help of SACCS/BBA he will be able to find him.

Table 5.12 Released Bonded Children (Carpet Weaving)

Year	*Total Children Released*	*Age Group %*			*Original Place of Residence (in %)*			
		Below 10	*10 to 12*	*12 to 14*	*Bihar*	*Allahabad*	*Mirzapur Bhadohi*	*Nepal*
1992	77	39	44	17	19	7	74	–
1993	236	27	36	37	8	34	19	39
1994	1	100	–	–	100	–	–	–
1995	75	17	53	30	81	–	19	–
1996	113	26	63	11	76	4	20	–
1997	147	15	50	35	86	6	8	–
1998*	11	55	45	–	100	–	–	–

Note: * Upto May 1998.

Source: Bachpan Bachho Andolan files. Reported cases signed by Magistrate for release.

There is no firm data on the extent of bonded child labour in the carpet weaving belt. The surveys conducted by various authors, lack sufficient evidence as these children are whisked away through back doors, before the surveyors could reach the spot. However raids conducted by Government officials along with BBA activists have yielded positive results. Several instances have been narrated by Juyal[38] highlighting the plight of bonded child labour. The committee appointed by Supreme Court of India is amazed, at the rampant presence of bonded child labour in the carpet industry. The discussions with several groups in the field indicated that due to the pressure of NGO's and Human Rights Commission of India, incidence of bonded child labour is on the decrease and majority of cases are only found in isolated areas.

A survey conducted in the NFE special schools run by local NGO's has identified 21 children, who were working as bonded child workers and were subsequently released by Govt./NGO's. These children are currently enrolled in NFE schools. (Table 5.13)

- About only 7% children surveyed, were identified as bonded/ migrant child weavers in 58 NFE special schools run by various NGO's. This indicates that either majority of released child weavers are not enrolled in the NFE schools, or the magnitude of bonded migrant child labour is being exaggerated by NGOs. The non-enrolment of these children may force them to go underground or back to work.
- Majority of children taken for weaving were in the age group of 8–12 years.

- Bonded children belonged mainly to land less families or families with very small land, scheduled caste, other backward classes or scheduled tribes.

Table 5.13 Bonded/Migrant Child Labour in NFE Special Schools- PROFILE (Composition at the time of Joining loom)

Total Children Surveyed	*Identified Bonded/ Migrated Child*	*% Bonded to Total Surveyed*	*Age Composition (%)*				
			<8	8–10	10–12	12–14	>14
311	21	6.75	5	39	38	14	4
Social Composition (% age Bonded Children)							
Brahmin/ Thakur	*Vaisya/ Kayastha*	*Schedule Caste*	*Schedule Tribe*	*Other Backward Class*	*Others*		
Nil	Nil	52	14	29	5		
Education Level at the Time of Joining Loom							
Illiterate without formal education	*Literate with formal education*	*Literate primary*	*Upto middle*	*Upto middle*	*Above*		
86	10	4	Nil	Nil	Nil		
Land Holding Size of Family (% age Bonded Children) (in acres)							
No Agriculture Land	<2	2-5	>5				
43	33	19	5				

96% of children were illiterate or literate without any formal schooling. This indicates absence of education and lack of agricultural land as major factors for sending children to work.

Inspite of the presence of child labour in the vicinity, children are brought from isolated/far away areas. They are preferred on two counts

i) Wages in the vicinity are higher.
ii) These children are bonded and hence can be pressurised and forced to do any work.

The manufacturers/exporters/established loom holders, in search for captive and cheap/docile child workers employ labour 'Scouts' to induct children from poor families. These middlemen (Dalals) have organised network, who procure the vulnerable children from far flung areas. (Palamau, Saharsa, Dharbanga, Samastipur in Bihar, Nepal, Sonbhadra, Banda,Ghazipur, Jaunpur in Uttar Pradesh). The agents pay an advance money to the cash starved parents. The parents were of the view, that lump-sum amount given as advance by the agent meet their immediate financial requirements like, marriage, medical expenses, litigation, repayment of earlier loans and repair of houses. The false promises of anticipated benefits in future after proper training to the child was stated as the main cause for sending children to work. Even children in schools dropped out and joined them.

The existing social & economic background of the family is exploited. The work conditions at looms are very poor. Dusty, dingy and light less rooms are used for the children to sit in for long hours in a couched position. They are made to sleep in the work place without any bedding. Long and arduous hours of work, without rest leads to extreme exhaustion. They are also engaged in household chores. The heavy implements used while weaving, are sharp, which often result in cuts and accidents. The treatment given is primitive. In some case; they explained that they apply lime and put the finger against the flame, thereafter dip the same in cold water and after an hour they are asked to resume work. The Bilwaria incident case bore visible marks of physical torture, such as branding with hot iron rods, was as a result of slow at work, made mistakes in weaving, asked for adequate food or even went to ease themselves without masters permission. At night they were locked up. If caught in the act of escaping, they are severely punished.

The children are also exposed to moral danger in a situation in which they are forced to live with unrelated, lone adults. Filthy and blatantly vulgar and obscure verbal abuses are the normal stock in trade.

The width assigned for weaving in the case of small children is not more than one foot, while the width assigned to the bigger children are 2-1/2 feet and all sitting in one row to finish the entire width length. This shows older children and elderly weavers, weave fast and better. The small children are only kept under their care and supervision. Thus the myth of nimble finger theory in fallacious.

Table 5.14 Bonded/Migrated Child Labour in NFE Special Schools

Factors	*% Respondents*
i) Who decided sending child for work	
i) Father	67.7
ii) Mother	3.8
iii) Both father and mother	17.0
iv) Other relatives	5.0
ii) Reasons for sending child for work	
i) Earning	36.0
ii) False promise of giving training to the child and later start self work	52.0
iii) To repay loan advanced	42.0
iii) Who motivated the family to send child for work	
i) Middle men (dalal)	75.0
ii) Self. After seeing others sending their children	15.0
iii) Poverty and starvation	30.0
iv) What was child doing before work	
i) No work (roaming aimlessly)	77.0
ii) Studying in school	5.0
iii) Worked in family loom	10.0
iv) Household work	8.0
v) Shepherd work	7.0
v) Who took the child to carpet loom	
i) Agent/Dalal	30.0
ii) Parent with agent/middlemen	23.0
iii) Along with other children of the same village	47.0
vi) Any advance received for sending child	
i) Yes	48.0
ii) No	15.0
iii) Do not know	37.0
vii) If yes, advance money received	
i) < Rs. 500	29.6
ii) Rs, 500-1000	26.0
iii) Rs. 1000-2000	8.4
iv) Above 2000	36.0
viii) Money used for	
i) Repayment of loan	35.0
ii) Keep family away from starvation	35.0
iii) Marriage & other social function	21.0
iv) House repair	18.0
v) Medical expenses	12.0
vi) Litigation	6.0

(*Contd*)

FAMILY LIFE & CIRCUMSTANCES	
i) Consumption of liquor/gamble	
i) Yes	26.8
ii) No	54.1
iii) No comment	19.1
ii) If yes, how often	10.5
i) Once a month	56.7
ii) Daily	73.7
iii) On festival days	
iv) Occasionally	72.9
iii) Does it result in family quarrels	
i) Yes	27.1
ii) No	72.1
iv) How did you feel then	
i) Very sad and scared	18.2
ii) Wanted to run away	8.9
iii) Did not bother	47.6
v) Did you have sufficient food at home to eat	
i) Yes	20.7
ii) No	15.0
iii) No comment	65.0
vi) Did you ever join school before joining loom	
i) Yes	28.0
ii) No	72.0
vii) If yes, Why did you leave it	
i) Uninterested	36.0
ii) No good education in school	49.0
iii) No comment	15.0
AT WORK PLACE	
i) Job assigned at loom	
i) Training along with other menial work	45.0
ii) Household work and other menial work	25.0
ii) Hours of work	
i) 4-6 hours	7.0
ii) 6-8 hours	85.0
iii) Above 8 hours	8.0
iii) Parent ever came to meet you	
i) Yes	35.0
ii) No	25.0
iv) Did you like the work place	
i) No	78.0
ii) Ever tried to run away	65.0

(*Contd*)

v) Work Conditions	
i) Free to roam anywhere	15.0
ii) Locked	56.0
iii) Ever given punishment	57.0
iv) Got hurt/sick during work	18.0
v) Medical treatment given	10.0
vi) Given rest during sick period	90.0
vii) Other domestic jobs undertaken	64.0
viii) Any Holidays given	
Yes	18.0
No	28.0
vi) Wages	
i) Payment sent to home	60.0
ii) Amount paid per month	
a) < Rs. 100	15.0
b) Rs. 100-150	65.0
c) No idea	20.0
vii) Food Given	
i) Sufficient & O.K.	26.8
ii) Insufficient & poor quality	45.0
iii) Sufficient but poor quality	28.2

5.11 OCCUPATIONAL HEALTH HAZARDS

Ihsan Dogramaci[39] pointed out "labour at young ages can have dire consequences on the child's development, both mental and physical. Physically, the children are not suited to long hours of strenuous, monotonous work. Their bodies suffer the effect of fatigue and exertion much more quickly than those of adults. Large number of them are already suffering from malnutrition, which lowers their resistance even further and makes them all the more vulnerable to disease"

Sample survey conducted by medical teams in the carpet belt reveal:

i) The evil consequence of remaining cramped up in damp pit looms result leg and back deformities or water retention in the knees, boils, swelling of lower limbs, aching joints, scabies, poor vision, night blindness and eye fatigue.

ii) A high incidence of tuberculosis, filariasis and enlarged lymph gland probably on account of fluff and dust in the ambient air. Complaints of breath lessness and asthama, due to regular body contact with chemicals and dyes.

iii) Worm infestation and sitting crouched with the stomach muscles pressed lead to less appetite, thus anaemic conditions are developed.

Majority of the respondents (Parents and children), also confirmed, several health problems like; night blindness, less appetite, worm infestation, aching Joints, scabies or skin diseases and eye fatigue. A survey conducted in the NFE centres reflected that 92.6% had normal vision, 7% had some problem and 3% had damaged vision.[40] This is probably because, the respondents were unaware of their state of vision and assumed every thing to be fine. Moveover the Surveyor could not conduct proper medical eye checkup to a ascertain their vision. The physical appearance of the children was found anaemic in among 60% children.

REFERENCES

[1] Agarwal, G.N. 1979: *Carpet-e-world*, vol. 1, p.100

[2] Abul-Fazal: *Aine-I-Akbari*

[3] Juyal, B.N; (1993): *Child Labour in the carpet industry in Mirzapur-Bhadohi A situational analysis & evaluation of government of India's National Child Labour Project*, ILO, New Delhi.

[4] Kanbargi, K; (1991): *Child Labour in Indian Sub-continent-Dimensions and Implications*, New Delhi, Sage Publications.

[5] Kanbargi, R; (1988): "Child Labour in India, the Carpet industry of Varanasi", in Aseefa Baquele & Jo Boyden, *Combating Child Labour*, Geneva, ILO.

[6] This training programme boosted induction of large number of children for training purposes and helped indirectly high drop-out rates in the schools.

[7] Juyal, B.N.; (1993): Op.Cit;

[8] Nandlal Ji; (1984): "*A study of labour problems and requirements in carpet industry*, unpublished Ph.D. thesis, Benaras Hindu University, Varanasi.

[9] *Ibid*.

[10] Juyal, B.N; (1993): Op. Cit;

[11] Nand Lal Ji; (1984): Op.Cit;

[12] Richard Anker, Sandhya Barge, Shahid Ashraf and Deborah Levison (1998): "Economics of Child Labour in India's Carpet Industry", in *Economics of Child Labour in Hazardous Industrics, Edited*, CORT, Baroda.

[13] Census of India—1981: *Bhadhoi Wollen Carpet Industry*, UP, Part-XC, Series-22.

[14] Kanbargi, R (1988): Op.Cit.

[15] Juyal, B.N.; (1993): *Child labour in the carpet industry in Mirzapur-Bhadhoi A situational analysis & evaluation of govenment of India's National Child Labour Project*, ILO, New Delhi.

[16] Gupta, M.; (1999): *Child Labour in hazardous work in India; Situation and Policy Experience* unpublished study of ILO.

[17] NCAER (1994): "Child Labour in Carpet Industry" Margin, October-December 1994.

[18] Juyal. B.N., (1993): OP. Cit;

[19] Sharma, V.R. (1998) "Economics of Child Labour in Carpet Industry" in Economics of Child Labour in hazardous Industries, Edited CORT, Baroda.

[20] Richard Anker, Sandhya Barge, Shahid Ashraf and Deborah Levison (1998): "Economics of Child Labour in Inda's Carpet Industry", in Economics of Child Labour in Hazardous Industries Edited CORT, Baroda.

[21] Burra, N. (1995): Born to work. Child labour in India, oxford University Press, New Delhi.

[22]*These 'Loom Owner' usually allow contractors to construct looms in their houses. The amount spent is given as loan against the work to be done by the loom owner. The loom owner is obliged to take orders only from the contractor for future. Hence wages fixed remain at the whims of contractor. A study conducted by (Nandlal Ji 1984) indicated that of the 446 loom owners, 39% were under mortgage and 52% were on the condition that they will work only for the financer.

[23] Nand Lal Ji: Op.Cit;

[24] Prem Bhai,; (1984): *Working condition of child labour in Mirzapur- Bhadohi Belt*, Banwasi Sewa Ashram, Govindpur, Mirzapur. P51

[25] Juyal B.N,: (1993): Op.Cit;

[26] Govt. of U.P. (1986): Report.

[27] Neera Burra; (1986): "Child Labour in India; Poverty, Exploitation and vested Interest", *Social Action*, July to September

[28] Katagade, 1984

[29] Anon; (1983): " Child Labour Abolition: Sivakasi Match Units Threaten To Mechanise", *Financial Express*, October, 11.

[30] Ibid.

[31] Shamshad, Khan; CREDA

[32] Nair,; (1961): *Child Labour in Carpet Industry*, pp 85-86.

[33] Juyal; (1980): *Child Labour the twice exploited*, Varanasi, Ghandhian Institute of Studies.

[34] Kategade; (1985): OP. Cit;

[35] Prem Bhai, (1985): *Working Conditions of Child Labour in Carpet Industry in Mirzapur-Bhadohi*, Banwasi Sewa Ashram, Mirzapur.

[36] Summary of Report of a fact finding committee appointed by the supreme court of India. In Mohd. Mustafa, Onkar Sharma, "*Child Labour in India. A Bitter truth 'ND Deep & Deep publication 1996.*

[37]*However it must be noted that some NGO's are of the opinion that these raids are dramatised to capture international attention and funds. They feel bonded child labour cases are blown out of proportion.

[38] Juyal, B.N. (1997): "The truth About Child Labour in the Carpet Industries" *Allalahabad Workshop*, proceedings Ankur Foundation.

[39] Dogmaci Ihsan: "Child Labour " An overview" in PM Shah and Nigel Contwell (eds) "*Child Labour: A threat to Health and Development*", Geneva.

[40] The selected sample only reflects children enrolled in the NFE centres. Since these centres are in operation for the last one to two years, hence the results may not reflect the health problems as envisaged by the children who were working full time in the weaving looms.

6 Non-Formal Education Centres — Profile

6.1 SIGNIFICANCE

A comprehensive strategy to combat child labour must begin with high quality schools and relevant educational programmes. The families should be willing to send their children for education to these schools. Primary education system in its present form is both unacceptable, unrealistic and unreachable to the children of poor, downtrodden and rural families. It is established that work can keep children away from school. At the same time, poor quality of education, often causes children to drop-out/'push-out'[1] of schools and start working at an early age. Our results testify that drop- out rates in Mirzapur-Bhadohi carpet belt is very high. Prof. Yash Pal, Chairman of National Advisory Committee in 1993, states joyless learning as a major problem for 'push-outs'. According to him,

> "both the teacher and the child have lost the sense of joy in being involved with educational process. Teaching and learning ... to the majority of our school going children are made to view at school as a boring, even unpleasant and bitter experience. They are daily socialized to look upon education as mainly a process of preparing for examination, no other motivate seems to have any legitimacy."

If schools are to attract and retain children, their courses have to be seen as relevant by both parents and children. One prerequisite of a successful State education programme is that it links the lessons taught to community life. Schools have to adopt to children's circumstances. The annual calendar and daily time table of a school must be adjusted according to the seasonal farming calendar in the area[2]. Schools also have to move towards children particularly in far flung and isolated rural areas, so that education is brought within easy walking distances. A simplified curriculum and locally produced learning materials must be evolved. Teachers with modest formal education have proven to be effective, when given concerted practical training and frequent in-service upgrades. Rigid traditional teaching methods must give way to child centered approaches. The National Policy of Education-1986 has reemphasized that the academic programme and school activities should be built around the child, and that the emphasis should be shifted from mere enrollment to retention, and quality of education.[3]

The sheer size of the population, non-availability of government school education in rural areas and non functoning of school education has lead to a growing realization among the people and policy and plan makers, that Non-formal Education (NFE) is the best alternative to inculcate educational awareness in the isolated, underdeveloped areas. The most significant step in this direction was the adoption of National Policy of Education (NPE-1986) and National Policy of Child Labour (NPCL-1987). Both these policies aimed at successfully rehabilitating child labour released from hazardous employment and to reduce the incidence of child labour progressively. The opening of special school for imparting NFE and vocational training was the major recommendation of the two policies.

It is generally admitted that government primary schools are not really appropriate to the needs of many rural children. Girls in the age group 6-14 are not attracted by the existing programme of education. On the contrary, NFE models have proved their efficacy in reaching to the poor and down trodden sections of the society. It has all the elements, which in the opinion of the policy makers constitute a "good" programme, and at the same time is cost effective. Its intended clientele would come from children of weaker section like, ST/SC/hilly areas/tribal areas/urban slums/ economically backward rural areas. The focus is to serve under privileged sections of the community, which remain unsettled by the existing government school system. Anil Bordia[4] urged "that expenditure on improving the facilities in government primary school, would do little to the poor, who drop-out, whereas the system of NFE is targeted to meet the needs of working children".

Almost all attempts to bring education to working children and children released from hazardous occupations, have been through non-formal education programmes, independent of the education system. Mirzapur-Bhadohi carpet belt was identified as one of the project based plan of action by NCLP-1987. Under this plan of action provision of non-formal education, vocational training, supplementary nutrition, and stipend for children released from prohibited employment was stipulated. The actual implementation were carried out by local non-governmental organisations. The successful literacy campaign have generally been found to be executed by NGO's, as they enjoy an element of enlightened voluntarism close to grass root reality with a requisite organizational strength.

6.2 GOVERNMENT SPONSORED NFE SPECIAL CENTRES

The Ministry of Labour, Government of India initiated three projects for rehabilitation of the working children. Two projects were started in Varanasi and Mirzapur-Bhadohi carpet belt. Several special NFE centres were started. According to Ministry of Labour, 130 such centres were in operation till 1995-96 in Uttar Pradesh. Nearly 9000 children were covered with a budget approval of Rs. 27.4 million.[5] The government initiative was supported by ILO and UNICEF in 1992. International Programme on the Elimination of child labour (IPEC) supported government Action Programme under NCLP and provided funds for NFE, nutritional health care and stipend for working children.

The special NFE centres under Labour Ministry and IPEC until 1996-98 were operated by the following NGO's:

i) *Bandhwa Mukti Samiti (BMS):* Implemented the Action programme in 1992-93. The NFE centres enrolled 150 children. An additional 250 children, not included in the Action programme, were provided with one hour NFE a day. 94 children were released from bonded labour. The children were provided with non-formal and vocational education, health care, daily meals and a stipend. Budget stipulated was U.S.$ 28,686.

ii) *Harijan Sevak Samaj (HSS):* NFE, health care, nutrition and vocational training was provided to 120 children in Garhwa. By the end of the 1992-93 programme, 50 children were going to regular centres. Budget stipulated was US. $ 22,775.

iii) *Centre for Rural Education and Development Action (CREDA) (1989 NCLP), IPEC (1992-95):* CREDA was founded in 1982, and since its inception, the issue of child labour has been a priority. NFE special centres under NCLP were started in 1989. Till 1995-96, CREDA had opened 50 special centres and a total of 2500 students had been enrolled in them.[6] CREDA gets an annual grant of Rs. 143,000 for each Special School. CREDA also opened several centres under the IPEC programme. Under this programme 18 such centres have been opened and 900 children were covered.[7] In addition the children were provided monthly stipend and mid day meal. The Action programme included an advocacy campaign for generating mass awareness and community participation against the exploitation of children. Budget stipulated for 1992-93 was U.S. $ 89,600 and in 1994-95 U.S. $ 97,338.

iv) *Saghan Kshetra Vikas Samiti (SKVS) (1992–93):* The NGO targeted 250 children in the Carpet Industry. It started well but could not be completed because of organizational difficulties. Budget stipulated was US $ 35,800.

v) *Bihar Khet Parishad (BKP) (1992–93):* Its target was 120 child labourers in the Palamau district of Bihar. Budget for the NFE Centres was US $ 13,600.

vi) *Shramik Vikas Sewa Ashram (SVSA):* During 1994-95, financial assistance was given to SVSA for providing NFE, Supplementary nutrition, health care and vocational training.

In a recent evaluation, done in connection with the progress of NCLP and IPEC, the following critical remarks have been made about NFE special centres.[8]

i) Awareness generation at the district level is very low.
ii) Development of teaching material for the special centres is totally inadequate. There is lack of training of implementing staff.
iii) Children often return to work after leaving the special centres.
iv) There is no impact seen on income generation activities for the benefit of parents of those child labourers, nor any integration with the work of the local education and women and child development department.
v) There is no reliable data base available.
vi) There is no proper evaluation and maintaining of these NFE Special Centres.
vii) Community acceptance level is not witnessed.
viii) Efforts for enrollment of children who have completed NFE in formal centres/vocational training is extremely limited.

6.3 CARPET EXPORT PROMOTION COUNCIL (CEPC)

The Carpet Export Promotion Council was established in 1982 by the government of India as an apex body of the carpet industry. Its primary objective is to promote the sale and exports of the Indian hand knotted carpets. In response to the widespread media reports about the use of child labour in India, the Council devised the "Kaleen – the Hallmark of Commitment" label. It acts as an assurance that no child exploitation has taken place in the manufacture of carpets. The scheme attempts to register all carpet weaving looms in the hope of bringing the industry under tighter control. This is however, a very ambitious task. The Council collects a cess of 0.25% from the export of each carpet and donates the money for welfare programme of weaver community.

Under this scheme CEPC sponsors NFE Special Centres run by local NGO's in the Mirzapur-Bhadohi carpet belt. 13 NFE Special Centres were sponsored by CEPC. The NGOs receiving funds from CEPC are;

i) Project Mala (4 special centres)
ii) Bandhua Mukti March (2 special centres)
iii) Child Labour Eradication and Welfare Society (2 special centres)
iv) CREDA (4 special centres)
v) Gramin Mahila Uthan Sasthan (1 Special School).

6.4 REHA SPONSORED NFE SPECIAL CENTRES

Several International donor agencies, supplemented the government initiatives for non-formal education in the Mirzapur-Bhadohi carpet region. SACCS (South Asian, NGO) played a catalyst role in expanding the NFE Centres to the released children from carpet weaving. SACCS, mobilized funds for these NFE centres through Bread for World, (Germany) BFW, Terra Des Homes (Germany) TDH, Misesior (Germany) and Christian Aid (U.K). The four donor agencies together formed Rehabilitation consortium (REHA). REHA committee of India recommends the projects from local NGO's (who identify the children for rehabilitation in the field) to REHA (Germany) and final sanction is granted by REHA (Germany). Monitoring of the project is undertaken by TDH (India).

The objective of these Special Centres is to provide non-formal education, nutritional diet, health facility and general awareness to the released children from carpet weaving. The funding was initially provided for 2 to 3 years. It is expected that after completing NFE, the children would be enrolled in formal education system. NGO wise list of Special Centres funded by REHA (Germany) is given in Table 6.1.

In addition to IPEC, CEPC and REHA funded NFE Special Centres, other national and international donor agencies have also started non-formal education in the carpet belt. These NGOs are:

Table 6.1 Non Formal Special Centres Funded by REHA

	Name of the centre	Numbers
i)	Shri Vivekanand Shiksha Samiti	5
ii)	Bachpan Bachho Aandolan	5
iii)	Manav Sansadan Avam Mahila Vikas	3
iv)	Yuva Vikas Sansthan	2
v)	Gramodaya Sansthan	5
vi)	Ankur Foundation	18
vii)	Gramin Vikas Kendra	4
viii)	Arpan Gram Vikas	12
ix)	Kosi Sewa Sadan	5
x)	Samudaya	12
xi)	SACCS/BBA	1
	Total	**82**

i) Project Mala (5 centres)
ii) Rugmark foundation (2 centres)
iii) Children Welfare Society. (16 centres).

6.5 NON-FORMAL EDUCATION, CENTRES-SPATIAL DISTRIBUTION, AND COVERAGE

Any comprehensive attack on hazardous child labour, must advance on several fronts. The aim must be to release children immediately from the most damaging situations, such as bonded labour and children under servitude condition. The rehabilitation of the released children and ensuring that new generation of children are not driven into the most hazardous forms of work should be tackled on priority basis. Both these aspects can only be tackled with active participation and co-operation of government, local communities, NGOs, spiritual leaders, employees and trade unions and child labourers themselves and their families.

Key initiatives undertaken in this regard was establishment of NFE Special Centres by government, national and international donor agencies and local NGOs. Mirzapur-Bhadohi carpet belt was divided into three zone, viz. Core zone, Peripheral Zone and Catchment zone, based on carpet weaving intensity and characteristics. (Refer Chapter 4). Core zone consisted of 2794 villages, Peripheral zone recorded 2299 villages and Catchment zone had 681 villages. The availability of government schools in these villages was found highly inappropriate (Table 6.2). 53% villages in peripheral zone, 47% villages in core area and catchment area, did not

Table 6.2 Bhadohi-Mirzapur Carpet Belt
(Villages without School facility 1991)

Area/Block		*Total Villages*	*% Villages* *With Govt. School*	*Without School Facility*
District CORE-AREA				
	i) Bhadohi	267	52.4	47.6
	ii) Gyanpur	234	40.6	59.4
Bhadohi	iii) Aurain	290	46.2	53.8
	iv) Sewapuri	188	49.5	50.5
	v) Araziline	227	51.5	48.5
	vi) Suriyawan	212	58.5	41.5
Mirzapur	vii) Kon	84	64.3	35.7
	viii) City Block	182	69.2	30.8
	ix) Lalganj	210	54.8	45.2
Allahabad	x) Handia	245	55.8	44.2
	xi) Goshia	173	48.3	51.7
	xii) Pipari	165	52.3	44.7
Jaunpur	xiii) Rampur	178	53.7	46.3
	xiv) Badshahpur	139	52.6	47.4
Total Core		**2794**	**52.76**	**47.24**
Peripheral Zone				
Mirzapur	i) Hallia	213	38.5	61.5
	ii) Marihan	140	49.3	50.7
Son-Bhadra	i) Dhorawal	354	34.7	65.7
	ii) Chatra	190	48.4	51.6
	iii) Chopan	93	74.2	25.8
	iv) Dudhi	124	63.7	36.3
Palamau	i) Garhwa	129	62.0	38.0
	ii) Daltonganj	78	69.2	30.8
	iii) Lesliganj	200	46.5	53.5
Banda	i) Mau	122	53.5	46.7
Allahabad	i) Chail	171	58.2	41.8
District	*CORE-AREA*			
Jaunpur	i) Kerakat	168	52.6	47.4
Ghazipur	i) Mohaumdabad	317	23.0	77.0
Total Peripheral Zone		**2299**	**46.94**	**53.06**
Child Labour Catchment zone				
Saharsa	i) Maheshi & Kosi Embankment Area	386	53.5	46.5
Samastipur	i) Rosera	116	69.6	30.4
	ii) Bhibuhutipur	44	93.2	6.8
Patna	i) Maner	45	80.0	20.0
Palamau	i) Gharwa	129	62.0	38.0
	ii) Daltongaunj	78	69.2	30.8
Total Catchment Area		**681**	**53.02**	**46.98**

Source: District Census Hand books, Census of India-1991.

possess any school facility. This signifies that school facility is not only in-operational but also inadequate, thereby pushing children to enter labour market. Thus provision of schools (both formal and non-formal) should be given top most priority, if children are to be protected from entering into carpet weaving.

The study area had 125 NFE Special Centres located. The core zone had 22 NFE special centres, 73 in peripheral zone, 29 in Catchment zone and 1 Vocational rehabilitation centre in New Delhi. (Refer Table 6.1) Thus the distribution of NFE Special Centres is comparatively less than the required, as the magnitude of villages without school facility is extremely high in the area. NGOs concentrating in Core areas were, RUGMARK, Children Eradication and Welfare Society, Manav Sansadan Avam Mahila Vikas Sansthan, Swami Vivekananda Shiksha Samiti (SVSS), Project Mala, Bachpan Bacchao Aandolan (BBA) and CREDA. Peripheral areas were served by Project Mala, CREDA, BBA, Ankur Foundation, Gramodaya Sansthan, Yuva Vikas Sansthan, Samangra Gramin Vikas Kendra, Children Welfare Society, Sampurna Gramin Vikas Sansthan, Bandua Mukti Morcha and SVSS. Catchment areas, which presently are being exploited by middlemen/agents for the supply of bonded child labour are only served by NGOs funded by REHA (Germany). The NGOs concentrating in these areas are Arpan Gramin Vikas, Kosi Sewa Sadan and SAMUDAYA. (Table 6.3).

Fig. 6.0 Mirzapur-Bhadohi Carpet Belt (1991)
%Villages-schools facility

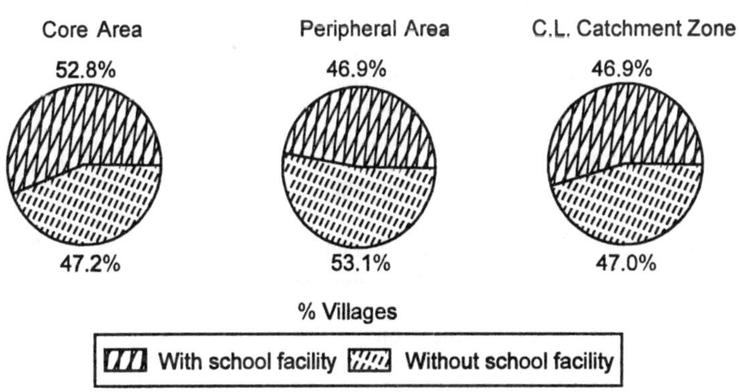

Table 6.3 Non-formal Education Special Centres Distribution (Block wise/NGO wise) 1997–98

Block	*NGO*	*Number NFE Centres*	*Number of NFE Centres selected for Survey*
Core Areas			
Bhadohi	1. Manav/Sansadan Avam Mahila Vikas Sansthan (MSAMVS)	1	1
	2. Children Eradication & Welfare Society (CE&WS)	2	1
Gyanpur	1. Bachpan Bacchao Aandolan (BBA)	1	–
	2. RUGMARK	2	1
Sewapuri	1. Project Mala	1	1
	2. MSAMVS	2	1
Kon	2. Swami Vivekananda Shiksha Samiti (SVSS)	3	3
Lalganj	1. CREDA	7	–
	1. BBA	2	1
	2. CREDA	1	1
Total Core Area	**22**	**10**	
Peripheral Areas			
Hallia	1. CREDA	3	1
	2. SVSS	2	1
	3. BBA	2	–
Marihan	1. BBA	1	–
	2. Project Mala	3	1
	3. CREDA	5	–
	4. CWS	3	1
Core Areas			
Dudhi	1. Bandua Mukti Morcha (BMM)	1	1
	2. Ankur Foundation (AF)	1	1
	3. BBA	1	1
	4. CREDA	5	2
	5. Sampurna Gramin's Vikas Sansthan	5	3
Dhorawal	1. Children Welfare Society (CWS)	13	2
Lesliganj	1. Samangra Gramin Vikas Kendra (SGVK)	4	3
Chopan	1. Ankur Foundation	17	9
Mau	1. Gramodaya Sansthan	5	3
Mohamadabad	1. Yuva Vikas Sansthan	2	2
Peripheral Areas		73	32
Catchement Area			

Maner	1. Arpan Gramin Vikas (AGV)	4	2
Bihata	1. AGV	8	4
Mahishi	1. Kosi Sewa Sadan (KSS)	4	3
Kohara	1. KSS	1	–
Rosera	1. SAMUDAYA	5	3
Bibhulipur	1. SAMUDAYA	1	1
Samastipur	1. SAMUDAYA	6	3
Cathhment Area		29	16
Delhi	1. SACCS/BBA	1	1
Total		**125**	**58**

The spatial distribution of NFE Special Centres, depicts highly concentrated pattern. Thus in order to bring other areas under NFE Special School influence, NGOs should widen its base to the new areas. The site selection of NFE Special centres, should be in the areas, which are generally not severed by govt. primary centres and where magnitude of child labour in carpet weaving is high. In fact NGOs should conduct a pilot survey to identify such areas, before locating NFE special centres.

The present survey found three instances where two or more than two NFE Special Centres are being opened in the same village by two different NGOs. The site selection of majority of NFE Special Centres is in-line with the objective like, areas with dominance of Scheduled caste/ Schedule tribe and backward population areas, without government primary school and areas located in isolated and inaccessible belts.

6.6 NFE SPECIAL CENTRES ENROLLMENT/ DROPOUTS/ATTENDANCE

Among the 58 Special NFE Centres surveyed, 3259 children were enrolled in 1997 September. This works out as 56 children per NFE Centre. Project Mala NFE Centres (Guria and Hasra) are the only centres enrolling new children every year.[9] Children enrolled per centre showed significant variations among the NGOs. Project Mala recorded highest enrollment followed by Child Eradication and Welfare Society, and Yuva Vikas Sansthan. The least enrollment was for Sampurna Gramin Vikas, Samanga Gramin Vikas Kendra, Children Welfare Society and Arpan. (Refer Table 6.4).

6.6.2 Girls Enrolment

The proportion of girls in these NFE Centres was 37%, which compared to all India level is good and significant. Most of the NGOs have been able to create conducive atmosphere in these rural areas for enrolling girls like; Arpan, Child Eradication Welfare Society, BBA, Samangra Gramin Vikas Kendra and Project Mala had enrolled very high percentage of girls in the NFE Special Centres. (Table 6.4).

Table 6.4 NFE Special Centres Enrolments

S.No	*NGO*	*NFE Centres Surveyed*	*Children Enrolled*			*% Girls enrolled*	*Children per Centre*
			Total	*Boy*	*Girls*		
1.	Project Mala	2	404*	217	187	46.28	202
2.	CREDA	4	246	226	20	8.13	62
3.	MS & MVS	2	123	78	45	36.58	62
4.	CLE & WS	1	152	74	78	51.31	152
5.	Bachpan Bacchao Andolan	2	101	52	49	48.51	50
6.	Child Welfare Society	3	97	70	27	27.83	32
7.	Ankur Foundation	10	346	185	161	46.53	34
8.	Yuva Vikas Sansthan	2	276	172	104	37.68	138
9.	Gramodaya Sansthan	3	250	167	83	33.20	83
10.	Swami Vivekananda Shiksha Samiti (SVSS)	4	313	211	102	32.58	78
11.	RUGMARK**	1	47	47	–	–	47
12.	SACCS/BBA**	1	52	52	–	–	52
13.	Arpan Gramin Vikas	6	214	104	110	51.40	35
14.	Kosi Sewa Sadan	3	251	200	51	20.31	83
15.	SAMUDAYA	7	257	139	118	45.91	86
16.	Sampurna Gramin Vikas	3	87	47	40	45.97	29
17.	Samangra Gramin Vikas	3	90	46	44	48.88	30
18.	Bandua Mukti Murcha	1	52	52	–	–	52
	Total	**58**	**3259**	**2040**	**1219**	**37.40**	**56**

* This includes the new enrolments in the year 1997–98.

** These are boarding vocational & NFE Centres, specially for children released from bondage or servitude condition, hence girls are not found in these NFE Centres.

6.6.3 Agewise Enrolment

The agewise enrolment of children in the NFE Special Centres depicts that 20% children were below 8 years of age, while 29% children were 8-10 years of age, 35% children were between 10-12 years, 12 % children were between 12-14 years and the rest 4% were above 14 years of age.

This indicates that a large proportion of siblings below 8 years also attend NFE Centres with elder brothers/sisters, who have been taken out of regular carpet weaving. Thus the objective of protecting younger children into weaving is being served. Children, who have devoted few years for carpet weaving are reluctant to attend these NFE Centres, as percentage of children above 12 years was small. However, it is encouraging to find that children between 8-12 years are encouraged for enrolment. BBA, Arpan Gramin Vikas and BMM are mostly concentrating on enrolling younger children below 8 years. (Refer Table 6.5)

Table 6.5 NFE Special Centres
Enrolled Children Sex & Age Composition

NGO	*Total Children*	*Percentage Children Age Groups*					*Percentage Sex Composition*		*Percentage Marital status*	
		<8. Yrs	*9–10 Yrs*	*11–12 Yrs*	*13–14 Yrs*	*15 +above*	*Male*	*Fem-ale*	*Marr-ied*	*Unma-rried*
1. Project Mala	6	–	16.7	83.3	–	–	50.0	50.0	–	100.0
2. CREDA	15	–	13.3	40.0	40.0	6.7	93.3	6.7	6.7	93.3
3. MS & MVS	13	15.4	53.8	30.8	–	–	69.2	30.8	–	100.0
4. CLE & WS	4	–	25.0	50.0	25.0	–	50.0	50.0	–	100.0
5. Bachpan Bacchao Aandolan	5	60.0	–	40.0	–	–	80.0	20.0	–	100.0
6. Child Welfare Society	17	17.6	29.4	29.4	17.6	5.9	82.4	17.6	5.9	94.1
7. Ankur Foundation	44	20.5	27.3	31.8	20.5	–	81.8	18.2	2.3	97.7
8. Yuva Vikas Sansthan	18	–	16.7	44.4	33.3	5.6	66.7	33.3	–	100.0
9. Gramodaya Sansthan	29	20.7	34.5	37.9	6.9	–	72.4	27.6	–	100.0
10. Swami Vivekananda Shiksha Samiti (SVSS)	32	9.4	25.0	65.6	–	–	78.1	21.9	–	100.0
11. Rugmark	5	–	20.0	60.0	20.0	–	100	–	–	100.0
12. SACCS/BBA	37	40.5	29.7	24.3	5.4	–	48.6	51.4	–	100.0
13. Arpan Gramin Vikas	13	15.4	38.5	38.5	7.7	–	38.5	61.5	–	100.0
14. Kosi Sewa Sadan	35	28.6	40.0	25.7	5.7	–	40.0	60.0	–	100.0

(Contd)

15. Samudaya	12	25.0	50.0	25.0	–	–	50.0	50.0	–	100.0
16. Sampurna Gramin Vikas	4	25.0	50.0	25.0	–	–	25.0	75.0	–	100.0
17. Samangra Gramin Vikas Kendra	7	57.1	28.6	–	–	14.3	85.7	14.3	14.3	85.7
18. Bandua Mukti Murcha	15	–	6.7	13.3	33.3	46.7	100	–	13.3	86.7
Total	**311**	**19.6**	**29.30**	**35.4**	**12.2**	**3.5**	**67.5**	**32.5**	**1.9**	**98.1**

Source: Sample Survey Conducted in 58 NFE Special Centres, September-1997 to November 1997.

6.7 SOCIAL COMPOSITION

The social composition of children enrolled in the NFE Special Centres indicates, 44% of children were scheduled castes, 36% children were from other backward Classes (OBCs), 12% children were from Scheduled tribes and the rest 6% were from higher castes. Thus, the major objective of these centres have been to cover weaker sections of Society, who are otherwise neglected in the education field. Majority of NGOs funded by REHA have achieved the objective of covering weaker and marginal sections of the Society. (Refer Table 6.6)

Table 6.6 NFE Special Centres
Surveyed Children: Social Composition

NGO	*Total Children*	*Percentage Child Religion*		*Percentage Child Caste*					
		Hindu	*Muslim*	*Brahmin/ Thakur*	*Vaisya/ Kayastha*	*SC*	*ST*	*OBC/ BC*	*Others*
1. Project Mala	6	100%	–	–	–	50.0	16.7	33.3	–
2. CREDA	15	100%	–	–	6.7	33.3	46.7	13.3	–
3. MS & MVS	13	100	–	15.4	7.7	30.7	7.7	38.5	–
4. CLE & WS	4	75.0	25.0	25.0	–	–	–	50.0	25.0
5. Bachpan Bacchao Aandolan	5	60.0	40.0	–	–	40.0	–	–	60.0
6. Child Welfare Society	17	100	–	5.9	17.6	17.6	47.1	11.8	–
7. Ankur Foundation	44	93.2	6.8	–	6.8	45.5	15.9	31.8	–

(Contd)

8. Yuva Vikas Sansthan	18	100.0	–	–	–	–	–	100.0	–
9. Gramodaya Sansthan	29	100.0	–	–	–	–	–	100.0	–
10. Swami Vivekananda Shiksha Samiti (SVSS)	32	100.0	–	–	–	81.3	12.5	6.3	–
11. RUGMARK	5	80.0	20.0	–	–	20.0	–	40.0	40.0
12. SACCS/BBA	37	94.6	5.4	–	–	62.2	–	32.4	5.4
13. Arpan Gramin Vikas	13	92.3	7.7	15.4	–	76.9	–	7.7	–
14. Kosi Sewa Sadan	35	100.0	–	–	–	71.4	–	28.6	–
15. Samudaya	12	100.0	–	–	–	91.7	8.3	–	–
16. Sampurna Gramin Vikas	4	100.0	–	–	–	–	50.0	50.0	–
17. Samangra Gramin Vikas Kendra	7	100.0	–	–	–	57.1	14.3	28.6	–
18. Bandua Mukti Murcha	15	100.0	–	–	13.3	6.7	40.0	40.0	–
Total	**311**	**96.8**	**3.2**	**1.9**	**3.2**	**44.4**	**12.2**	**35.7**	**2.6**

Source: Sample Survey Conducted in 58 NFE Special Centres, September-1997 to November 1997

6.8 DROPOUT AND ATTENDANCE RATE

Drop-out rates and attendance records of the ever enrolled children are significant to infer the quality of education provided to the children. However, these two indicators are affected by incentives provided to the children like, provision of mid-day meals and stipend. Therefore, the high drop-out rates and low attendance rates are found in those centres who do not offer incentives like mid-day meal and stipend. On the other hand drop-out rates were low in those centres which provide these incentives.

6.9 NFE SPECIAL CENTRES-BUDGET

Annual budget spent by the NGO's for the NFE centres was worked out to examine the per child per annum expenditure.[10] Expenditure incurred under various head viz; staff salary, teacher's salary, rent for school building, teaching aid materials, supplementary nutritional diet, health care, awareness campaign, travel etc; has been worked out. (Refer Table 6.7).

Table 6.7 NGO's Annual Budget Under Various Heads

NGO's Names	*Total Budget Per/ Annum*	*Enrolled Child*	*Staff Salaries*	*Teacher Salaries*	*Rent*	*Teaching Aid*	*Mid day Meals*	*Health Care*	*Camping Program awareness*	*Admi-nist ration Exp.*	*Budget Per centre Per/ Annum*	*Budget Per Child*
Ankur Foundation	573.0	600	48000	216000	15000	100000	–	–	20000	22000	28650	955
Gramodaya Sansthan	971500	200	76800	43200	–	22000	480000	–	210000	61000	242875	4857
MSAMVS	139300	250	36000	28800	9000	15000	–	–	7500	28000	464333	557
SVSS	388800	250	82800	96000	12000	12500	165000	8000	–	30000	77760	1242
SACCS/BBA	1375800	200	694000	24000	75000	–	–	240000	273800	687900	6879	
Yuva Vikas Sansthan	205000	246	30600	19200	9600	10000	120000	–	–	6000	102500	742
AGVS	466000	500	6000	88500	18000	97250	–	48000	64000	36000	466600	932
KSS	392000	250	60000	96000	–	75000	25000	49000	15000	72000	78400	1568
Samuday	710100	600	108000	158400	–	119000	180000	–	55800	70000	71010	1184
Project Mala	3190000	720	761000	40000	46000	789000	62000	–	74000	797500	4431	

Source: Data collected from NGOs.

Per child per annum expenditure was highest for SACCS /BBA i.e; Rs 6879. This includes expenditure incurred on campaigns, release of children from bondage and provision of vocational training at Mukti Ashram. SAMUDAYA NGO also spends RS. 4858 per child per annum. The per child per annum expenditure by Project Mala was Rs. 4431. Other NGO's have less budget for the NFE programme. Teachers' salary expenditure was high for Project Mala and SACCS/BBA.. The budget expenditure reflects, the priorities of the NGO. SACCS/BBA spends high proportion of budget on awareness campaigns and travel. Budget on campaigning by other NGOs did not show appropriate returns from the field study. Some NGOs have shown health care expenditure, but in the field, such facility given was limited like; in case of Kosi Sewa Sadan. Per child expenditure on the whole does reflect performance level attained by the NFE centres.

6.10 NFE SPECIAL CENTRES-ACTIVITIES AND FACILITIES

The (NPE-1986) and (NPCL-1987) envisaged Non-formal Education to provide basic primary educational, vocational training, supplementary nutrition for children, stipend for children to compensate their earnings and health care for all the children attending the NFE centres. The basic objective was to create general awareness for education and provide other child welfare programmes.

Majority of NFE special centres, under study in Mirzapur-Bhadohi carpet weaving belt, do not provide the above stated activities satisfactorily. Even the NFE Programme provided by some centres is only for 2 years. Project Mala, RUGMARK and NFE Centres funded by CEPC and IPEC have multiplicity of activities viz., NFE, vocational training, mid-day meals, stipend, uniform for children and health care for children. Other NFE centres funded by REHA (Germany) provide NFE, uncooked meals and some stipend money. Mukti Ashram (SACCS) RUGMARK School (Balashry, Gopiganj) are the only boarding centres, providing all activities and facilities to the enrolled children.

Full vocational training is provided by Mukti Ashram and four centres of Ankur Foundation. The time devoted is 24 hour per week. The vocations taught at Mukti Ashram include textile weaving, welding, motor winding, electric repairs, tailoring, and carpentry. Vocations taught at Ankur's Centres are cycle repair, wood carpentry, durry making and tailoring. Each centre provides one of the above stated vocations. Vocational training of 6 hours per week is provided, along with NFE in Project Mala and RUGMARK NFE Centres. The vocations taught at Project Mala are carpet weaving

Table 6.8 NFE Special Centers (Activities and Facilities)

NGO	*NEE Years Devoted*	*Voctional Training Vocation*	*Weekly Time Devoted*	*Boarding School*	*Mid day Meals*		*Health Care Provision*	*Stipend Monthly*	*Uniform*	*School bags*
					Cooked	*Uncooked*				
1. Project Mala	3Years	CW/TAL	6Hours	–	Yes	–	Good	Rs 100*	Yes	Yes
2. CREDA	3Years	TAL	6	–	Yes	–	Poor	Rs 100	yes	No
3. MS & MVS	2 Years	–	–	–	–	–	–	–	–	–
4. CLE & WS	2 Years	–	–	–	Yes	–	Poor	Rs 100	Yes	–
5. B.B.A.	2 Years	–	–	–	–	–	–	–	–	–
6. Child Welfare Society	3Years	–	–	–	–	–	Poor	–	–	–
7. Ankur Foundation	3Years	CR/DW/ WCXX TAL	24	–	–	–	–	–	–	–
8. Yuva Vikas Sansthan	2 Years	–	–	–	–	–	–	–	–	–
9. Gramodaya Sansthan	3Years	TAL@	6	–	–	Yes@	–	100@	–	–
10. SVSS	2 Years	–	–	–	–	Yes@X	–	35	–	–
11. Rugmark	3Years	CW/TAL/ WC/MI/SC	6	YesA	Yes	–	Good	–	Yes	Yes
12. SACCS/BBA	3Years	–	–	–	–	–	OK	3D	–	–
13. Arpan Gramin Vikas	2 Years	–	–	–	–	–	–	–	–	–
14. Kosi Sewa Sadan	3YearsE	–	–	–	–	–	–	–	–	–
15. SAMUDAYA	2 Years	–	–	–	–	–	–	–	–	–
16. Sampurna Gramin Vikas	2 Years	–	–	–	–	–	–	–	–	–
17. S. G. V. K.	2 Years	–	–	–	–	–	–	100	–	–
18. B. M. M.	2 to 6 Months Z	TX/MR/ WIT-AL/WL	24	YesA	Yes	–	Good	(8)	–	Yes

Note: CW: Carpet Weaving, TRA: Tailoring, WC: Wood Craft Carpentry, CR: Cycle repair, DW: Durry weaving, WT: Welding, MR: Motor rewinding, TX: Textile Machine, SC: Screen Machine, MT: Music.

*Rs 100 is set aside as Rehabilitation fund to be given after completion of NFE.

**Ankur Foundation gives, only vocational training at four centres viz; Cycle Repairs/Durry weaving/Wood Carpentry/Tailoring.

@Gramodaya provides tailoring vocational/uncooked meal and Rs 100 stipend only in one centre (Balapur) and tailoring. Advance carpet weaving training centre has been recently started at Guria school of Project Mala. Looms have been scientifically modified to suit the working postures. Such looms could provide significant inputs for development of carpet weaving scientifically in the belt. RUGMARK School (Balashry at Gopiganj) teaches carpet weaving, screen making, music, wood carpentry and tailoring. One centre of Gramodaya Sansthan teaches tailoring.

Cooked midday meals are provided at NFE centre of Project Mala and Some Centre of CREDA,[11] CLE & WS, Bandhua Mukti Morcha, and one NFE centre of Gramodaya Sansthan. Provision of health care was extremely poor in majority of NFE Centres except for Project Mala, RUGMARK and Mukti Ashram. They maintain regular health cards for the enrolled children and regular visits by doctors are ensured. Arpan Gramin Vikas also provides basic health check-up and awareness to the children and their parents. Uniform and school bags are also supplied by few NFE Centres. Uniform is only provided by Project Mala, CLE & WS and RUGMARK. (Refer Tab No.6. 8). Mukti Ashram, after the completion of vocational training supplies, tool kits to the outgoing adults for starting self employment. This scheme has been applauded by adults and has helped them to earn for themselves. Project Mala also maintains rehabilitation fund for the enrolled children (Rs 100 per month per child) and gives the fund after the completion of NFE, so that they can start their own work. Children enrolled in formal centres are provided all necessary school expenditure by the NGO. (Refer Table 6.7)) Adult education programme is undertaken by Guria Centre of Project Mala. The programme has invoked good response from the community. It has improved the child/teacher/ parent contacts. Perhaps high attendance rate and lower drop-out rates could be also attributed to adult education programme.

6.11 NFE SPECIAL CENTRES-INFRASTRUCTURE

If the NFE Special Centres are to attract and retain children, the infrastructure in terms of building, basic amenities, teaching aids, sports equipment and school environment must be provided satisfactorily. Due to initial heavy capital investment, majority of centres in India lack basic infrastructure facilities.

In a survey conducted by Ministry of education, 40% centres have no pucca building, 9% have no building at all, 40% have no black-boards, 60% have no drinking water, 70% have no library facilities, 53% without play grounds, 89% lack toilets and 35% have only single teacher to teach three or four different classes. Many of these centres remain without any teacher for varying periods of time. Even teachers are sub-contracted for teaching work.[13]

The study conducted for the NFE Special Centres in Mirzapur-Bhadohi belt, depicts the following results (Table No.6. 9)

i) Nineteen per cent Centres have pucca building, 10% centres semi-pucca and 71% centres kutcha building. Pucca building are only in centres of Project Mala, CREDA, RUGMARK and at Mukti Ashram.

ii) Only 12% buildings were self owned and the rest were on rent. Again self owned building were mostly centres owned by Project Mala, CREDA, RUGMARK and SACCS/BBA.

iii) Fifteen per cent Centres had no building, the classes were held in open fields. During extreme heat, cold and rainy season, no classes were held.

iv) On an average each centre had 1.5 rooms. Two to three classes are taught simultaneously in each centre. Two classes are made to sit side by side and taught different courses. This diverts the attention of the students. On the contrary Project Mala centres had 6 rooms, RUGMARK 11 rooms[14] and Mukti Ashram 8 rooms.

v) Classes are generally held is the open fields, as rooms are congested and extremely small to accommodate all children. Therefore in majority of centres, classes are not held during rainy days and extreme weather conditions.

vi) Ventilation is very poor in majority of centres and is not fit for the teaching environment. Some rooms are only fit for live stocks.

vii) Only 32% centres have play grounds and 52% centre have drinking water facility. Toilet facility was only available in centres of Project Mala, RUGMARK and Mukti Ashram.

The NFE special school infrastructure facilities are poor in majority of the centres. It is important that one time grant for the basic infrastructure is given to NGOs, so that the centres are attractive for the children. In fact surroundings around the majority of centres are not conducive for NFE education. Stagnant water pools breeding mosquitoes were found in front of some NFE centres. Therefore adequate attention must be provided to site selection of NFE Centres. Local community/Panchayats must be involved, so that proper building is earmarked for the NFE Centres.

Table 6.9 NFE Special Centers Infrastructure (Based on field Survey)

NGO	*Nature of building*			*Building ownership*		*% NEE Centres without building*	*Number of Rooms per centre*	*Sitting Arrangement*	*Room light*	*% Play ground*	*% of centres with drinking water facilities*
	Pucca	*Semi Pucca*	*Kutcha*	*Own*	*Rented*						
1. Project Mala	100	–	–	100	–	Nil	6	Mats & table	Good	100	100
2. CREDA	100	–	–	–	100	Nil	2	Tat pati	OK	80	80
3. MS & MVS	–	–	100	–	100	Nil	1	Tat pati	OK	70	100
4. CLE & WS	–	50	50	75	25	Nil	2	Tat pati	OK	20	100
5. Bachpan Bacchao Aandolan	50	50	–	–	100	Nil	1	Tat pati	Poor	20	100
6. Child Welfare Society	–	–	100	–	100	Nil	1	Tat pati	Poor	20	60
7. Ankur Foundation	–	30	70	–	100	40	1	Open air & Tat pati	V.Poor in some	30	30
8. Yuva Vikas Sansthan	–	50	50	–	100	Nil	2	Open air & Tat pati	OK	50	50
9. Gramodaya Sansthan	–	25	75	25	75	30	1	Open air & Tat pati	Poor	30	60
10. Swami Vivekananda Shiksha Samiti (SVSS)	25	–	75	25	75	25	1	Open air & Tat pati	Poor	50	50
11 RUGMARK	100	–	–	100	--	Nil	14	Table & Chairs	Good	100	100

12. SACCS/BBA	–	25	75	–	110	50	1	Open air & Tat pati	OK	50	50
13. Arpan Gramin Vikas	25	–	75	25	75	50	1	Open air & Tat pati	Poor	25	25
14. Kosi Sewa Sadan	25	25	50	25	75	25	1	Open air & Tat pati	Poor	50	50
15. SAMUDAYA	–	–	100	–	100	50	1	Open air & Tat pati	Poor	–	–
16. Sampurna Gramin Vikas	–	–	100	–	100	50	1	Open air & Tat pati	Poor	–	–
17. Samangra Gramin Vikas Kendra	–	100	–	–	100	Nil	1	Tat pati	V. poor	100	100
18. Bandua Mukti Morcha	100	–	–	100	–	–	8	Chair/Tab	Good	100	100
Total	19	10	71	12	88	15	1.5			32	52

Source: Field Survey.

6.12 NFE-SPECIAL SCHOOL-TEACHERS

Teachers are the key to education. They often represent the only positive role model, which children talk about for future. One pre-requisite of a successful education programme is the teaching methods and techniques adopted by teachers. The high drop-out/push-out rate is the outcome of improper teaching staff, who lack basic teaching skills. Therefore right choice of teachers selection and regular in- service up-grade through training programmes are basic key to a successful NFE programme. The methods of teaching have to be joyful, demonstrative and participatory. Rigid traditional teaching methods must give way to child-centred approaches.

Children must enjoy education, if it is to have a powerful effect. Unfortunately, most of the educational programmes suffer due to less attention given for the recruitment of teachers. Wages given to teachers are exceptionally low. Many of them are forced to abandon teaching, or take second or even third job to survive. Teachers need to be retrained or replaced, if the education imparted is not relevant to children's needs. Teacher/children ratio also needs proper guidelines. High Teacher/Children ratio may not provide sufficient required guidance to the children. The regular practice of teaching two different batches of students at the same time will also be counter productive for the education programme.

> Shri Sopadilal (B.A.) was teaching in a private primary school at Mirzapur and had to travel 20 kms up and down everyday. The salary paid was meagre and could hardly make two ends meet. An advertisement by CWS for teaching in one of the their NFE centres changed his future. He was selected and asked to go though a training programme of 4 weeks. The training programme changed his whole out look. The methods learnt at the training centre helped him to teach better to the NFE children. He is now rated as one of the best teachers. He explains things through practical demonstration. He explains, various skills to the children within a natural set up. Children are attentive. He encouraged participatory education. He is now certain that his method of teaching earlier was boring and defective. He suggests that making teaching a joyful activity depends a lot on the methods of teaching and usage of teaching materials and tools. He feels push out rates/Drop-out rate are to a large extent due to defective teaching. If a student does not come to school three to four days continuously, he makes it a point to visit the parents of the child and enquire about the reason for his absence. This helps to create a good rapport with the parents.

The 58 NFE Special Centres have recruited 151 staff (both teachers and Supervisory Staff) member. However majority of NFE centres had one or two staff members per centre. Total teaching staff excluding vocational teachers were 103 is these 58 NFE centres, registering an average of 1.77 teachers per centre. The NFE centres of Mukti Ashram, RUGMARK, Project Mala and CLE & WS have 5 or more teaching staff per NFE centre. Teacher/Child ratio was extremely low in Mukti Ashram and Balashray (RUGMARK). These two centres are providing NFE and vocational training to only released children from bondage. Therefore intake of children is limited.

Project Mala NFE centres take students regularly on year to year basis. All other NFE centres have only one batch of students. Sex ratio of the teaching staff was 43 female teachers per 100 male teachers. However centres of Project Mala, YVS, Ankur and Arpan have significant female teachers also. Vocational teaching staff was only available at centres of Project Mala, CREDA, four centres of Ankur, RUGMARK and Mukti Ashram. (Refer Tab No.6.10)

The teaching staff available and Teacher/Child ratio, reflects that several NFE centres funded by REHA needs more recruitment of teachers. At least 2 teacher per NFE centre with 50 children each must be maintained as a norm to cater properly for the children's needs.

6.12.1 NFE-Special Centres-Teaching Staff Education Levels

The experience of several NFE centres throughout the country have shown that even with a low level of formal education of the teachers but with sufficient in-service training has helped to create proper education environment. It is difficult to find highly qualified formally educated teacher in these isolated and far flung areas, as the present wages paid to them are very low. Therefore teachers with minimum formal education level, but trained properly are necessary for the successful NFE Programme.

Sixty two per cent teachers were educated up to 10+2 levels, twenty three per cent teachers up to graduation level and fiftan per cent above graduation level. Only seventeen per cent teachers were either experienced or trained, at the time of recruitment and fourty one per cent have joined at least one short term teacher's training course. The distribution pattern of education levels and training attained by the teachers among the NFE Centres, varied from NGO to NGO. The NFE Centres funded by REHA have provided in-service training to some teachers, while 40 to 50 teachers were neither trained nor did they receive any training.

Table 6.10 NFE Special Centers Staff Pattern

NGO	*Total Centres*	*Total Staff*		*Teaching Staff*		*Vocational Staff*	*Teaching staff per centre*	*Vocational staff per centre*	*Children per teacher*
		Male	*Female*	*Male*	*Female*	*Male*			
1. Project Mala	2	12	9	6	6	4	6	2	25
2. CREDA	4	8	2	8	2	4	2	1	17
3. MS & MVS	2	–	2	–	2	–	1	–	62
4. CLE & WS	1	7	1	5	–	–	5	–	31
5. Bachpan Bacchao Aandolan	2	2	–	2	–	–	1	–	51
6. Child Welfare Society	3	13	3	6	–	–	2	–	16
7. Ankur Foundation	10	10	5	6	5	4	1.1	0.40	23
8. Yuva Vikas Sansthan	2	1	3	1	3	–	2	–	69
9. Gramodaya Sansthan	3	5	–	5	–	–	1.66	–	50
10. Swami Vivekananda Shiksha Samiti (SVSS)	5	9	1	9	1	–	2	–	39
11. RUGMARK	1	11	6	6	1	3	7	3	4
12. SACCS/BBA	6	–	6	–	6	–	1	–	36
13. Arpan Gramin Vikas	3	4	1	4	1	–	1.66	–	50
14. Kosi Sewa Sadan	7	4	3	4	3	–	1	–	37
15. SAMUDAYA	3	3	–	3	–	–	1	–	29
16. Sampurna Gramin Vikas	3	3	–	3	–	–	1	–	30
17. Samangra Gramin Vikas Kendra	1	3	1	1	1	–	2	–	26
18. Bandua Mukti Morcha	1	12	1	3	–	4	7	4	5
Total	58	107	44	72	31	19	1.77		31

Table 6.11 NFE Special Centres
(Teaching Staff Education Levels)

NGO	*Total Teachers*	*Teachers Education Level %*			*Teachers %*		*Teachers attended short training %*
		Up to 12	*Up to B.A*	*Above B.A*	*Trained*	*Untrained*	
1. Project Mala	12	58	33	9	42	58	25
2. CREDA	10	50	50	-	20	80	50
3. MS & MVS	2	50	50	-	50	50	-
4. CLE & WS	5	60	-	40	-	100	-
5. Bachpan Bacchao Aandolan	2	50	-	50	-	100	-
6. Child Welfare Society	6	83	17	-	17	83	67
7. Ankur Foundation	11	91	9	-	-	100	27
8. Yuva Vikas Sansthan	4	100	-	-	-	100	75
9. Gramodaya Sansthan	5	60	20	20	-	100	75
10. Swami Vivekananda Shiksha Samiti (SVSS)	10	40	10	50	20	80	40
11. RUGMARK	7	29	42	29	29	71	43
12. SACCS/BBA	5	60	-	40	-	100	40
13. Arpan Gramin Vikas	6	100	-	-	-	100	-
14. Kosi Sewa Sadan	7	86	14	-	-	100	-
15. SAMUDAYA	3	100	-	-	-	100	100
16. Sampurna Gramin Vikas	3	100	-	-	-	100	-
17. Samangra Gramin Vikas Kendra	2	75	25	-	25	75	-
18. Bandua Mukti Murcha	7	25	50	25	100	-	100
Total	**103**	**62**	**23**	**15**	**17**	**83**	**41**

* Mukti Ashram teachers teach general awareness to the released children. The teaching programme is for 2 to 6 months.

REHA (India) have so far organised two in-service teachers training courses for the teachers. The training given was found useful and appropriate.

The NFE Centres of Project Mala, RUGMARK and Mukti Ashram have recruited high proportion of trained or experienced staff and regular training is being provided by trained professionals from NCERT/State Training Institute or District Training Institutes.

The results of the study depict, that training to recruited teachers must be given top priority, as still sixty per cent teachers in NFE centres are without adequate training. Again the training courses should be organised by competent authority, who have wide ranging experience. Staff from NCERT and State Training Institutes, should be engaged. The funding agencies should ensure proper in-service training of teachers and this condition should be made mandatory for the release of further funds. Several NFE centres, still follow old and traditional teaching methods which are boring and encourage drop out/push out rates.

Training is one of the important component envisaged in the NFE scheme. Paradoxically, the training component was lacking in the implementation process. It is rare to find teachers who have been specially trained for NFE programme. The question of commitment and renunciation is problematic. Impulsiveness, hyperactivity, deficit attention disorders, poor speech pattern, inconsistency are familiar to teacher without basic training or in-service training. There are no easy remedies, though flexibility, creativity, humour, patience and a variety of curriculum based activity can help. Training is an essential ingredient to improve their ability.

6.13 NFE SPECIAL CENTRES CURRICULUM

The curriculum adopted and subjects taught in the NFE centres were diverse and ranging from basic skills of counting, alphabets learning to reading skills and numeric skills. Majority of NFE Centres were following self devised curriculum by the teachers and basic books on counting, and learning Hindi language. Environmental science and general knowledge awareness was restricted to few NFE Centres only.

Project Mala Centres were following Minimum Learning Levels devised by NCERT for the Non-formal Education. Other Centres of RUGMARK, CREDA, CLE & WS, CWS were following Uttar Pradesh Board curriculum for Primary Centres. Majority of NFE Centres funded by REHA were following self devised basic level curriculum to teach basic skills of counting, learning and alphabets.

Subjects taught also varied from NGO to NGO. Project Mala emphasised on maths, hindi, environmental science, spiritual learning and general health and hygiene related knowledge. (Refer table 6.12)

Table 6.12 NFE-Special Centers Curriculum Adopted

NGO	*NFE Years of teaching*	*Curriculum Adopted*	*Subjects taught*	*Time Devoted per day*	*Stationery /Books supplied*
Project Mala	3 Years	MLL (NCERT)	Maths, Language, General Science	6	Books, Note books, pen, pencil
CREDA	3 Years	U.P. Board	Maths, Language, General Science	6	Books, Note books, pen, pencil
CLE & MVS	2 Years	U.P. Board	Math, Eng., Hindi	6	Books, Note books, pen, pencil
CLE & WS	3 Years	U.P. Board	Math, Environment, Hindi	6	Book, Notebook, pen, Slate.
BBA	2 Years	Up to teacher	Maths, Hindi	4	Books, Notebooks
CWS	3 Years	U.P. Board	Maths, Environment Science, Hindi	4	Books, Slate, Notebooks
Ankur	3 Years	Up to teacher	Maths, Hindi (only basics)	4	Slates, Books
YVS	2 Years	Up to teacher	Maths, Hindi (only basics)	4	Nil
Gramodaya	3 Years	U.P. State Board	Maths, Hindi, Social Science	6	Books, Notebooks
SVSS	2 Years	Self devised by NGO (Monthly work sheet given)	Maths, Hindi	4	-
RUGMARK	3 Years	U.P. Board	Maths, Hindi, Environment, G.S.C	6	Books, Stationary, Pen, Pencil, Slate
Arpan	3 Years	Self devised	Maths, Hindi, Environment, G.S.C	4	Slate and few books
KSS	2 Years	Self devised up to teacher	No particular Books followed	4	Nil
SAMUDAYA	3 Years	Self devised up to teacher	Maths, Hindi, No particular books followed	4	Books, Slates
Sampurn Gramin Vikas	2 Years	Basic Skills only	Counting, alphabets, tables	2	Books, Slates
Samangra Gramin Vikas	2 Years	Basic level only	Counting, alphabets, tables	2	Books, Slates, Notebooks
BMM	2 Years	Basic only	Maths/Hindi	4	Notebooks, Pen, Pencil
SACCS/BBA	3 Months	Basic only	Maths, General Science, Awakens (Basic only)	2	Notebooks, Pen, Pencil

The curriculum followed and subjects taught in majority of NFE Centres lacked, proper guidance from NGOs and everything was left up to teachers initiative. In the absence of trained teachers, and lack of proper guidance, the effective NFE teaching programme was suffering. This requires immediate attention from NGOs and funding agencies as the purpose of NFE is self defeating without appropriate curriculum followed. Basic education should be one component of education curriculum. Other aspects should include, environment, basic human needs, training ensuring self esteem like; crafts, SUPW, games, singing, story telling, basic hygiene and knowledge of laws governing children. The curriculum on these subjects were found very weak in majority of NFE Centres, except for centres of Project Mala, RUGMARK, SVSS and Arpan.

Although majority of centres, do provide basic books, slates and stationery, but these items are provided only once in the beginning of the term. Children enrolled at later stages do not possess these stationery items.

6.14 NFE-TEACHING AIDS AND METHODS ADOPTED

NFE special centres have adopted several teaching aids and methods to inculcate the educational levels. Project Mala and RUGMARK Centres have adopted varied aids and methods. Practical demonstration, out door surveys, remedial classes for children, constant usage of charts, and posters are significant features. These teaching aids, have shown positive impact on the children's educational understanding. The NFE centres funded by REHA, IPEC and CEPC have been using black boards, charts and posters to explain and teach the children. However majority of NFE Centres, still follow the traditional and unimaginative methods of education. Teachers with in-service training courses, were trying to adopt the new techniques. Students were found attentive and engrossed in these classes, where practical demonstration of skills were shown. (For example weights and measures in Guria School of Project Mala was practically illustrated through weighing scales. The children were found enthusiastic to grasp the skills). Other methods followed were group discussions, out door tours, group songs and encouraging questions from children. (Refer Table 6.13)

Humour is an important teaching tool. If a child can begin to see the funny side of bad situations, he can often find his way out of it. So joyful teaching methods should be encouraged. Motivation is also a powerful aid to generate attention from students. To increase motivation, teachers should set up goal in the mind of children. The learning should be related to local living conditions and aspects around the child. Text books may not be an ideal teaching tool. A series of booklets, containing demonstrative pictures could make learning more interesting.

6.15 SKILL TEST PERFORMANCE

During the decade 1990-2000 there have been considerable efforts to bring learning achievements under systematic investigation.

Table 6.13 Teaching Methods/Aid Adopted

NGO	*Teaching Aids/Methods used*
1.	Black-board, Charts, Posters, Practical demonstrations, Out door survey, Group song, Reading books, Environmental field surveys. Group discussion, Encouraging question from children, Remedial teaching classes, Class tests, Sports, Library, Music.
2.	Black-board, Charts, Poster, Group songs, Rigid & traditional methods, Sports
3.	Black- board, Poster, Charts, Book reading, Sports
4.	Black- board, Charts, Story reading, Group songs, Sports
5.	Black-board, Charts, Posters, Book reading, Group songs, General child labour awareness, Sports
6.	Black-board, Charts, Book reading, Sports
7.	Black-board, Charts, Book reading, Rigid & Traditional methods
8.	Black-board, Charts, Book reading, Group songs, General child labour awareness
9.	Black-boards, Charts, Book reading, Group songs, Posters, Sports
10.	Black-boards, Book reading, Charts, Posters, Group songs, Plays, Environmental out door surveys, Sports, Drill
11.	Black-boards, Book reading, Practical demonstration, Out door surveys, Group songs, Plays, Environmental surveys, Group discussion, Regular tests, Remedial classes. Sports activities, Drill, Music, Library.
12.	Black-board, Book reading, Practical demonstration, Group songs, Sports Book reading
13.	Black-board, Charts, Book reading.
14.	Black- board, Charts, Poster, Book reading
15.	Block-board, Charts
16.	Black-board, Charts
17.	Black-board, Charts, Poster, Book reading, Practical demonstration, Group songs, Sports, Drill, Music, Play, Out door trips, Environment projects.

In an earlier study conducted by NCERT in 1992-93, in 46 low literacy districts across eight states, result showed;[16]

i) Among class V students, the maximum student achievement was 20 out of 40 in word meaning and 17 out of 44 in reading comprehension.
ii) Learning achievements in mathematics were even lower than in reading. More than four-fifth of the students studying in class IV or V, could not achieve a minimum score of 40 percent. Jacob Aikara Conducted a study in 1997 in four states to assess the levels of learning achievements in language, Mathematics and Environment studies.[15]

Table 6.14 Teachers Assessment
(Method adopted to test Children learning Skill)

NGO		*Observation*	*Weekly/Monthly Six Monthly Test*
1.	Project Mala	–	100.0
2.	CREDA	12.5	87.5
3.	MS & MVS	74.5	25.5
4.	CLE & WS	..	100.0
5.	Bachpan Bacchao Aandolan	33.3	66.6
6.	Child Welfare Society	–	100.0
7.	Ankur Foundation	25.0	75.0
8.	Yuva Vikas Sansthan	50.0	50.0
9.	Gramodaya Sansthan	50.0	50.0
10.	Swami Vivekananda Shiksha Samiti (SVSS)	–	100.0
11.	RUGMARK	50.0	50.0
12.	SACCS/BBA	35.7	64.3
13.	Arpan Gramin Vikas	100.0	–
14.	Kosi Sewa Sadan	100.0	–
15.	SAMUDAYA	100.0	–
16.	Sampurna Gramin Vikas	–	100.0
17.	Samangra Gramin Vikas Kendra	–	100.0
18.	Bandua Mukti Murcha	25.0	75.0
	Total	**38.7**	**61.3**

In order to examine and assess the skills learned by children in the selected NFE centres, a skill test was conducted, covering skills related to understanding, arithmetic, general awareness, civic sense, environmental science, history and geography of local area, language reading and language writing. Simple age appropriate and learner specific questions on the above aspects were prepared keeping in view the local and community understandings. The selected children were asked to write the anowers on separate sheets. (See in set answer sheets). Reading tests along with verbal questions-answers were also conducted.[17]

The results of the tests conducted by the research team established that;

i) only 11% children have good level of understanding 39% were O.K in understanding and the rest 49% were poor

ii) Arithmetic skills were good only for 13% children, where as it was poor for 34% and O.K. for 53%.

iii) General knowledge skills were poor-for 60% children and O.K for 34% children

iv) Civic sense skills were comparatively better, probably due to regular infusion of these values by teachers.

v) Environmental Science skills were found extremely poor for 83% children, where as 15% children were found O.K in this skill.

vi) The knowledge of local history and geography was also found below the mark for majority of children.

vii) The reading and writing skills were found better among majority of children.

The performance of boys and girls did not show significant variations. In fact girls scored better in terms of reading, writing and environmental science skills. Boys performed better in arithmetic and general understanding. Performance of other skills was similar between boys and girls.

The results of the test varied among the NFE centres. Majority of children from Project Mala centres scored either good or satisfactory Rank is based on the number of skill tests. It establishes a clear relationship between levels of understanding and infrastructure, teachers training and methods adopted for teaching. Civic sense skills were found exceptionally good in the NFE centres of Project Mala and RUGMARK, establishing significance of missionary teaching among the children.

Table 6.15 Survey as Assessment: Learning Assessment

NGO	*Skill learnt & level of understanding*			*Arithmetic Skill*			*General Knowledge*			*Civic Sense Skill*		
	Good	*OK*	*Poor*	*Good*	*OK*	*Poor*	*Good*	*OK*	*Poor*	*Good*	*OK*	*Poor*
1. Project Mala	80	20	-	50	50	-	-	100	-	100	-	-
2. CREDA	20	80	-	53.3	46.7	-	40	46.7	13.3	46.7	13.3	40.0
3. MS & MVS	-	23.1	76.9	-	45.5	54.5	-	7.7	92.3	-	9.1	90.9
4. CLE & WS	-	100	-	25	75	-	-	75	25	-	50	50
5. Bachpan Bacchao Aandolan	-	-	100	-	75	25	-	50	50	-	25	75
6. Child Welfare Society	35.3	7.6	47.1	35.3	5.9	58.8	11.8	17.6	70.6	11.8	64.7	23.5
7. Ankur Foundation	6.8	61.4	31.8	4.5	59.1	36.4	2.3	27.3	70.5	29.6	11.1	59.3
8. Yuva Vikas Sansthan	5.6	33.3	61.1	5.6	33.3	61.1	-	27.8	72.2	5.6	22.2	72.2
9. Gramodaya Sansthan	-	44.8	55.2	-	48.3	51.7	-	31.0	69.0	-	-	100
10. SVSS	40	30	30.0	6.3	56.3	37.5	-	12.5	87.5	90.6	6.3	3.1
11. RUGMARK	40	-	60	40	20	40	-	60	40	40	60	-
12. SACCS/BBA	-	3.4	96.6	13.3	86.7	-	6.7	53.3	40	-	61.5	38.5
13. Arpan Gramin Vikas	41.7	41.7	16.7	46.2	38.5	15.4	15.4	30.8	53.8	23.1	23.1	53.8
14. Kosi Sewa Sadan	17.1	60.0	22.9	8.6	62.9	28.6	8.8	47.1	44.1	3.0	18.2	78.8
15. SAMUDAYA	66.7	33.3	-	-	100	-	-	-	100	-	100	-
16. Sampurna Gramin Vikas	-	100	-	-	75	25	-	-	100	-	-	-
17. Samangra Gramin Vikas Kendra	-	42.9	57.1	-	71.4	28.6	-	14.3	85.7	-	-	10.0
18. Bandua Mukti Murcha	8.3	50.0	41.7	9.1	45.5	45.5	8.3	83.3	8.3	8.3	66.7	25.0
Total	11.8	39.1	49.1	13.4	52.9	33.7	5.8	33.8	60.4	24.0	23.6	52.4

Table 6.15 (Contd.)

NGO	*Environmental Science*			*History and Geography*			*Language Spoken*			*Language Writing*		
	Good	*OK*	*Poor*	*Good*	*OK*	*Poor*	*Good*	*OK*	*Poor*	*Good*	*OK*	*Poor*
1. Project Mala	50.0	50.0	–	–	16.7	83.3	–	–	–	40.0	60.0	–
2. CREDA	6.7	13.5	80.0	13.3	–	86.7	30.0	70.0	–	30.0	70.0	–
3. MS & MVS	–	–	100	–	7.7	92.3	–	100	–	–	66.7	33.3
4. CLE & WS	–	25.0	75.0	–	–	100	75.0	25.0	–	25.0	75.0	–
5. Bachpan Bacchao Aandolan	–	–	100	–	–	100	–	100	–	–	75.0	25.0
6. Child Welfare Society	–	41.2	58.8	–	–	100	70.6	29.4	–	–	64.7	35.3
7. Ankur Foundation	–	3.7	96.3	–	22.2	77.8	29.5	61.4	9.1	25.0	63.6	11.4
8. Yuva Vikas Sansthan	5.6	27.8	66.7	5.6	72.2	22.2	5.6	66.7	27.8	5.6	55.6	38.9
9. Gramodaya Sansthan	–	–	100	–	24.1	75.9	–	79.3	20.7	–	58.6	41.4
10. SVSS	–	–	100	–	–	100	87.5	12.5	–	21.9	65.6	12.5
11. RUGMARK	–	60.0	40.0	–	20.0	80.0	60.0	20.0	20.0	40.0	20.0	40.0
12. SACCS/BBA	–	38.5	61.5	–	53.8	46.2	–	30.8	69.2	–	15.4	84.6
13. Arpan Gramin Vikas	–	15.4	84.6	–	41.7	58.3	23.1	53.8	23.1	15.4	23.1	61.5
14. Kosi Sewa Sadan	–	6.1	93.9	–	3.0	97.0	–	27.3	72.7	–	39.4	60.6
15. SAMUDAYA	–	–	100	–	100	–	–	–	100	–	100	–
16. Sampurna Gramin Vikas	–	–	–	–	–	–	25.0	75.0	–	–	100	–
17. Samangra Gramin Vikas Kendra	–	–	100	–	–	100	–	57.1	42.9	–	57.1	42.9
18. Bandua Mukti Morcha	–	58.3	41.7	–	25.0	75.0	–	83.3	16.7	–	42.9	57.1
Total	2.0	15.0	83.0	1.2	20.2	78.6	25.4	50.8	23.9	10.5	55.8	33.7

REFERENCES

[1] Weiner, Myron; (1991): *The Children and the State in India*, Oxford University Press, New Delhi.

[2] This has been one of the strategy adopted in Kerela and Himachal Pradesh, where very low school drop-out rates are matched by low incidence of child labour.

[3] National Education Policy; (1986): *A programme of Action, New Delhi.* Government of India.

[4] Anil Bordia; (1977): "*Working paper on child labour in India*", pp 11-12 & 99, Ministry of Education & Social Welfare.

[5] Ministry of Labour; (1996): Government of India.

[6] Administrative Staff College of India; (1994): *Eliminating Child Labour Through Community Mobilisation*, CREDA Efforts, Hyderabad.

[7] During our survey majority of centres were closed, due to stoppage of funds from the Labour Ministry. Hence the assessment could not be effectively studied.

[8] V.V.Giri National Labour Institute; (1996): *Towards Eliminating Child Labour*.

[9] Other NGOs enrolled children at the beginning of session for two/three years period but facilities like stipend, supply of books, mid-day meals is only given to the children officially enrolled in the beginning of the first year. Project Mala enrols new children every year. It started NFE programme in 1992.

[10] Annual budget spent by the NGO's could be ascertained only for Ankur Foundation, Gramodaya Sansthan, MSAMVS, SVSS, SACCS/BBA, Yuva Vikas Sansthan, Apran Gramin Sansthan, SAMUDAYA, and Project Mala. Information from other NGO's could not be ascertained.

[11] Due to stoppage of funds, majority of CREDA centres were closed during our field survey period.

[12] Ministry of Education Report-p36.

[13] This include rooms meant for boarding, library, staff and kitchen.

[14] Yadav, H.S. and others (2000), *Education for All,* Learners Achievement in Primary Schools, MHRD, GOI ad NIEPA.

[15] UNICEF (1996): *Progress of the States*

[16] The ratings given are

- Poor less than 40 score out of 100
- OK 40-60 score out of 100
- Good above 60 score out of 100

The results are subjective analysis of the investigators' views.

7 Non–formal Education Centres Performance Levels

7.1 NFE SPECIAL SCHOOLS-RESCUE, AND FORMAL SCHOOL ENROLMENT

The performance of NGOs in the field of NFE is also related to enrolment, rescue of children from exploitative work, completing successfully the non-formal education, enrolment of children in formal schools and providing self employment on the basis of skills learnt. 7187 children were ever enrolled for NFE by these NGOs in the carpet belt. Of these 25% of the children were enrolled by project Mala alone.

Release of migrant and bonded children was mostly accomplished by SACCS/BBA, RUGMARK and Kosi Sewa Sadan. However in the absence of proper rehabilitation schemes for these released children, it is possible that these children will be again pushed into the labour force. So rehabilitation of released migrant and bonded children should be taken up, on priority basis, so as to protect these children from entering the labour force once again.

More than 12000 children have been rescued by NGOs from exploitative work. SACCS/BBA have contributed significantly for the rescue of these children (77% children were rescued by SACCS and its affiliated NGO's) (Refer Tab 7.1)

731 children have completed NFE from these special schools, out of which 78% children were from Project Mala and 22% children from CWS. All other NGOs (except CREDA} have started NFE only in 1995-96 and have yet to complete NFE for the first batch enrolled in 1995-96. All the NGOs have contributed significantly for enroling children in formal schools. This was achieved through awareness campaigns, making parents agree to send the children back to schools, who had initially dropped out. Project Mala after completing NFE for various batches have consistently

tried to enrol the children in formal schooling, by providing school fees, stationery, books and uniform charges to the enrolled children. Significant attempts were also made by BBA and SACCS to enrol the children in formal schools. Actual results would be only seen after the NGOs complete the NFE programme for the first enrolled batches. (Refer Table 7.2).

Table 7.1 NFE Special Schools Performance-Ever Enrolment, Rescued from Work

S.No	*NGO*	*Total Children Ever enrolled in NFE*	*Total Children Rescued from Exploitative Work*	*Per cent Rescued Type*		
				Family	*Local Non-family*	*Migrant*
1.	Project Mala	1807	1807	100	–	–
2.	CREDA*					
3.	MS & MVS	71	111	10.8	80.18	9.0
4.	CLE & WS	287	287	100.6	–	–
5.	B.B.A	401	7500	–	35.0	65.0
6.	C.W.S	275	292	94.0	6.0	–
7.	Ankur Foundation	996	175	100.00	–	–
8.	Yuva Vikas Sansthan	276	177	8.47	91.53	–
9.	Gramodaya Sansthan	648	648	81.00	19.00	–
10.	SVSS	313	202	54.45	45.54	–
11.	RUGMARK	115	115	–	–	100
12.	Arpan Gramin Vikas	214	32	94.0	6.0	–
13.	Kosi Sewa Sadan	444	157	–	64.96	35.03
14.	SAMUDAYA	257	–	–	–	–
15.	Sampurna Gramin Vikas	87	250	100.0	–	–
16.	Samangra Gramin Vikas	150	150	50.0	50.0	–
17.	BMM	96	96	35.0	65.0	–
18.	SACCS/BBA**	750	7500		35.0	65.0
	Total	**7187**	**12053**			

* Data from CREDA could not be collected due to non co-operation from CREDA.

** SACCS/BBA and BBA work together.

Providing employment to the educationally weak children, now aged above 15 years after completion of NFE is acid test for success of NFE programme. The community expects immediate return after NFE in terms of job opportunity. Only four NGOs viz. (Project Mala, CREDA, RUGM-

ARK, SACCS/BBA[1] & Ankur Foundation[2]) are providing vocational training. 506 grown-up children aged above 15 years were absorbed in employment after successful completion of NFE/vocational training in these special centres. Majority of the persons had joined carpet weaving, welding, cycle repairs, carpentry etc. after achieving proper skills and understanding through these centres. Sixtyeight per cent of children had learnt these skills from *Mukti Ashram*, in New Delhi and 22% children had learnt from Project Mala. (Refer Table 7.2).

Table 7.2 NFE-Completed NFE, Joined Formal School and Entered into Employment

S.No	*NGO*	*Children completed NFE*	*% to total*	*Joined Formal School*	*% to total*	*Entered into Employment*	*% to total*
1.	Project Mala	567	78.0	155	22.0	109	22.0
2.	CREDA*	–	–			–	–
3.	MS & MVS	–	–	42	6.0	–	–
4.	CLE & WS	–	–	15	2.0	10	2.0
5.	B.B.A	–	–	56	8.0	–	–
6.	C.W.S	164	22.0	48	7.0	–	–
7.	Ankur Foundation	–	–	35	5.0	24	5.0
8.	Yuva Vikas Sansthan	–	–	66	9.0	–	–
9.	Gramodaya Sansthan	–	–	60	8.5	8	2.0
10.	SVSS	–	–	22	3.0	–	–
11.	RUGMARK	–	–	28	4.0	5	1.0
12.	Arpan Gramin Vikas	–	–	56	8.0	–	–
13.	Kosi Sewa Sadan	–	–	12	2.0	–	–
14.	SAMUDAYA	–	–	14	2.0	–	–
15.	Sampurna Gramin Vikas	–	–	6	1.0	–	–
16.	Samangra Gramin Vikas	–	–	5	1.0	–	–
17.	BMM	–	–	6	1.0	–	–
18.	SACCS/BBA	–	–	78	10.5	350	68.0
	Total	**731**		**704**		**506**	

*No data was collected due to non-co-operation from CREDA

Source: Sample Survey.

7.2 NON-FORMAL EDUCATION CENTRES: PERFORMANCE LEVELS

A multivariate analysis of all the selected NFE centres in the study area was worked out to assess and evaluate the performance of these NFE centres. 18 major indicators and 64 sub-indicators were selected to examine and analyse the performance levels. The indicator selected, covered wide range of activities (Refer Table 7.3)

Table 7.3 Level of NFE Performance Selection of Indicators and sub Indicators with Weights assigned

S.No.	*Name of Major Indicator and Sub Indicator*	*Criterion Selected with Weights*
1.	**Site Selection, Coverage and Extent**	
	i) Approach to the NFE Centre	Pucca (1), SemiPucca (2), Kutcha (3)
	ii) Existing School facility	Govt. School (1), NFE (2), No School (3)
	iii) Number of villages covered by NFE	Actual number of villages
2.	**Students Enrolment & Teacher/Student Ratio**	
	i) Total Students enrolled	Actual Number
	ii) % of Girl Students enrolled to total students	Actual percentage
	iii) % Teachers to enrolled Students	Actual Percentage
3.	**Students Admitted in formal Schools, released from work and Employed**	
	i) % Students admitted in formal schools to total enrolled	Actual Percentage
	ii) % Children released from Carpet weaving to total enrolled	Actual Percentage
	iii) % Children employed to total enrolled	Actual Percentage
4.	**Attendance & Drop-out rates**	
	i) Percentage attendance (Monthly Average)	Actual Percentage
	ii) % Drop-outs to total enrolled	Actual Percentage
5.	**Teachers Profile**	
	i) Total teachers per centre	
	ii) Education level of teachers	Up to 10+2 (1), Graduate (2), Above Graduate (3),
	iii) Training level of teacher	Trained (4), Experienced (3), In-service training (2) No training (1)

(*Contd.*)

6.	**Vocational Teaching**	
	i) Trained Vocational teachers	Trained (5), InService training (3)
	ii) Quality of Vocational training given	Good (3), OK (2), Poor (1)
	iii) Training Equipment's available	Good (5), OK (3), Poor (2)
	iv) Hours devoted for vocational training per day	Actual
7.	**Teaching Aids used**	
	i) Prepare Daily lessons	Yes (3), A bit (2), No (1)
	ii) Teaching Aids used (Black board, posters, charts)	Yes (3), Sometimes (2), No (1)
	iii) Practical Demonstration	Yes (3), Sometimes (2), Occasionally (1), No (0)
	iv) Songs taught	Yes (4), Sometimes (3), Occasionally (2), No (0)
	v) Equipment available	Yes (3), Same (2), Few (1), No (0)
	vi) Remedial Classes held	Yes (3), Sometimes (2), No (1)
8.	**Testing Methods Employed**	
	i) Conduct Regular Examinations	Yes (3), Sometimes (2), Yearly (1), None (0)
	ii) Regular copy checking	Yes (3), Sometimes (2), Nil (1)
	iii) Regular Weekly test	Yes (3), Sometimes (2), Nil (1)
9.	**Curriculum Taught**	
	i) Curriculum taught	NCERT (5), U.P. Board (3), Self devised (2), According to teacher (1)
	ii) Subjects taught (Math level)	Good (3), OK (2), Poor (1)
	iii) Language	Good (3), OK (2), Poor (1)
	iv) General Science	Good (3), OK (2), Poor (1)
	v) Environmental Studies	Good (3), OK (2), Poor (1)
10.	**Teachers Salary**	
	i) Salary of teacher (Monthly)	Above 1500 (4), 1000-1500 (3), 500-100 (2), Less than 500 (1)
11.	**Other Activities Provided**	
	i) Sports Activities	Good (3), OK (2) Poor (1)
	ii) Some useful productive work	Good (3), OK (2) Poor (1), No (0)
	iii) Craft learning	Good (3), OK (2) Poor (1), No (0)
	iv) Drill & Physical education	Good (3), OK (2), No (1)
	v) Environmental visits & field visits	Good (3), Sometimes (2), Nil (1)
	vi) Parent Teacher Meetings	Yes (3), Sometimes (2), Nil (1)
12.	**School timing & Hours**	
	i) School timing & Hours devoted	Actual hours per day

(*Contd.*)

13.	**Special Activities**	
	i) Adult Education	Yes (3), Sometimes (2), No (0)
	ii) Hostel & Boarding facilities	Yes (5), No (0)
14.	**Child Labour Awareness & Health**	
	i) Join Rallies & Participation	Yes (3), Sometime (2), No (1)
	ii) Health of Children (Surveyors personal observation)	Weight/Height/Physical injury
15.	**Facilities Provided**	
	i) Uniform	Yes (3), No (0)
	ii) School bags	Yes (3), No (0)
	iii) Book & Stationery	Good (3), OK (2), Poor (1)
	iv) Mid-day meals	Cooked (5), Uncooked (3), No (0)
	v) Stipend given	Rs. 100 (3), Rs 50-100 (2), Less 50 (1), No (0)
	vi) Vocational training Kit	Yes (5), OK (3), No (0)
16.	**Infrastructure (Building & Seating)**	
	i) Building	Good (5), O.K (4), Poor (3), V. Poor (2) No (1)
	ii) Number of rooms	Actual
	iii) Furniture	Good (5), O.K (3), Poor (1)
	iv) Seating Arrangement	In rooms (5), Sometimes (3), Open (2), Poor (1)
	v) Drinking Water	Yes (1), No (0)
	vi) Open space for play ground	Yes (5), O.K (3), Poor (1), No (0)
	vii) Ventilation	Good (3), O.K (2), Poor (1)
17.	**School Surroundings & Internal Environment**	
	i) Clean Education Centre	Good (5), O.K (3), Poor (2), V. Poor (1)
	ii) Plantation Activities	Good (5), Poor (3), No (0)
18.	**Children's Skill tests**	
	Skill test results conducted by Research team	
	i) Maths	Good (3), O.K, (2), Poor (1)
	ii) Language	Good (3), O.K, (2), Poor (1)
	iii) Vocational Skill	Good (3), O.K, (2), Poor (1)
	iv) Social Science & Environment	Good (3), O.K, (2), Poor (1)

Weights were assigned to various indicators, to give the relative importance and significance to each sub-indicator. Weights assigned was given, keeping in view the importance and prevailing levels among the centres. (In case of approach to NFE centre, weights were assigned on the basis of the principle that more the isolation and difficult the approach road, higher the weights. Similarly villages already provided with government primary school, or any other NFE centre was given lesser weights, compared to village without government school or NFE centre).

7.3 COMPOSITE INDEX

In order to work out composite index of the sub-indicators, within the major indicator, sub-indicators were made scale free, so as to obtain a composite index. Negative indicator (like percentage drop-out rate to total enrolled students) was treated separately, before working out the scale free index.[3] The scale free values were later added together to derive composite score, known as standard deviates.[4] These score measure the departure of individual observations, expressed in comparable form. Technically speaking, the standard scores are the linear transformation of the original data. The standard score of any observation is calculated as:

$$Zi = \frac{X_i - \overline{X}}{\text{s d of X}}$$

Where as Zi = Standard Score of any observation i

X_i = Magnitude of condition X for observation I territory

X = Mean

Sd. Of X = Standard Deviation of Variable

The composite index for each level of function has been worked out by the following method:

$$\Sigma Ii = Z_{ij}$$

Where as I_i = Composite Index of I level of function for territory (i).

Z_{ij} = Standard Score of i to i, Number of functions fur territory (i)

Composite index values for all the major 18 indicators selected was found separately. The composite values were grouped into four levels of performances, based on magnitude of the composite scores derived (The level of performance derived were High, Medium, Low and Very Low). (Table 7.4).

Table 7.4 Non Formal Education Centres Levels of Performance

Levels	*1* *Site Selection Coverage & Extent*	*2* *Students Enrolment and Teacher/Student Ratio*	*3* *Students Admitted in Formal School Released & Employed*	*4* *High Attendance and Low Drop-out Rates*	*5* *Teachers Profile*
HIGH	Hasra	Guria Nawada Kalan Bhogan Balashrya	Media Ka Dera Narayanpur Seelam-pur Balapur, Matiyara Guria Newada kalan Bikna Mujhera Khurd Lalli, Balashrya	Balashrya Guria Mukti Ashram	Balashrya Guria Mukti Ashram
MEDIUM	Mukti Ashram Binka Dhanlabthan Narayanpur Bhogan Bahuti Balapur Gidhya Bahpur Media Ka Dera Chukka Nawadakalan Jhataki Koylasthan Mujhera Khurd Milky, Maheshi	Mukhti Ashram Mujhera Khurd Seelempur Narayanpur Maner Mujhera Kalan Mahishi Hasra	Cheekwaheed Amva Khurd Lakhania Karsauta Binka, Bala-shrya Balapur Mura dpur Nimyacheehi Dyal Chak, Keval Seelampur, Bahpur Nawada Kalan Puri Katra Mukti Ashram Dhuma, Paniyara Parsona, Muhali Hasra	Ghabi Ghat Mujhera Kalan Puri katra Paniyara Bank Bhogan Bihata Dyal Chak Karsota Maner Gheevehi Dhuma Amva Khmd	Hasra Bhogan Nanda Kalan Lakhania Bikna Mujhera Kalam Bahuti
LOW	Ghabi Ghat Dyal Chak Bihata, Guria Nimayachee Dhuma, Bihata Bajeetpur Puri Katra Paniyara Ghee-vehi Jharia, hatiyra Longa Mithunia Lakhania Amva Khurd Jorukhad(BM)	Lalli Dhuma Bahuti Jharia Gheeve Media Ka Dera Bihata Sasachiya Matiyara Gidhya Dyal Chak Bajeet Pur Lunga Muhali Simha	Jorukhad Mujhera Khurd Mujhera Kalan Media Ka Dera Keval Gheevehi Mithunia Bahuti Dhuma Lalli Maner Mithunia Simha Ghabi Ghat	Kaval Kon Bhahpur Ramgrah Lakhamia Dhuna Jorukhad Kurian Patra Parsona Jorukhad (BMM) Kala Pahar Chakka Keval	Mujhera Khurd Puri Katra Paniyara Karsota Mattiyara Maner Bahpur Dyal Chak Narayanpur Seelampur
VERY LOW	Rest All	Rest All	Rest All	Rest All	Rest All

Table 7.4 (Contd.)

Levels	6 Vocational Teaching	7 Teaching Aids used	8 Testing Method Employed	9 Curricuum Taught	10 Teachers Salary
HIGH	Mukti Ashram Guria Balashya	Balashrya Mukti Ashram Guria Hasra	Guria Hasra Balashrya	Guria Hasra	◦ Mukti Ashram Guria Balashrya Hasra
MEDIUM	Hasra Ramgrah Chekwakeed Kon	Bhogan Bank, Bahpur Maner, Bihata Dyal Chak Bajeetpur Mujhera Kherd Bahuti	Mukti Ashram Puri Katra Nawada Kalen	Balashrya Maner Bikna Bahpur Dyal Chak Bajeetpur Mukti Ashram	Media Ka Dera Nawada Kalan Kon, Matiyara Ramgrah Lalli, Gheveehi Balapur Jarukhad
LOW	Bilura Bikna Lakhania Keval Dhuma Balapur	Puri Katra Mujhera Kalan Seelampur Narayanpur Kon Nawada Kalen Balapur	Bhogen Bahuti Bank Maner Paniyara	Bahuti Puri Katra Mujhera Khurd Media Ka Dera Balapur Mattiyara Bhogen Mujhera Kala Seelampur	
VERYLOW	Rest All	Rest All	Rest All	Rest All	Rest All

Table 7.4 (Contd.)

Levels	*11* *Other Activity Provided*	*12* *School Teaching Hours*	*13* *Special Activites*	*14* *Child Labour Awarness*	*15* *Multiple Facilities*
HIGH	Balashrya Mukti Ashram Guria Hasra	Guria, Hasra Bala Shrya Mujhera Kalan Mujhera Khurd Bahuti, Mattiyara Bhogan, Balapur Seelampur Dhuma, Kavel Lakhania, Bikna Narayanpur Media Ka Dera	Mukti Ashram Balashrya	Mukti Ashram Balashrya	Guria Hasra Mukti Ashram Balasherya
MEDIUM	Bhogan Keval Dhuma Balapur Bahuti		Guria Ghabi Ghat Jornkhad Purikatra	Puri Katra Jornkhand Koylasthan Mahishi Binka Lakhania Kavel, Bahuti Bhogan, Jhataki Narayanpur Seelampur MujheraKalan Guria, Hasra Ghabi Ghat Mujher Khurd Puri Katra Nawada kalan	Keval Dhuma Binka Lakhania Nawada Kalan
LOW	Mujhera Khurd Mujhera Kalan Media Ka Dera	Mahishi Dhaulabatan Kala Pahar Amva Khurd Paniyara			Balapur Jorukhad

Levels	*11*	*12*	*13*	*14*	*15*
	Dyal Chak Bajeet pur Bank Maner	Koylasthan Kurian Patra Muthunia, Longa Jharia,Neemayachi Nawada Kalan Puri Katra, idhya Jorukhad, Chhaka Ghabi Ghat Jhataki, Singha Sarchiya, Muhali Muradpur, Milky Bahpur Jorukhd (BMM) Bajeetpur, Maner Dyal Chak, Bank Bihata, Koksha			
VERY LOW	Rest All	Rest All	Rest All	Rest All	Rest All

Table 7.4 (Contd.)

Levels	*16* *Infrastructure Bulding*	*17* *School Surroundage Internal Environment*	*18* *Children Skill test*	*19* *Composite Index*
HIGH	Balashrya Mukti Ashram Guria Hasra	Mukti Ashram Hasra Balashrya Guria Amva	Guria Balashrya Mukti Ashram Harsa Kavel Dhuma Puri Katra	Guria Balashya Mukti Ashram Hasra Binka
MEDIUM	Nawada Kalan Lakhania Bikna Dhuma Kavel Lalli Paniyara Amva Khurd	Khud Bikna Lakhania Kavel Dhuma	Paniyara Lakhania Maner Bank Amva Khurd Balapur Bikna	Nawada Kala Lakhania Bhogen Dhuna Kavel Balapur Puri Katra Bahuti Media Ka Dera Mujhera Kalan Maner Paniyara
LOW	Balapur Parsona		Bihata Bahuti Mujera Khurd Mujera Kalan Bhogan Lalli Nawada Kalan Seelampur Karsota Mattiyara Naraya- pur Parsai Media Ka Dera Simha Muradpur Keval Gheevhi Koksha Ghabi Ghat Jorukhand Sarachiya Neemyachi Mohishi	Paniyara Maner Narayarpur Dayal Chak Bahpur Seelampur Bank Bajeetpur Matiyara Bihata
VERY LOW	Rest All	Rest	Rest	Rest

7.4 LEVELS OF PERFORMANCE

The result derived indicate, four NFE centres of Guria, Hasra, Balashrya and Mukti Ashram recorded high level of performance in the overall composite index for 18 indicators together. The composite score obtained by these four centres were high, with extremely wide gap, compared to next level of centres. 15 NFE centres recorded the next level of performance. 10 NFE centres registered low level of performance in the overall composite score, while the rest of 29 NFE centres had very low level of performance (Refer Table 7.4).

A majority of indicators, related to multiple functions, like building infrastructure, school surroundings and environment; the NFE centres of Guria, Hasra, Balashrya and Mukti Ashram ranked high in performance levels. In terms of teachers profile, teaching aids adopted, testing aids used, teachers salary and facilities and other activities, the NFE centres of Guria, Balashrya and Hasra ranked top in majority of these indicators. The vocational training's performance was found high in Mukti Ashram, Guria and Balashrya.

The performance for curriculum taught was recorded top for Guria and Hasra centres, as both these centres have adopted Minimum Levels of learning course devised by (NCERT). Balashrya, Maner, Bikna, Amva Khurd, Bahpur, Dyal Chak, Bajeetpur and Mukti Ashram recorded second level for the curriculum taught. The courses devised by these centres are either State Education Boards or self devised by teachers.

The skill test performance conducted by the research team on the selected sample students in the NFE centres, reflect high performance by Guria, Balashrya, Hasra and Mukti Ashram. These four NFE centres have also recorded high level of performance in case of teachers profile and teaching aids adopted and methods of testing tools used. Thus indicating strong correlation between teachers performance, school environment and infrastructure with students skill level test performance.

Keval, Dhuma, Puri Katra, Paniyara, Lakhania, Manèr, Bank, Amva Khurd, Balapur and Bikna recorded second highest levels in the skill test performance. Very poor levels of performance was recorded by NFE centres of Ankur Foundation, Kosi Sewa Sadan, Samudaya, Bandhua Mukti Morcha and few centre of Arpan. (Refer Table 7.4).

Site selection and coverage for NFE centres was found high for Hasra. (The centre is located in isolated area covering several villages without educational facility). Other NFE centres recording second highest level in case of this indicator were NFE centres of Gramodaya (Mau Block of

Banda District), SVSS (Bahuti, Bhogan), Kosi Sewa Sadan (Saharsa District) and Samudaya (Samastipur district).

Students enrolment, girl students enrolment and teacher/student ratio was found high in Guria, Nawada Kalan, Bhogan and Balashrya. The second level of performance for this indicator was recorded by Mukti Ashram, Hasra, Mujhra Khurd, Seelampur, Narayanpur, Maner, Mujhera Kalan and Mahesi.

High attendance percentage (Monthly Average) and low drop-out rates were found for Guria, Hasra, Balashrya, Narayanpur, Seelampur, Balapur, Matiyara, Newada Kalan, Bikna, Lalli, Bahuti and Media Ka Dera. These results indicate that in addition to inducements like mid-day meals and stipends given to children, motivation by teachers have also helped in high attendance rate and low drop-out rates. Although majority of these NFE centres do provide mid-day meals and some stipend, yet few centres without these inducements registered high performance like, Seelampur and Narayanpur of Yuva Vikas Sansthan, which provides Channa, Bananas to children.

Children admitted in formal school, were released from carpet weaving and provided some employment was found high for Guria and the vocational centres of Mukti Ashram, Kon and Ramgarh (Ankur Foundation).

The levels of performance derived from the study indicate NGOs with high funding from international donor agencies have definitely contributed for NFE development in the carpet belt. However, the performance of the NGO is also related to its mission, dedication, hard labour put by the field workers and teachers.

7.5 LEVELS OF PERFORMANCE-CORRELATION ANALYSIS

Co-efficient of correlation matrix was worked out for all the selected indicators, to examine the level of correlation and relationships among the indicators. (Refer Table 7.5)

i) Majority of the selected indicators recorded very high coefficient of correlation among themselves, which was significant at 99.9 percent level. This reflects a close association and relationship among the majority of selected indicators for providing NFE programme.
ii) Skill test performance level conducted by surveyors were highly correlated at 99.9 percent levels with majority of indicators (except for site selected and students admitted in formal schools and released from carpet weaving). This reflects that students' performance is

Table 7.5 Coefficient of Correlation Among Indicators

Correlation	*IND1*	*IND2*	*IND3*	*IND4*	*IND5*	*IND6*	*IND7*	*IND8*	*IND9*	*IND 10*	*IND 11*	*IND 12*	*IND 13*	*IND 14*	*IND 15*	*IND 16*	*IND 17*	*IND 18*	*Total*
IND1	1.000	-	-	-	-	-	-	-	-	-	-	-	-	-	-	-	-	-	.393*
IND2	.328*	1.000	-	-	-	-	-	-	-	-	-	-	-	-	-	-	-	-	.576**
IND3	-.231	-.331*	1.000	-	-	-	-	-	-	-	-	-	-	-	-	-	-	-	.277
IND4	.256	.367*	.146	1.000	-	-	-	-	-	-	-	-	-	-	-	-	-	-	.451**
IND5	.386*	.729**	.073	.299	1.000	-	-	-	-	-	-	-	-	-	-	-	-	-	.925**
IND6	.105	-.024	.568**	.060	.502**	1.000	-	-	-	-	-	-	-	-	-	-	-	-	.647**
IND7	.293	.456**	.279	.435**	.736**	.504**	1.000	-	-	-	-	-	-	-	-	-	-	-	.842**
IND8	.361*	.669**	.072	.428**	.898**	.381*	.774**	1.000	-	-	-	-	-	-	-	-	-	-	.912**
IND9	.395*	.591**	.112	.520**	.762**	.272	.749**	.845**	1.000	-	-	-	-	-	-	-	-	-	.830**
IND10	.258	.264	.425**	.470**	.620**	.639**	.695**	.641**	.523**	1.000	-	-	-	-	-	-	-	-	.770**
IND11	.392*	.607**	.126	.357*	.910**	.534**	.874**	.868**	.782**	.705**	1.000	-	-	-	-	-	-	-	.923**
IND12	.375*	.518**	-.229	.375*	.437**	-.108	.289	.471**	.521**	-.190	.353*	1.000	-	-	-	-	-	-	.405**
IND13	.165	.323*	.144	.064	.652**	.624**	.560**	.524**	.362**	.559**	.669**	.011	1.000	-	-	-	-	-	.663**
IND14	.321*	.324*	-.014	.279	.424**	.112	.456**	.412**	.426**	.354*	.421**	.353*	.432**	1.000	-	-	-	-	.476**
IND15	.323*	.479**	.276	.291	.845**	.687**	.664**	.812**	.705**	.663**	.764**	.408**	.525**	.353*	1.000	-	-	-	.916**
IND16	.259	.422**	.366*	.336*	.825**	.700**	.626**	.792**	.648**	.757**	.755**	.233	.660**	.403**	.895**	1.000	-	-	.911**
IND17	.283	.387*	.299	.146	.838**	.785**	.616**	.779**	.612**	.657**	.782**	.243	.694**	.252	.894**	.912**	1.000	-	.885**
IND18	.161	.605**	.076	.357*	.792**	.342*	.576**	.834**	.725**	.504**	.711**	.464**	.490**	.435**	.762**	.773**	.711**	1.000	.811**

closely associated with teaching quality methods employed by teacher for teaching and school environment, as well as facilities and infrastructure provided by NFE centres.

iii) Teachers profile was significantly correlated with majority of indicators related to teaching methods employed and testing methods used. This reflects strong influence of teachers efforts in inculcating quality education.

iv) Attendance and drop-out rates were also significantly correlated with performance in multiple activities and inducements in terms of mid-day meals and stipends, provided by NFE centres teachers profile, teaching aids used and curriculum taught.

The composite index was significantly correlated with all selected indicators, except for site selection, coverage and children released, admitted in formal schools and employed in self employment.

7.6 STEPWISE REGRESSION ANALYSIS

Stepwise regression analysis for two dependent variables were examined to find out the percentage explained by other selected indicators on these two dependent indicators. The dependent indicators identified were:

i) Children skill test performance levels (based on tests conducted by research team).

ii) Percentage children attending schools (monthly average) and % drop-out rates to total enrolment.

The hypothesis to be tested through stepwise regression was:

i) Children skill test performance levels are explained by teachers profile, curriculum taught, teaching aids used and school infrastructure and facilities.

ii) High percent children attendance and lower drop-out rate are dependent on multiple facilities provided by NFE centres especially mid-day meals, stipend and health care, quality of education, teaching aid adopted, vocational teaching, building infrastructure and facilities in NFE centres.

The results show that all the variable considered in selection (i) and (ii) are found to be statistically significant. The results obtained through stepwise regression proved both the hypotheses (Table 7.6) with some new indicators explaining the dependence of these two indicators.

Table 7.6 Stepwise Regression Analysis

Explained Variable Derived	*Multiple R Values*	*Percentage explained*
Dependent Variable: Children Skill Test performance (Surveyor's Test)		
1. Testing methods employees	.50.63	5
2. Building Infrastructure and facilities	.65470	20
3. Curriculum Taught	.85470	
4. Teachers Salary	.86999	1
5. Teachers Profile	.87973	1
6. Teaching aids used	.89223	2
7. Rest Indicators together	.90339	1
Dependent Variable: Percentage Attendance and drop-out Rates		
1. Facilities Provided	.460741	46
2. Curriculum taught	.52051	56
3. Teachers Salary	.57012	5
4. School Environment & surrounding	.68831	11
5. School Hours	.74260	6
6. Building Infrastructure	.76168	2
7. Vocational teaching	.80093	4
8. Rest of Indicators		

Children skill test performance level was explained largely by:

i) Testing methods employed by teachers (65%),
ii) building infrastructure (20%),
iii) teachers salary (1%),
iv) curriculum taught (1%),
v) teachers profile, (1%)
vi) and teaching aids used (1%).

This proves that regular testing methods, building infrastructure along with salary of teachers (which is highly related to teachers profile, training and methods adopted for teaching) explains the skill test performance. Thus demand and response of quality education is the result of teachers role and good infrastructure available in the NFE centres.

ii) High percentage of attendance and low drop-out rates is largely explained by facilities provided by centre, curriculum taught, teachers salary (indicating indirectly teachers motivation), school environment, school timings, building infrastructure and vocational training given in the centre. Thus multiplicity of activities like providing NFE, mid-days meals, uniform, stipend, would ensure low dropout and high attendance rates. However curriculum taught and teachers motivation, methods of teaching were also factors for improving regular attendance and decrease in drop-out rate. The involvement of NGOs activities was also found as an important component for this dependent variable.

7.7 GENERAL COMMUNITY AWARENESS

Attempts were made to examine the impact of NFE programmes, in inculcating community general awareness related to social, economic and child labour problem. Parents of the children in particular and community members in general were examined. The results of the study depicts; (Refer Table No 7.7)

Table 7.7 General Awareness Performance

i)	**Know Child Labour Act?**	
	Yes	25.7
	No	71.9
	Has heard of it	1.8
	Came to know of it as loom owner caught in the village	0.6
ii)	**Know Bonded Labour Act?**	
	Yes	17.5
	No	82.5
iii)	**Know Govt. programme for elimination of rehabilitation**	
	Yes	18.7
	No	79.5
	Not much	1.8
iv)	**Know about various Govt. schemes for rural development**	
	Yes	31.0
	No	65.5
	Has heard of it but no knowledge	3.0
	Has rough idea of it	0.5
v)	**Schemes known?**	2.9
	IRDP	5.3
	JRY	
	IAY	1.2
	Money for Daughter's marriage	0.6
	IRDP & JRY	20.5
	Not known	69.5
vi)	**Got Any Loan/Assistance from the Schemes?**	
	No	100.0
vii)	**Money given after child released**	
	No	100.0

viii) Know about Govt. loom owner are supposed to pay if your child is released from bondage ?	
Yes	9.2
No	90.1
Not much	0.7
ix) Do children work in Looms?	
Yes	37.5
No	62.5
x) Can NCLP eliminate child labour?	
No	93.8
To Some extent	6.2
xi) Reaction towards NFE centre	
Ever satisfied/happy/hope kindled	50.0
Very helpful	36.7
Have no time for child	13.3
xii) Who motivated you to take out child from loom?	
NGO Activists	83.6
No one	6.1
Just took him out	10.3
xiii) Should Child work in Carpet Weaving?	
Yes should help parents after schools	70
Yes should be allowed to work full-time	20
No work for children	10
xiv) Why don't you send children for Education	
No School Available	45
Inappropriate Education in Schools	52
Have no money to give education	3
xv) Improvement of NFE Centre	
Vocational training be started in all NFE Centre	65
Three years course should be enhanced to 5 years	75
More such centres should be opened	58

i) Majority of the respondents were ignorant about the child labour issues and steps taken by government to eradicate child labour. Respondents (72%) were ignorant about child labour act 1986 and its significant features. This shows that government machinery and the NGOs activists have not been able to campaign and create mass awareness about child labour issues. Similarly community were not aware of any government rehabilitation programmes for the release of child labour from exploitative work. However, some discernible attitudinal change in the rural comm-unity, specially among those who are decision-makers in the villages was observed.

ii) Several govt. schemes for poverty alleviation programmes have been in operation since decades. It is ironical that majority of respondents were not aware of any of these poverty alleviation schemes. 66% respondents have not heard of these schemes. Only 31% respondents were knowing that these schemes exist. These schemes seem not to be functioning. On a limited scale, some NGOs try to organise people into self-help groups through savings and credit, but the number is far below the required level. People want NGOs to play important role for pressurising govt machinery to make these government schemes operative.

iii) Knowledge of specific schemes was extremely poor among the respondents. Some respondents knew about IDRP & JRY scheme (21%). The NGOs seem to play very limited role in the general awareness and mass education programme for poverty alleviation schemes in the area. The benefits of such schemes seem to be concentrated among some section of society only. No respondent had received any loan from these schemes.

iv) None of the respondents had received any money after the child was released from carpet weaving, neither they had any knowledge about the scheme. Respondents were completely ignorant about recent Supreme Court's direction on child labour issue. Except for BBA, other NGOs were hardly concerned about the arrangement of funds for the released children.

v) A majority of the respondents were praising NGOs efforts in motivating the families for removing the children from carpet weaving. They were satisfied that adequate awareness was created among the families, highlighting the ill effects of the child labour.

vi) However majority of respondents were also of the opinion that children should be allowed to help their parents in weaving after school time and at intervals. But were against the full time child labour. They felt they were the victims of the carpet manufacturers/exporters on the one hand, and NGOs on the other hand. They were unanimous about the need for the elimination of child labour, but majority felt the efforts of government and NGOs only addressed the symptoms, and not the real issue, which is poverty, non-availability of education facilities, adult unemployment and low adult wages. They were critical of some NGOs highlighting the problem of child labour disproportionately there by harming carpet industry.

Saroj aged 12 years D/o Jaggilal belongs to Mallaha caste. Her own brother forced her to work on a carpet looms at the age of 7, on a monthly salary of Rs. 70. She accepted the carpet weaving under in-human work atmosphere as the only options before her. Fortunately due to the awareness programme by REHA, her brother agreed to send her to SVSS school at Bahuti. Today she talks confidently and is well acquainted with basic knowledge of Hindi and Maths. She even participated in cultural programmes held at Mirzapur and won several awards. She wants to pursue her education. However, she is uncertain as she feels after completing NFE at Bahuti, she may not be allowed to study further. The Govt. high school is far away from her village. Her vision is changed and looks forward to becoming teacher herself and teach the children of her village. Her revolutionary songs carries the message to fight slavery and exploitative Child Labour.

vii) A sizeable respondents blamed non availability of school facilities for not sending the children for education. Inappropriate teaching environment was indicated as major cause for not sending children to schools.

viii) Most of the respondents were extremely, happy with NFE centres run by local NGO's. They wanted more and more centres to be opened. The duration of three years period for NFE was found to be less. Majority of respondents want further education in these NFE Centres, instead of stipends. Parents are concerned that they may not be in a position to pay cost of education in the formal school after completion of NFE. They fear Children might have to return to the looms, in the absence of schools and funds to finance the expenses for education from class VI onwards.

ix) Vocational teaching in these NFE centres were highly praised. It provides viable confidence to the child to start his/her work . Rehabilitation fund after the NFE programme by Project Mala was highly acclaimed. Respondents were vehemently demanding that all the NFE centres should have voca tional training especially, Carpet weaving, Welding, Electric repairs etc. Vocational teaching after NFE for one year was major demand from the parents. The vocational training should include basic teaching of trade.

Thus NGO's efforts for starting NFE centres were acclaimed, where as awareness about child labour issues were lacking.

Jai Kumarj who is 10 years old, D/o Hariram belongs to a very poor family. Her life revolved around lack of awareness and education facility, accompanied by acute poverty. She had to work in carpet looms in her village for two years in lieu of Rs. 60 per month. Her day started at 6 A.M. She had to attend to the household chores before rushing off for carpet weaving. Initially she was asked to do cleaning of the area and prepare woollen balls. After six months she was introduced to weaving. She felt the work was boring, monotonous and tiring. The master's, strict vigil would stop her from any complaints, but in her hearts, she always wanted to go to school for education. She even once confided to her parents that she would like to go to school, but the parents refused to send her. Teachers from project Mala succeeded in making her parents agree to send her to Mala School of Guria. The parents only agreed because she would get, Rs. 100 as stipend every month. Now she is completely transformed, upright with full of confidence. Her parents, now want her to pursue her education. They feel, she is intelligent and has good grasp power in Maths. She has learnt tailoring as well. She holds her Project Mala teachers in real high esteems. She feels proud to show off her books, school bags and her work to her younger siblings and parents at home.

Shri Durgawati Namki and Kailashi, mothers of Renu and Chanpier of Village Choursi (Mirzapur) spoke about their initial reluctance in sending their children to attend NFE Centres run by BBA/and Ankur Foundation. They agreed later as the kids got hurt in looms while weaving carpets. The Children also refused to go back to the looms again out of fear that they may not be able to return for a long period. So the children were loitering all through the day without any activities. Once they joined these Schools they seemed to have changed a lot. They feel confident and are willing to continue learning in the NFE centre. The parents were now also happy to send them. But once the NFE programme will be over, they will have to continue to do the household job or will be forced to join carpet weaving in order to earn money for their sustenance of life.

7.8 CHILDREN COMPLETED NFE PROGRAMME

25 Children, who had completed NFE programme from various NGO's were selected to assess the performance. Majority of the respondents have completed NFE programme during 1994-95. Three respondents were females and 22 respondents were males. 22 respondents were from scheduled caste/schedule tribe and other backward class, where as 3

respondents were from higher castes. 21 respondents were un-married and 4 were married (Table 7.8). Sixty percent of respondents were enrolled in formal schools after NFE programme and 28% have entered into labour force. The 12% respondents were still unemployed, depending on subsidiary occupations like, agricultural labour. Those entered into labour force, 57% have joined back in carpet weaving and 14% each were employed as teachers (vocational teachers in Guria School of Project Mala), agricultural labours and in trade activities (Table 7.8 and 7.9).

Table 7.8 Children Completed NFE Programme Social Composition

NGO	*Number Children Surveyed*		*Social Composition*				*Married*	*Unmarried*
	M	*F*	*SC*	*ST*	*OBC*	*Others*		
Project Mala	2	–	2	–	–		1	1
CREDA	1	1	1	–		1	1	1
CLE &Ws	1	–	–	1	–	–	–	1
CWS	2	–	1	–	–	1	–	2
Ankur Foundation	7	–	6	1	–	–	1	6
UVS	2	2	4	–	–	–	–	4
KSS	2	–	2	–	–	–	–	2
Gramodaya	4	–	4	–	–	–	–	4
SACCS/BBA	1	–	1	–	–	–	–	1
Total	**22**	**3**	**21**	**2**	–	**2**	**3**	**22**

Source: Sample Survey conducted in October 1997 to November 1997.

Table 7.9 Children Completed NFE Programme

NGO	*Admitted in Formal School*	*Joined Work*	*Unemp–loyed*	*Main Occupation*			
				Carpet Weaving	*Teacher*	*Agri. Labour*	*Trade*
Project Mala	1	1	–	–	1	–	–
CREDA	2	–	–	–	–	–	–
CLE &Ws	1	–	–	–	–	–	–
CWS	2	–	–	–	–	–	–
Ankur Foundation	1	4	2	3	–	1	–
UVS	4	–	–	–	–	–	–
KSS	1	1	–	–	–	–	1
Gramodaya	3	–	1	–	–	–	–
SACCS/BBA	–	1	–	1	–	–	–
Total	**15(60)**	**7 (28)**	**3 (12)**	**4 (57)**	**1 (14)**	**1 (14)**	**1(14)**

Source: Sample Survey conducted in October 1997 to November 1997.

Table 7.10 Child Labour in Surveyed Looms

Block	*Total Looms*	*Total Workers*	*%Child worker to total worker*
1. Kon	85	42	11.63
2. Dudhi	10	42	16.66
3. Chopen	24	87	6.89
4. Ghrawal	1	5	–
5. Mau	57	282	4.25
Total	**177**	**777**	**8.62**

Respondents enrolled in formal schools were of the opinion that:

i) teaching aids and methods applied in formal school are different than in the NFE centres. Respondents from Project Mala and CLE & WS indicated that teaching was better in NFE centres compared to formal schools. However respondents of other NGO centres were of different opinion. They praised the formal schools.

ii) Behaviour of formal school teachers was considered good and similar to NFE school teachers according to the respondents.

iii) Children's behaviour was found better in NFE Centres, compared to the formal schools.

7.9 NFE & IMPACT ON CHILD LABOUR IN CARPET WEAVING

Non-formal Education Centres in the study area seems to have played a significant role in controlling full time child labour in Carpet weaving. A survey conducted in 177 looms of Kon, Dudhi, Chopen, Ghorawal and Mau block in October, 1997, indicates that there were only 8.62% child workers in these looms, compared to 30% estimated by various studies. This indicates that NFE programme have significantly contributed in reducing the full time child labour component in carpet weaving. However children helping parents after school hours was a common feature.

Thus the presence of education facility, appropriate to child's needs, have reduced demand for child labour. Raising school attendance and decline in child labour seems to go together. It is difficult to say, which is the effect and which is the cause.

The variation in the proportion of child labour in looms was found probably due to performance of various NFE centres. Several looms surveyed in SVSS, BBA, and Gramodya Sansthan influence zone indicated,

The story of Amai, from Maner Potna, is slightly different. An extremely cheerful and talkative eleven year old, worked in a brick klin for a meagre sum, in order to support her parents. Carrying heavy loads of bricks seemed to be the only way out to earn her bread. By sheer luck, she came across Ram Babu, incharge of Arpan Grameen Seva who wished to put her in the school. Convincing the reluctant parents to allow Amai was only possible after assuring that they would not loose their regular earnings through Amai. But instead of a brick klin, she would work as a maid to clean utencils after school. Her morning hours from 8 to 12 noon were to be spent attending the Maner City NFE school. Her life became totally transformed she was excited about her visit to Delhi organised by SACCS and Bachpan Bachao Andolan for school children. They studied at Mukti Ashram. She claims to have seen "unchi unchi building" (Tall building) and eaten "Tamatar" (tamatoes) and "achcha Khana" (good food). She enjoyed visiting Red Fort, Qutub Minar and other places. She has a good command over her Hindi languge and recites poems very well. Washing utencils after school does not dampen her spirits in the least. Given the opportunity she would love to become a teacher in the same school at Maner. She feels there's no harm in working after school in order to support the family. She the all praises for Ram Babu whom she considers as her saviour.

very high success rate. This could be related to the objectives and mission of NGO in eradicating child labour. The provision of mid-day meals, stipend, vocational training and quality education in the Project Mala schools reflected less proportion of children engaged in full time carpet weaving.

Therefore strong established positive relationship was found between NFE and decrease in child labour component in carpet weaving. Thus the NFE experiment will go a long way in eradicating child labour.

REFERENCES

[1] Mukti Ashram is the main rehabilitation centres run by BBA/SACCS for the released children through raids conducted jointly by BBA/SACCS activities with government officials.

[2] Only four centres of Ankur Foundation provide vocational trasining. These four centres do not provide NFE program.

[3] In case of this indicator mean of this observation was divided by actual observation to make the observations positive.

[4] Smith, D.M, (1977): *Where the Grass is Greener Croom Helm, London* p. 365-67.

8 Evaluation and Assessment of Local NGOs

The evaluation and assessment of the NGOs is based on the performance of the NFE schools managed by them. An extensive field survey was conducted (between August 1997 and November 1997) to secure first hand information on the functioning of the schools. A brief analysis of the NGOs surveyed is given in the following text:

8.1 MANAV SANSADAN AND MAHILA VIKAS SANSTHAN (MS & MVS)

MS & MVS has head-office located at 128 Sheodaspur, Manduadih Road, Varanasi. The NGO was formally registered in the year 1990, but has been working much before. It is a small organisation. Its basic thrust is to impart craftsmanship training in pottery to potters. Khadi-Gramudyog, CAPART, DRDA and REHA provide funds for different projects. Three NFE centres were started from June, 1996 to rehabilitate released child labour. Funds for these three centres are provided by REHA. The centres are:

1. Amva Khurd (Bhadohi Block, District Bhadohi)
2. Paniyara (District Varanasi)
3. Jogapur (District Varanasi)

(Out of the three, two centres Paniyara and Amva Khurd were surveyed during the month of October, 1997).

1. *Paniyara:* The village is 40 kilometre away from the main city of Varanasi. Bus facility to the village is not available. Only jeep facility is available from the main city to village Paniyara main road. The road is very rough. From the main road, the village is accessible only by foot. The centre has rented Pucca building with two rooms and a verandah at a rent of Rs. 250 per month. The children are given one large DURRI for seating. The school has one blackboard and few

charts. The centre provides books to the children. The books taught in Class III, IV, and V are usually prescribed by UP Education Board. The Centre does not provide any other facility like, mid-day meal, stipend, uniform, medical facility, vocational training and out-door sports.

The centre has one teacher. The teacher has long experience in teaching, as he was teaching in a high school, before joining this school. His method of teaching is different than the traditional one, which is being appreciated by the students. There are 58 children enrolled in the centre, out of them 42 were child workers especially from carpet weaving and agriculture. The people of the village are aware about the child labour problem. They give full support to the centre. However, they feel that stipend, mid-day meal and vocational training should be given to the children.

2. *Amva Khurd:* Amva Khurd village is comprised of 14 hamlets and from 5 to 6 hamlets the children are coming to the village school. The village is located on Bhadhoi- Banaras route. From the main road at Lachhapur bazaar stop, one has to travel by foot for 1 kilometre to the main village. The centre has rented one room and verandah. The rent is Rs. 250 per month. On the day of visit to the centre, the room was found stuffed with fodder and other accessories. The class was taken in verandah, but it is a small place for 70-80 children. Both teacher and children find it very congested. The classes are mostly held under the shade of tree. Jute matting (Tat-pattis) are provided for seating. The centre has two chairs. Water is available from tube well but the centre has no toilet facilities. No teaching aids are provided.

NFE is given to the children. Books, slates, chalks, school bags, notebook and pencil were given to fifty children. The centre does not provide mid-day meal, stipend, uniforms, medical facilities and vocational training. The school has one lady teacher (Ms.Sushila Verma). The teacher has attended a workshop for training, organised by REHA. The teacher feels the training was very useful. The books prescribed are by U.P. Board.

This year 90 children were enrolled, out of which 40 are girls. Last year 150 children were enrolled, out of which 77 were girls. Most of the children were from loom owners families and those working in carpet weaving. Most of the children enrolled last year have left the school and new admissions have taken place this year. Twentyfive children enrolled were from carpet looms. The children can at best write their name in Hindi and can do simple additions and subtractions. The parents appreciate the work of the teacher, but feel medical facilities, mid-day meals and vocational training should be given by the centres.

Last year a loom owner's survey revealed that nearly 75% workers in the looms were children, especially brought from Bihar and Nepal. However, due to raids conducted by government, children were sent back. Now very few children are engaged in weaving as per the villagers.

8.2 YUVA VIKAS SANSTHAN (YVS) (GHAZIPUR)

The organisation was established in 1988, for rehabilitation of child labour. It has opened two centres for child rehabilitation in June, 1996. The centres are:

1. Salimpur (Mohammadabad Block, District Ghazipur)
2. Narayanpur (Mohammadabad Block, District Ghazipur)

1. *Salimpur:* Salimpur village is located 23 kilometres away from Mohammadabad. Bus service is available from Mohammadabad. The centre has its own building, land being given by Pradhan. The centre has one big room, the building is semi pucca. The centre has two black-boards, one table and 4 chairs.

   The centre provides mid-day meals to the children. The menu comprises of Channa/Banana/other seasonal fruits. The centre does not provide books, stationery to the children. However, during exams, register and pens are given to the children. No stipend, medical care and vocational training is given to the children.

   The school has two lady teachers, both have participated thrice in workshop training. Both draw salary of Rs. 500 per month each. For teaching, the curriculum is based on the syllabus from formal schools. Same pattern of teaching is adopted, though style of teaching is different. Local people appreciate the efforts of the NGO in creating mass educational awareness, especially among the poor and down-trodden sections. They want to establish the centre effectively. People donate willingly for the establishment of the centre.

2. *Narayanpur:* The centre is located in Mohamadabad Block of Ghazipur District. The centre was started in 1996. The centre is 7 kilometres away from Mohamadabad town across river Ganga. The centre runs classes in thatched rooms. The house was built by villagers. The room has no walls and floor is of mud. There are three blackboards and 4 chairs in the school. There are two teachers, both have studied up to class XII. Both have participated in Workshop organised by

REHA. The teachers are paid Rs. 500 as salary. 149 children are enrolled in the school, out of which 98 were child workers both from carpet weaving and agriculture. The school provides mid-day meal for the children. The school does not have any provision for books, uniform, school bags, stipend and medical aid. No vocational training is given.

The percentage of attendance is high and drop-out rates are very low in both the schools. Community response was found positive, as more children want to get enrolled in these two schools. The NGO has created mass awareness and government has been pressurised to open primary school in Saleempur. The NGO feels vocational training should be part and parcel of the NFE programme. Skill test performance of children did show positive impact, as children although first time school goers, have medium level understanding of the language and maths. Village people are appreciative of the efforts of NGO.

8.3 GRAMODAYA SANSTHAN

The head office of the NGO is at Kanpur. The office has all modern amenities and facilities like computers, books, stationery, research team etc. Gramodaya Sansthan is the out-come of a prolonged struggle and mass movement to secure legal and constitutional rights to displaced tribals, harijans, and others belonging to the disadvantaged backward communities and to secure them social justice and equality.

The major activities of the NGO include rehabilitation and prevention of child labour, women education and skill development. The NGO has been working in urban slum and rural areas of Kanpur. Non-formal education for working children and school drop-out children is given. Vocational training is also given to these children.

Six NFE centres in Mau block of Banda district are run by this NGO for carpet weaving children. The funds have been provided by REHA (Germany) and the centres were started in 1995. REHA provided funds for 4 centres, but the funds are being utilized for 6 centres. The NFE centres are at Balapur, Matiyara, Media ka Dera, Chivli, Bhatta, Biki Ka Dera. Three NFE centres viz. Balapur, Matiyara and Biki Ka Dera were surveyed.

The centres are located in the isolated and highly inaccessible area, which were prone to child labour for carpet weaving. Enrolment for these working children were given priority. This area developed as peripheral carpet weaving belt to capture cheap child labour. Significant contribution has been made by this NGO in eradicating and release of child labour from looms. In fact majority of looms have been shut down due to lack of child labour.

The NFE centres have generated tremendous awareness and high enrolment is found in these centres. Girl's enrolment is given top priority. Children have attended school for the first time. Hence skill tests conducted reflected poor results, which could be explained by poor educational infrastructure in the area. The centres have kutcha buildings with two to three rooms. Basic teaching aids like, blackboard, posters, charts were used for teaching purposes. Curriculum is based on formal schools. Teaching method is joyful and appreciated by children. Attendance rate is high and drop-out rates are low.

Quality of teachers is of medium level, as teachers lack modern approach of teaching. They need regular in-service training. NGO'S regular monitoring, has helped to create, sense of responsibility among the teachers.

Mid-day meals and stipend is provided by only one NFE centre (Balapur). However, books and basic stationery is provided to few students of other centres also.

In terms of levels of performance the NFE centres are ranging between medium to low. Infrastructure facilities in the schools are poor. Classes are held in open, as the present accommodation is not sufficient. Attention for infrastructural development is needed.

The awareness created by the NGO for child labour problem is generally appreciated by the community. NGO organises meetings to generate awareness and consciousness. People are appreciative of the efforts of NGO in creating mass awareness. They voluntarily support the programmes run by NGO and contribute money for its success. The people feel that in addition to NFE, other activities like nutritional midday meals, and vocational training must be started for the children. Currently the vocation of tailoring is only provided by Balapur centre. Loss of income due to NFE for children was not given much importance by parents of enrolled children. The people wanted more schools with better infrastructures and quality teaching.

8.4 RUGMARK FOUNDATION

SACCS efforts with the help of United Nation Human Right Commission, UNICEF, Indo German Export Promotion Council (IGEP) and other carpet manufacturers, resulted in the creation of independent, monitoring and labelling system-RUGMARK. The label certifies carpets made without the use of child labour. The children found weaving in the registered looms under RUGMARK are released and provided rehabilitation.

RUGMARK runs one boarding school at Balashrya and one primary school at Jagapur. Balashrya school at Gopiganj stands prominent from the main road. It has big buildings with many rooms. The field in the front is well maintained.

The boarding school provides shelter for children and helps to facilitate their reintegration into mainstream of society. It is an integrated project to provide formal, non-formal, vocational training. The school is geared to accommodate 75 children and provide adequate emphasis on Non-formal education, vocational training, social and human rights awareness, cultural training and physical and spiritual activities. In order to make the children conversant with the art of management, during their stay at the centre, the students are assigned several responsibilities like, kitchen & store, campus maintenance, discipline, sports and games and cultural events on a rotating basis.

During our visit at Balashry, 47 children- all boys were enrolled. The children are grouped into three classes according to age and level of understanding.

The curriculum taught is of Uttar Pradesh Board Syllabus, teaching of English language is done from the initial stage. Teachers are highly trained and qualified with regular in-service training. The curriculum is children centred providing skills for maths, hindi, English, and general science. Teachers adopt several teaching aids for imparting skills. The skill test on children conducted, indicates high level of understanding and grasp by the children. However, comprehension skills were poor.

The centre provides vocational training in carpet weaving, wood carpentry, tailoring, screen making, mechanic and music. Regular medical check up and maintenance of medical records were found. Quality training is provided to the children, as trained teachers are employed. The centre got highest rank in vocational teaching and equipment provided to children.

The centre provides multiple facilities like full boarding, clothing, stationery, books, uniform, shoes and educational material. Great significance is attached to personal hygiene and cleanliness. The school is well maintained with good infrastructure like library, music room, high quality sports equipment, recreation room. One child of the centre was chosen to participate for state level athletes. Significant importance is given to cultural aspects especially songs, drama, music and dance.

Physical education is the part and parcel of the curriculum. Several children have established themselves after getting vocational training. Ecological landscape has been preserved and developed with clean atmosphere. Good hygiene and public health measures are adopted in the living room, kitchen and class rooms. Nutritional diet based on local available vegetables and cereals are provided to children.

However, complete isolation is maintained as outsiders are not allowed to the centre without permission. The impact on the community was found minimum.

8.5 PROJECT MALA

Project Mala was established in 1989, "to educate and rehabilitate working children." It hopes to help eradicate the use of child labour on the carpet looms by providing a three year non-formal education to children between the ages of 10 and 14, who are involved in the carpet weaving. This education is equivalent to 5 years in the formal primary system (levels I-V). The idea is that on completing the NFE, the children would either join labour force, with more favourable terms as skilled workers or will continue further education in the formal schools. Project Mala currently runs four NFE schools at Guria, Hasra, Pathera and Amoi. The site location of schools are in line with the objective of serving isolated carpet weaving areas without primary education facilities. The enrolment is done on year to year basis, after a thorough survey of the village. Adequate attention is paid to enrol girl students. Enrolment performance, attendance percentage and low drop-out rate are major achievements of Mala schools. Marginal sections of children are given priority in enrolment as children from SC / and backward classes were largely enrolled.

Along with NFE, the project Mala schools have made reputation in providing technical skills by way of vocational training in the field of carpet weaving and tailoring. The one hour daily course on carpet weaving and tailoring has been applauded by the parents. They consider the training as an asset, generating confidence among the children. Recently, Advance Weaving Academy has been started at Guria centres for the children, who have completed NFE at Mala Schools. The Weaving Academy is using modified and scientifically developed looms for the artisans, which could provide ease and comfort at work. The modified loom can be adjusted according to the work demands. Project Mala schools adopt Minimum Learning Levels (MLL) curriculum designed by NCERT for non-formal Education. It has inducted some aspects along Gandhian lines and is in accordance with guidelines laid down by the government of India. It combined productive work with other forms of learning. The curriculum is child centred, providing basic primary skills for maths, language, general awareness, social science and general sciences. Time taken is divided into four periods-maths, hindi, vocational training and recreational activities. Teachers attach significant importance to using teaching aids like, charts, posters, story, songs, practical demonstration of skills, outdoor field tour, remedial teaching for children. The skill tests conducted on children by research team found Mala children ranking top in the level of understanding, analysis and comprehension skills. Mala teachers are trained and full of enthusiasm. They work hard and have missionary zeal to promote education in the rural areas.

Project Mala provides multiple activities to its students viz. non-formal education, mid-day nutritional meals, vocational training, regular medical check ups, uniform, books & stationery, school bags and some useful productive work (SUPW) crafts, games, gardening, singing and dancing. Importance is attached to school environment, cleanliness, and good moral training. The schools were clean and congenial for educational atmosphere. Great significance is attached to personal hygiene and cleanliness. The schools are well maintained and offer a contrast to surrounding environment. Each school has 5 or 6 class rooms open but shaded verandahs. The landscape development is in conformity to the local surrounding plantation, flower beds, growing fruits and vegetables are common in all Mala schools. Building structure, amenities and facilities provided are of good standard, comparable to any public schools in major cities of India. The campus environment has undoubtedly played significant part in attracting children enrolment.

An integral part of the school is monthly stipend of Rs. 100 per child which is contributed and set aside as Rehabilitation Fund to be given only after completion of NFE. The fund is utilized to provide instruments for self employment or for higher education.

The in-depth survey conducted at Guria and Hasra centres ranked both Guria and Hasra at top rank for majority of selected indicator. The over all composite index also recorded high rank for Guria and Hasra centres. Teachers profile, teaching aids adopted, curriculum taught, testing methods utilized, school environment, teacher salary, infrastructure recorded were the highest for Mala schools.

A discussion with parents and community members of the Mala school students indicated that they see a change in the children behaviour, since they began at Mala schools. Their health and physical appearance had changed for the better, their personal hygiene habits had improved, they had become more alert, learnt things quicker and had confidence to face the challenges and spoke better. The influence was also found on their friends and siblings, as they also expressed motivation for teaching. Mala schools have played significant role in creating more demand for schools, as more and more children want to get enrolled in Mala Schools. Parents feel instead of stipend, children should get more years of schooling, as in Govt. schools.

The administrative set up of Mala has provided significant input for the development of schools. Regular monitoring of administration has helped to create good rapport with the teachers, students and parents. The efforts of administration are highly praised. The initiation of adult education centre at Guria has created significant general awareness for children education.

8.6 SWAMI VIVEKANAND SHIKSHA SAMITI (SVSS),MIRZAPUR

SVSS was set up in 1970, to serve the society by creating education infrastructure in Mirzapur City. The organisation runs a crèche, a middle school and a junior high school in Mirzapur City. The school is recognised by the state government. Five NFE special schools were started by SVSS in June 1995 with the help of REHA funds. These five centres were Mujehra Khurd, Mujera Kalan /Mathia, Bhogan, Bahuti and Mawai Kalan. All the five centres were surveyed during September 1997 to November 1997. The location of the centres is in line with the objectives, as these centres are dominated by scheduled caste, scheduled tribe and backward communities. All the five villages are without government primary schools. Children from these villages were either staying at home or doing weaving and other households jobs. Thus there is strong positive response from the community for these NFE centres. Though officially 50 children are enrolled, other children, especially siblings are also attending schools. Each NFE centre has two teachers. The average attendance in most of the centres range between 80 to 90%. Curriculum for the NFE centre is designed by SVSS, which includes basic hindi, mathematics, general studies, social studies and spiritual and moral education. Books followed are prescribed by U.P. Board meant for formal schools. The books and stationery are provided by the SVSS out of the grant sanctioned under the project. Classes are held in the open under the shade of tree, as the present accommodation is not sufficient enough for the enrolled children, especially in Bhogan and Mavaikalan. Surrounding environment in Bhogan was found un-hygienic with stinking water in front of the class. The schools are equipped with basic teaching aids /material i.e. black board, chalk sticks and charts. However, the regular display of teaching materials/aids was not done in the centres. The sports material is limited and sports activities are not organised regularly.

The teaching staff appointed have modest formal education. The methods of teaching are rigid and traditional. Children have been grouped in two classes according to their performance. Most of the children were attending school for the first time. The school environment is informal and free. SVSS has significantly contributed in raising the child labour awareness issues in these villages. Group songs were encouraged portraying ill effects of Child labour. SVSS, currently pays Rs. 35 to each child enrolled (only 50) in cash as stipend per month. In addition Rs. 20 per month, per student is utilized to provide refreshment i.e. roasted grains, biscuits and banana etc. The arrangement is quite successful in attracting children to schools.

The response from the community was encouraging, as more and more demand for such schools were raised. Community considered these schools as their own schools. The parents wanted children to continue education in these schools even after two years. The loss of earnings due to NFE to children was not considered important, instead the education of children was given priority.

The areas of concern were inadequate and inappropriate methods of teaching by teaching staff, lack of funds for teaching aids and infrastructure were the main hurdles. Non use of teaching aids and materials, inadequate building infrastructure and furniture were the other concerns.

Teachers' in-service training needs more attention. Regular monitoring by SVSS administration has helped to create sense of responsibility among teachers.

The community appreciated the NGO's efforts in creating general education awareness. However, lack of vocational training in the schools was major lacunae considered by the community. They want vocational skills to be taught.

8.7 BACHPAN BACHAO ANDOLAN (MIRZAPUR) (BBA/SACCS)

BBA is a NGO, based in Delhi. The organisation is working for the release for bonded child labour and children in servitude conditions. The objective of the NGO is the total elimination of child labour and restoring children right to education. BBA believes in direct action through raids in co-ordination with government officials, legal bodies and individuals. After winning confidence of local population, child's captive place of identification is revealed to government officials for conducting raids. The NGO claims to have released 7500 children from captivity in Mirzapur-Bhadhoi carpet belt. Other methods followed are mass awareness campaigns against child servitude, domestic consumer boycott campaigns against the materials prepared by children and NFE centres providing education to the released children. The released bonded child labour is provided transitory rehabilitation at Mukti Ashram in New Delhi. The released children unable to get immediate relief due to bureaucratic apathy are enrolled in the Ashram. The children released are transported from released areas to Delhi for immediate rehabilitation.

BBA is currently running six NFE centres in Mirzapur and Son-Bhadra district and one transit rehabilitation centre in New Delhi (Mukti Ashram) The six NFE centres are Purikatra, Ghabi Ghat, Baruedeo, Parsi Tola in Mirzapur district, Hinshinpur in Bhadhoi and Jorukheda in Son-Bhadra district. The NFE centres in Mirzapur- Son- Bhadra have been started in 1996-1997. The research team visited Purikatra and Jorukheda in October 1997.

The NFE centres provide NFE and basic stationery items like, notebooks, slate and chalk to the children. Number of children working in family carpet looms is high especially in Purikatra (Mirzapur).

Purikatra

The centre was started in July-August,96. It is located in Laldiggi, Gosaitola, Mirzapur. There are number of carpet loom owners in this municipality area and children work in their family looms.

The classes are held in Ms. Sangeeta Dube's house. The centre does not have a building of its own. It is run in teacher's house, in her bed room. In winters classes are held upstairs in a room that has tin roof. The room does not have window and there was no adequate sunlight. No tat-patti are there. Water and toilet facilities are available. Room size is small. No furniture except for two chairs were found.

The school does not provide any facilities like, books, uniform, mid-day meal and stipend to the children. However slate and chalks were given to the children. 90 children were enrolled in 1966, out of which 35 were girls. This year 55 children were enrolled, out of which 27 were girls. On the day of visit 22-25 children were present, mostly in the age-group of 5-8 years. Some children had dropped out. From the current year government schools have started giving 3 kilograms of wheat to each child, hence children from this school have dropped-out.

The centre has only one teacher. She is paid Rs.600 per month. Although not trained, she has an innate ability to handle the children. Children were very fond of her. She has no set curriculum and no teaching aids are provided to her. She has helped parents to make them agree to send children for education. Students initially were shy, but now they are free. The children can count, write names and alphabets. But on the whole writing skills were of poor quality. But children sing songs, play and seem to enjoy in these special schools.

People in the area were aware about the child rights. The people felt that government schemes were not in-operative in the area. Benefits of these schemes are not being utilised by these people.

8.8 MUKTI ASHRAM

It is situated in village Ibrahimpur, Block Alipur in North Delhi. The Centre was established in 1990 by SACCS and BBA. These two NGOs have been rescuing children from bondage and servitude. The two NGOs felt the need for immediate rehabilitation of the freed children from various hazardous industries. As an effort to provide transitory help for the released children, Mukti Ashram was established.

The Ashram has built up its own building, plantation is sufficiently done to create good ecological atmosphere. The whole campus is developed to replicate village atmosphere, which is soothing to eyes. The building constitutes several rooms, some rooms are kuchha, but most of the rooms are pucca. Three dormitories for the students are quite big to accommodate the released children. The rooms are not airy. The Ashram has electricity, drinking water, toilet and telephone facility. The Centres also maintain one health unit and a small library. The Centre has boarding facility for more than 50 children at a time. Demonstration material on child labour issues is well stacked and posters are displayed. However, reading material for children are few. Approach road to the Ashram from the main road is Kuchha and it becomes muddy during rains.

The Ashram is a residential centre, as both boarding and lodging is provided to the released children. The children are also given two pairs of clothes, chappals, soap and oil, bedding, writing material. The centre also provides vocational training in the following crafts viz; Cloth weaving, tailoring, Motor winding. welding and carpentry. All the necessary equipment required for the training purpose is provided to the children after proper training, thereafter, a tool kit is provided to few children. There are at present 52 children living in the Ashram. The children above 16 years are taught vocational training. The class for vocational training is of four hours duration which is being held daily. The children below 16 years are given NFE, where they are taught reading, writing and counting skills. Most of the children are fresh from the release, hence they require tremendous effort to get interested in NFE. Few students who have completed NFE have been admitted in formal schools and all the expenditure is borne by the Ashram. The training in the Ashram initially is for three months, but if needed it is extended for further three months. Some released children are regularly brought from villages for training in the Ashram. The levels of performance derived from the study, puts Mukti, Ashram in high rank for majority of indicators, including the composite index. The dedication of teachers and workers is highly acclaimed by children. Children are regularly taken out for field trips. Some children visited few foreign countries in connection with International Global March for child labour eradication.

The children in the Ashram are brought after release from various hazardous industries by activists. They are provided vocational training and general awareness in this centre. Apart from vocational training and NFE classes, social education is also held. The class is compulsory for all the students. In this class general awareness about child labour, rights of child, exploitation in society, class segregation, gender issues, etc. is discussed. Group activities are also encouraged and each child is given responsibility for separate work in the Ashram. The Ashram has 5 teachers for vocational training, one teacher for NFE and one teacher for social education. Two of the ex-students are employed in the Ashram, one is NFE teacher and other is manager cum social education teacher. The craft teachers are diploma holders and have long experience in their respective fields. The teachers are very clear in their perspective on child labour. There is no set curriculum. On the whole the approach of teaching is highly appreciated by the children. However children feel such training should be for longer period. The enrolment of the children should also be increased, so as to accommodate more children in the Ashram.

8.9 ANKUR FOUNDATION

This organisation has been working since 1976, but was perhaps registered later. It grew from a decade long involvement with the problems of

Banwasis, particularly in the Vindhyan/Kaimer region of Son-Bhadra and palamau. The funding from REHA for Non-formal education & vocational training has started in July,1995. It is of three years duration. The NGO has started working on the issue of child labour during last five years.

The NGO has opened 14 NFE centres, mostly in Kon area in Duddi Block of Son- Bhadra district. 4 centres are for vocational training in four different crafts viz; carpentry, tailoring, bicycle repairs and Durri weaving. It has also organised training programmes for the parents of child labour. Its annual budget is Rs.14 lakhs.

Its head-office is in Allahabad. It has regional office at Gurumara in Son-Bhadra. Gurumara is 50 kilometres away from the major rehabilitation centres. Hence the supervision work is of poor nature, which has hampered the quality of NFE programmes. A list of villages with school facility was provided to us but on scrutiny it was found that some centres have been closed and instead new centres were opened namely :

1. Bilurua	2. Longa	3. Mitihinia
4. Singa	5. Asna Bandh	6. Kachnarwa
7. Gaura Singa	8. Barvahikholi	9. Gidhiya
10. Nimiyarhidi	11. Ammarola	12. Ramgarh
13. Kon	14. Cheerwaheed	15. Kishanpurwa
16. Karail.		

On the day of our visit to these centres, the number of children found was very small. Most of the centres remained closed for three to four days continuously. Only 30-35 children are enrolled in each of these schools. On enquiry we found that only 10 to 15% children attending the schools were from carpet weaving. All the schools are providing NFE only. No facilities are being given to the children. The rooms are highly un-hygienic with no ventilation, no drinking water and toilet facility. Each school has one teacher. The teachers are irregular, who lack imagination and do not have teachers' training. Methods of teaching are traditional. Since no supervision is there from the organisers, hence the job is taken lightly. During our entire stay, schools were not functioning. The students had to be brought by force by the teachers. Educational aids were absent with no poster, blackboards, picture charts etc. The NGO does not provide mid-day meal, books, uniform, vocational training in these special schools. Hence no incentives are provided for regular attendance. Drop-out rates are very high. Some of the centres are run in residential houses in the village, which can hardly accommodate the children.

1. *Ramgarh:* This centre provides durri weaving training to adults/ children. Women work on daily wages.
2. *Kon Bicycle Repair Centre:* The centre is located in the main market, and seems to be a regular commercial bicycle shop. Although a register was maintained, but we found only adults were working or learning the repairs. No record of children given training was maintained. The selection of children for training purpose was not based on any criteria. It was up-to the master to admit the people for learning. The shop did not seem a training workshop, instead it looked like a normal commercial shop. The master claimed that he is paid Rs. 1000 as salary for the training, but on scrutiny we found, no such training was imparted during last three months.
3. *Kishanpurwa:* Tailoring is taught to women. The centre has two machines and 8-10 women were learning the tailoring skills.
4. *Cheerwaheed Carpentry Workshop:* The carpentry workshop has modern equipment, which the owner has purchased after getting loans from government. Interested children/adults get enrolled with him for learning the skill. We found 4 adults were working with him. Cost of wood for learning/practice is provided by Ankur Foundation. No record was maintained to show that children/adults were trained by the centre.
5. *Mithinya:* The village is sparsely populated with several hamlets. Each hamlet is away from each other. Children have to come from far distances. Classes are held in open field, as the centre has no building. One blackboard, with no other teaching aids are provided. Water is not available and children have to get their own water. No other facilities are given by the school. The school has one teacher. She is paid Rs. 800 per month, while other teachers in other schools are paid Rs. 500 per month. People are ignorant of the working of the centre. Students are very irregular. Out of 35 enrolled students, only 5-10 attend the classes, as they have to travel for 2 hours to reach the school.

The team visited other centres like Longh, and Karail. All the centres were below standard, as very few children were attending the schools. The classes are held in open spaces. Classes are highly irregular. Teachers are paid Rs.500 per month as salary. Teaching methods are traditional and remote. No innovative methods are employed. Except for provision of books to some students, no other facilities are given to students. The people are unaware about the working of schools. Due to lack of supervision by the officials, the working of these centres are far below the standard. Most of the schools were closed due to festivals.

8.10 ARPAN GRAMIN VIKAS KENDRA

Arpan Gramin Vikas Kendra was registered in 1991. The NGO has head-office at Maner (Patna),which is about 25 Kilometres away from Patna City. The NGO is running 12 schools, out of which 2 schools are in Maner city and the rest in rural areas. The NGO has admitted 182 children in formal schools. Its objectives include creating awareness among the population for the eradication of child labour. The NGO provides books, slates, pencils, for the students. In addition one rupee each is given daily to students for attending the schools. The classes are held for three to four hours in the morning. The special schools have generated tremendous awareness, as the attendance was found good. Parents were participating with the activities of the schools.

Most of the schools lack building facilities, however small rooms were rented for this purpose. Classes are usually held in open spaces. The schools lack basic amenities like tables, chairs, Posters, charts. Other teaching aids are used by teachers. Children were highly appreciative of teachers.

Each school has one teacher. Curriculum is based on Bihar Government school. Teachers help students to get admitted in formal schools. On an average 30-50 children are enrolled in these schools. Very few children were working in carpet weaving. Most of the children were working in agriculture field, brick kilns and as casual labourers. Attendance is above 90% in most of the schools. Other methods like songs, dramas are also encouraged.

The NGO runs the following schools:

1. Maner City	2. Dyal Chak	3. Bajeetpur
4. Bank	5. Manergarh	6. Bihata City
7. Lodipour	8. Nagwa	9. Pandechak
10. Sikandarpur	11. Balipur	12. Patsa
13. Musepur		

Of these, 10 centres were visited and detailed survey was conducted in 9 centres.

8.11 SAMUDAY (SAMASTIPUR)

The NGO is running 20 centres, 10 centres are being officially funded by REHA. However, these funds are utilised for 20 centres. The centres for rehabilitation were started from April, 1996. The project is for three years duration. The centres run by the NGO are:

1. Muradpur 2. Nathudwar 3. Modipur
4. Kanker 5. Udaipur 6. Govindpur
7. Shankarbasa 8. Rajmara 9. Milky
10. Samastipur City

The NGO only provides NFE, no other facilities are provided to the children. In fact in the Milky centre, children complained that they were charged Rs. 5 every month to meet teachers salary. The organisers feel parents can ask for accountability if they are charged a small token fee. The teacher gets only Rs. 200 as salary per month. The school did not have any blackboard, teaching aids. The parents are not aware about the centres' objectives. The school runs only for two hours in the morning. Curriculum followed is from formal schools. During our visit all the schools were closed due to some technical difficulty with REHA. The NGO was willing to restart the school after clarifications from REHA.

8.12 KOSI SEVA SADAN

It was registered in 1978. The founders were associated with J.P. Narayan Movement. The organisation has been fighting for rehabilitation of people displaced due to construction of Kosi dam and are involved with the flood rescue operation. The project on rehabilitation of child labour was started in August, 1996. This NGO has freed 117 children from bondage. At present it is running 5 centres. The centres are:

1. Mahashi 2. Jhataki 3. Koylasthan
4. Kothia 5. Arapatti

The schools provide books, slates and pencils to the children. No other facility is given to the children. Classes are held in open spaces, as 3 centres do not have rooms. No teaching aids are provided. Teachers are paid salary of Rs. 400 per month. They do not have a set curriculum, but they try to follow formal school books. Students are least interested as traditional methods of teaching are followed. In Mahishi 117 children are enrolled, out of them 32 are girls. In Jhataki 85 children were enrolled, out of which 25 were girls. Perhaps the NGO entered all the children in the register, who did not go to schools. The attendance is very poor. The schools have inadequate facilities.

In brief, the survey revealed that performance of the NGOs is rather mixed, not only with effect to the NFE but also with regard to other tasks performed by them. Some NGOs provide good infrastructure in schools, provide good vocational training, train children to be accommodated in formal education, provide enough fellowship; while others are not in a position to provide bare minimum roof for the school. But there is an enthusiasm observed both among the teachers and the students and also among the parents for non-formal education. The community feels that some day NFE would change the fate of their children and the community as a whole.

9 Conclusion

The present study encompasses an in-depth study of child labour issues confronting the society. Policy initiatives undertaken by government and voluntary sector for eradication of child labour have been examined and evaluated. An assessment of non-formal education programme undertaken by several NGOs in the carpet weaving belt has also been made.

- The observations reveal that international pressure and sustained movement generated by voluntary sector have contributed significantly to compel the government to address the child labour issues and problems in India during the last one decade. The government and non-governmental agencies have jointly launched concerted attack to eradicate exploitative use of child labour especially in hazardous industries. The efforts of Labour Ministry (Government of India), supplemented by South Asian coalition on Child Servitude (SACCS), UNICEF, ILO, REHA (Germany), Project Mala (UK) and Child Welfare Society have contributed significantly in achieving progressive elimination of child labour in hazardous industries especially the carpet weaving. Child Labour Act 1986, NPCL - 1987, NACEL-1994 and supreme Court directions - 1996, were the commendable steps undertaken in the right direction. The role of Human Rights Commission, social activists, intellectuals, grass root workers, especially activists from Bachpan Bachhao Aandolan and Bandhua Mukti Morcha have infused greater vigour and enthusiasm to release children under servitude and bonded conditions. The release of children is achieved through raids and rescue operations with the help of government agencies.

Some of the main conclusions of the study are as follows:

- The magnitude of child labour in India is underestimated, due to inadequate and unreliable data base. The proportion of children not enrolled in school (Aged 5–14 years) was 50.35% as per 1991 Census. Even the children enrolled in schools may not be attending the schools, as drop-out/push-out rates are extremely high. This indirectly indicates a high presence of child labour (Aged 5–14 years) in the work-force. However majority of working children can not be contoured as exploitative and abusive, since it is carried out under the protective guidance of parents/family members.

- Child labour in carpet industry has generated strong international attention as 95% of carpets are being exported. SACCS with the help of United Nations Human Rights Commission, UNICEF and Indo-German export promotion has generated strong international consumer awareness campaign in United States and European countries, compelling the exporters and manufacturers to subject their carpet weaving looms to RUGMARK or KALEEN certification. The child labour issue in carpet weaving belt has been sensitised on a large scale, leading to raids and rescue of bonded child labour. This has created mass awareness campaign among loom owners and exporters against the open use of child labour.
- The increased demand of carpets in the international market from India on the one hand and the promulgation of the provision of Child Labour Act - 1986 on the other hand, has lead to both, the processes of concentration and dispersion in the carpet weaving. The traditional carpet weaving belt in Mizapur-Bhadohi region has far outgrown its geographical spread. It now extends approximately twice to thrice the area that it commanded in 1960s. Core Zone has witnessed high concentration of loomage and induction of migrant child labour from labour catchment areas, where as, peripheral zone experience wide dispersal of looms and child labour from family and local non-family segments. This acts as "reach out" zone for the child labour to avoid provisions of Child Labour Act - 1986.
- The carpet weaving belt is agriculturally under-developed, due to lack of irrigation. The area is prone to recurrent floods and drought conditions. Inadequate educational infrastructure, relative isolation due to poor road and communication network is generally common in the carpet weaving belt. These factors have significantly contributed to high level of unemployment, social under-development, lack of awareness and exploitation of labour force.

- The structure of carpet industry constitutes a large line of "intermediaries" in between loom holders and exporters. These intermediaries in the form of a series of commission agents and non-artisan loom owners have siphoned away maximum benefits leaving behind very low wages for the weavers. Thus induction of child labour-family, non-family and captive or bonded is encouraged to avail low labour cost, advantages or quiet submissiveness and uncomplaining acceptance of harsh working conditions. Advance payments to the "cash starved" parents by the loom owners with the connivance of agents/middlemen and carpet manufactures have strengthened their hold over the child worker.
- Loom owners have emerged from backward and non-artisan class, with the help of loans provided by manufacturers. Thus "captive looms" are created by manufacturers, even though they are not located in their premises or sheds. This is to circumvent the legal hurdles due to the provisions of Child Labour Act – 1986. The onus of employing children is shifted to loom owners. Child carpet weavers belong mostly to marginalised groups viz., scheduled caste/scheduled tribe and other backward classes.
- The working conditions prevailing in these looms are highly inappropriate. Children have to work in couched positions during extreme weather conditions, with poor ventilation, congested working space, long and continuous hours of arduous work of weaving. Other basic amenities like safe drinking water and toilet facilities are absent. Majority of respondents confirmed several health problems like night blindness, less appetite, worm infestation, aching joints, skin diseases and eye fatigue. The wage received by the children are extremely low, with drastic cuts imposed for slight defect in the weaving.
- The incidence of bonded child labour in the carpet weaving has decreased significantly, due to pro-active approach adopted by NGO's and government agencies. About 7% children surveyed were bonded or migrant weavers. These children were either from land-less families or families with very small land. Majority of Children were in the age group of 8–12 years; 96% children were illiterate or literate without any formal schooling. This indicates absence of agricultural land and inadequate educational infrastructure as major factors for sending children to work.
- Mirzapur-Bhadohi carpet weaving belt recorded very high drop-out/

push-our rates from the government schools. Of every 100 children enrolled in Schools, only 33 reached up to class V, 10 reach up to class VIII and only 1 child reached up to class X. In addition, the availability of government primary schools in the carpet weaving belt was found highly in-adequate as 49% villages in the study areas did not posses any school facility. This indicates that school facility is not only inappropriate but also inadequate.

- Non-Formal Education Schools have been sponsored by Labour Ministry, (Government of India under NPCL-1987, supported by IPEC, ILO) REHA (Germany), Project Mala (UK), Carpet Export Promotion Council (CEPC), CRY and Child Welfare Society in the carpet weaving zone and Labour Catchment zone of Mirzapur-Bhadohi. 125 NFE schools are currently run by local NGO's in the region.
- The spatial distribution of Non-formal schools (sponsored by government and voluntary sector) in the carpet weaving belt is highly concentrated and comparatively less than the demand. Hence magnitude of villages without school facility is extremely high in the area. This has helped in the induction of child labour in carpet weaving. Thus more concerted efforts on part of government and non-governmental agencies are needed to expand Non-formal education schools in the region.
- The site selection of NFE schools is in line with the objectives like; dominance of scheduled caste/scheduled tribe and backward population areas. Majority of these schools are located in isolated and inaccessible belts.
- The NGO's have been able to create conducive atmosphere in these rural areas of enrolling large proportion of girls. Along with working children their younger siblings have been also enrolled, thereby serving the objective of protecting entry of younger children into weaving.
- The objective of enrolling children from weaker sections in these NFE schools is achieved, as 44% children enrolled were from scheduled castes, 32% were from other backward classes and 12% were from scheduled tribes.
- Drop-out rates and attendance records of the ever enrolled children in these NFE schools were related to provision of multiplicity of activities especially mid-day meals, stipend to children and quality of education provided by teachers. Several NGO's like Project Mala, SVSS, Yuva Vikas Sansthan, Arpan Gramin Vikas and Gramodaya Sansthan have recorded high attendance records and low drop-out

rates. The provision of books, stationery, slates etc., is restricted only once in the beginning of session. Majority of NFE schools funded by REHA (Germany) only provide Non-formal education.

- Mukti Ashram (SACCS/BBA) and Balashrya (RUGMARK) provide full boarding facilities to the enrolled children. These centres also provide high quality vocational training to the enrolled children. The vocational training includes, carpet weaving, welding, wood carpentry, tailoring, textile weaving, electric repairs etc.
- Project Mala schools have multiplicity of quality activities. These activities include NFE, vocational training, nutritional mid-day meals, regular health care for children and rehabilitation fund after the completion of NFE programme. The vocational training includes carpet weaving and tailoring. Recently Advanced Weaving Academy has been introduced in Guria centre, which teaches advanced weaving to selected children who have completed NFE. The looms are scientifically modified providing comfort for weaving. Adult education programmes are also conducted by Guria centre of Project Mala. This has strengthened teacher/student/parent participation.
- The infrastructure facilities among majority of NFE schools in the Mirazpur-Bhadohi carpet belt were extremely poor, except for Project Mala, Rugmark, Mukti Ashram and CLE & WS NFE schools. Classes were held in open fields as rooms were highly congested and extremely small to accomodate all children During extreme weather conditions and rainy season classes were not held. Ventilation was poor in majority of centres and not fit for teaching environment. Even the basic facilities like, safe drinking water, play grounds and conducive hygienic locations were absent. Stagnant water pools breeding mosquitoes were found in front of some NFE centres. The site selection for NFE school must be given due weightage.
- Average number of teachers per NFE school is 1.77 teachers. However the NFE schools of Mukti Ashram, Rugmark, Project Mala and CLE & WS have 5 or more teaching staff per centre Sex ratio of teachers was 43 female teachers per 100 male teachers. The teacher/child ratio reflects that REHA funded schools need more recruitment of teachers. At the least norm 2 teacher per 50 children must be maintained to cater properly for the child's educational needs.
- 62 percent teachers were educated up to 10 + 2 level, 23% up to graduation level and 15% above graduation level. Only 17% teachers

were either experienced or trained at the time of recruitment and 41% had joined at least one shortterm teachers training course. The education level and training attained by teachers varied among NFE centres. NFE centres funded by REHA have provided in-service training to some teachers, while 40 to 50 teachers were neither trained nor received any training. The results depict that training to the recruited teachers must be given top priority. Paradoxically the training component was lacking in the implementation process.

- The curriculum adopted and subjects taught in the NFE schools were diverse, ranging from basic skills of counting, alphabet learning to reading skills. Project Mala schools were only schools following Minimum Levels of Learning (MLL) devised by NCERT of NFE programme. Other schools were following UP Board/Bihar Board curriculum for primary education Majority of NFE schools were following self devised curriculum by teachers. Curriculum adopted and subjects taught lacked proper guidance from NGOs and everything was left up to teachers initiative in the absence of NFE schools. This requires immediate attention from NGOs and funding agencies as the purpose of NFE is self defeating without appropriate curriculum.
- NFE schools have adopted several teaching material and aids to inculcate educational skills among children. The teachers of Project Mala and Rugmark are adopting practical demonstration, outdoor surveys, remedial classes, constant use of charts and posters. However majority of NFE centres still follow rigid traditional and unimaginative methods of education. Teachers with in-service training course, were trying to adopt new teachniques. Students were attentive and engrossed where practical demonstration of skills taught were shown. Other methods followed were group discussions, out-door tours, group songs and encouraging children's direct participation.
- The skill test performance conducted established that only 11% children have good level of understanding, 39% were okay in understanding and the rest 49% were poor. Arithmetic skills were good for 13% children, okay for 53% children and poor for 34% children. General knowledge skills were poor for 60% children and okay for 34% children. Environmental skills were found extremely poor for 83% children and okay for 15% children. The knowledge of local history and geography was also found poor in majority of children. The reading and writing skills were found satisfactory in majority of children. The reading and writing skills were found satisfactory in majority of

children. The performance of boys and girls did not show significant variations. In fact girls scored better in terms of reading, writing and environmental skills. Boys performed better in arithmetic and general knowledge and general understanding.

- The results of test varied among NFE centres. Majority of children from Project Mala scored either good or okay rank in a number of skill tests. It establishes clear relationship between level of infrastructure, quality of teachers in terms of in-service training usage of teaching aids and materials and the skill acquired by children enrolled in NFE.
- Release of migrant and bonded children was mostly accomplished by SACCS and BBA activists. However in the absence of proper rehabilitation schemes for these released children, it is possible that these children are again pushed into labour force. So rehabilitation of released migrant and bonded child labour should be taken up on priority basis 731 children have completed NFE programme and 78% of these children were from Project Mala schools.
- All the NGO's have contributed significantly for enrolling children into formal education in government schools. This was achieved through awarenes programme. Employment to children who have completed 'NFE programme/vocational training was major achievement of the NGO's However REHA sponsored NFE centre which do not provide vocational teaching may, face large unemployment rate after completion of NFE programme. Therefore vocational training must be included in NFE centres which do not provide vocational teaching.
- The performance level of NFE schools, based on composite index derived for selected 18 indicators indicate NFE centres of Guria, Hasra, Balashrya and Mukti Ashram recorded highest level of performance in a number of indicators as well as for the final composite index. In case of indicators related to availability of multiple functions, building infrastructure, school surroundings and environment, teachers profile, teaching aids adopted, teachers salary, these four centres again ranked top. the performance of curriculum taught was recorded top for Guria and Hasra the NFE centres of Project Mala.
- The skill test performance again reflects high performance by Guria, Balashrya, Mukti Ashram and Hasra NFE centres. Thus reflecting strong correlation between teachers performance, school environment and infrastructure level with children's skill test performance.

- The levels of performance derived indicate NGO's mission, objectives and dedication have significantly contributed to the high level of performance Annual budget spent per child was also related to the performance of NFE centre.
- Majority of selected indicators recorded very high coefticient of correlation, which was significant at 99.9% level. Skill test performance of children was significantly correlated with teachers profile, teaching methods employed and testing tools used. This reflects strong influence of teachers efforts in inculcating quality education. the composite index was significantly correlated with all selected indicators except for site selection coverage and children released from carpet weaving.
- Stepwise regression analysis for two dependent indicators viz. I) children skill test performance level and ii) Percentage children attendance and percent drop-out rate was worked out. It indicates that skill test performance of children was largely explained by testing methods employed by teachers, building infrastructure, teachers salary, curriculum taught, teachers profiles and teaching aids used. thus demand and response of quality education is the result of teachers roles and good infrastructure available in NFE centres.
- High percentage of attendance and low drop-out rates is largely explained by multiplicity of functions provided by NFE centre like (mid-day meals, medical care and stipend), curriculum taught, teachers salary, school environment and vocational training given in NFE centres. Thus presence of multiplicity of activities, would ensure low drop-out rates and high attendance percentage.
- The impact of NGO activities and NFE programme in creating general awareness in the community reflects that majority of respondents were ignorant about the child labour issues. Seventy two per cent respondents were ignorant of Child Labour Act., 1986. Community was not aware of any government rehabilitation programmes for the released child labour from carpet weaving However some discernible attitudinal changes in the rural community was observed especially among community leaders.
- The government poverty alleviation schemes are in-operation for the last two decades, yet 60% respondents have not heard of these schemes. People want NGO's to play important role for pressurising government machinery to make these government schemes operative.

The NGO's seem to play very little role in the general awareness and mass education programme for poverty alleviation schemes in the area.

- Teaching aids and methods applied in formal schools were found less attractive, compared to NFE schools.
- Non-formal education had significant impact in reducing child labour in carpet weaving. Only 8.26 child weavers were found in looms currently operating in those villages with NFE schools. However, children helping parents after school hours was a common sight.
- NGO's efforts have been praised in motivating the families for removing children from carpet weaving. Adequate awareness has been created highlighting ill effects of child labour. Parents were also of the view that children should be allowed to help family, in weaving carpets after school time. They felt, they were the victims of carpet manufacturers on the one hand and NGO's on the other hand. They were unanimous on the needs of eliminating exploitative and abusive use of child labour. They feel NGO's and government machinery only address the symptoms and not the real issue, which is poverty, non-availability of education facilities, and low adult wages. They were critical of some NGO's highlighting the child labour issue disproportionately, as it harms the carpet weaving, the only source of income in the region.

RECOMMENDATIONS

The recommendations derived were related to:

1. Generation of employment opportunities.
2. Co-ordination to integrate government efforts, with voluntary organising for the effective utilisation of poverty alleviation programmes and general development programmes.
3. Strengthening, monitoring and evaluation of NFE special schools.
4. Awareness generation programmes.

I. Generation of employment Programmes

- The income decreased due to the withdrawal of children from looms and has also closed a source of taking loans/advances. Thus job opportunities for adults must be created. There are sizeable number of grown up children and parents having adequate knowledge of the art of carpet weaving. Number of families also possess looms, but they don's have requisite knowledge of acquiring credit facilities and marketing expertise. *Promotion of Co-operatives for carpet manufacturing would ensure full employment and higher adult wages.* The study conducted by Raju Damle of RISCB could provide relevant inputs for operation of co-operatives in carpet manufacturing.

- Training and financial aid for parents of enrolled children in industrial crafts like; sewing and dress making, candle making, machine weaving, tufted carpet weaving, food processing, agro based activities like; dairy farming should be started in the NFE centres. The training and financial aid should be arranged through government sponsored poverty alleviation programmes. The emphasis should be on self-employment, income supplementation through development plans for informal sector as a part of anti-poverty strategy.
- Parents of enrolled children should get priority under various poverty alleviation programmes of government. These programmes include, Employment Assurance Scheme (EAS), Integrated Rural Development Programme (IRDP), Jawahar Rozgar Yojana (JRY), Development of Women and children in Rural Areas (DWCRA), District Primary Education Programme (DPEP), Integrated Child Development Services (ICDS), National Literacy Campaigns (NLCs), School Health Projects (SHP), Training for Rural Youth for Self Employment (TRYSEM), Indira Awas Yojana (IAY), Prime Minister's Rozgar Yojana (PMRY), Mid-day meal scheme etc.; NGOs must help the parents to get loans and other entitlements under these programmes. This would help in bringing confidence building measures with the community.

II. Co-ordination committee

- Co-ordination between government agencies, representatives of NGOs and parents of enrolled children in the NE special schools is the basic pre-requisite condition for successful implementation of government programmes. *District level committees for convergence of services should be set up for this purpose.*
- The Committee should be headed by district collector, other members should include representatives of related government departments associated with above stated poverty alleviation programmes, representatives of NGOs associated with child labour eradication programmes and Non- formal education programmes, representatives of parents of enrolled children in NFE schools and representatives of

village Panchayats. The representatives of village panchayats should include weaker sections and women.

- The committee should accord priorities to the affected families under the above stated, poverty alleviation programmes.

III. Straightening, Monitoring and Evaluation of NFE Programme

- The magnitude of villages without schooling facility is high in the carpet weaving belt. Instead of opening new government schools (which are currently ineffective and incapable of imparting relevant education for the rural needs), more Non-formal Education schools must be opened by providing funds to the NGO's with proven record of NFE. It would ensure proper educational environmenta in the carpet weaving belt and would stop entry of younger children into weaving as well as provide required education to the children withdrawn from carpet weaving.
- The location of NFE schools should precede with proper survey for the identification of areas. Areas with high incidence of child labour in carpet weaving must be selected for NFE school location. The site location of the school should consider the accessibility of villages to be covered for NFE programme. Location of the NFE school should be central, so that majority of children from surrounding villages could get enrolled in the schools. Other considerations for site location should include areas dominated with scheduled caste/other backward castes/ economically weaker sections and scheduled tribe population. Funding agencies should ensure that sites selected are hygienically sound and appropriate. NGOs should also approach village panchayats for providing building facility for the school. Separate class rooms/sitting place for teaching different level of classes must be provided.
- To wean away children from work and motivate them to join NFE programme, camp schools should be organised for four to eight weeks in the block/tehsil headquarters in a pleasant or child friendly environment, before the academic session. Social workers/teachers should visit regularly to the children in work place and develop positive relationship with parents before motivating them to send children for such camps. The motivation requires highly oriented, talented and trained staff. These camps should remain open full time and should provide books, stationery, shelter and food.

- Non-formal Education strategy in the present form will prove ineffective, unless children, who have completed NFE are not enrolled in formal schools or are not provided apprenticeship training to avail self employment. Thus children should be either enrolled in formal schools or be retained by these NFE schools till 15 years of age. The Two/three years of NFE programme may not be suitable for a child who has entered the schools at the age of 7/8 years.
- Preference in enrolment in these NFE schools should be given to working children from scheduled castes /scheduled tribes/other backward classes and economically weaker sections. However other children or siblings of these children should also be encouraged to get enrolled in formal schools or these NFE schools. Adequate steps must be taken to enrol girl children in these NFE schools.
- NFE schools must provide multiplicity of functions viz, Non-formal education, nutritious diet, medical care, supply of books stationery (slates, chalks, notebooks etc.;) At least one vocational training course should be area specific depending upon local crafts, resources and demand. After the completion of three years of NFE, relevant apprenticeship training and trade training information must be given to the children not enrolled in formal schools. (including information regarding credit facilities available and further training programmes conducted by government.)
- NFE school timings and vocation period should be fixed in consultation with community members. It should be conductive to the agriculture calendar of the area.
- Adult education programme once in a week for the parents of enrolled children at the time suitable to them must be undertaken by the teachers of NFE school. It will create child/teacher/parent rapport, improve children attendance and will discourage drop-out rates.
- The stipend for the enrolled children should be restricted to one child per family, while other children from the same family should be encouraged to join schools. The stipend should be converted into rehabilitation fund to be given only after the completion of NFE programme. The rehabilitation fund must be regularly deposited in bank/post office against the child's name. The rehabilitation fund could be used either for further schooling or for the purchase of equipments for self employment. The stipend value may vary from NGO to NGO, depending upon funds available for the purpose.
- Transitory rehabilitation centres must be opened in the carpet weaving

belt for the children released from bondage on the same pattern as is done in Mukti Ashram in New Delhi (SACCS/BBA) . The maintenance and operational funds for this purpose should be collected from the employers (Supreme Court directions must be followed to collect funds). The transitory camp should provide basic NFE and vocational skills for 6 to 12 months.

- A minimum norm of two teachers per NFE school for 50 children must be implemented. Teachers recruited for the NFE programme hold the key fro the success of programme. To procure talented teachers, salaries of teachers must be increased to minimum of Rs. 1200 per month. Committed teachers (both males and females) preferably from local areas and from dominant social groups, even with less formal education level should be recruited. NGO's must ensure that all recruited teachers are provided teaching training programme at the beginning of the session. Regular in-service training up-grade, should be conducted by experts from NCERT/State Educational Training Institutes. The training up-grades should be at least once in a year.
- The aim of the in-service training is to enhance the quality of the work of teachers/ supervisors. The training should be based on "activity based instructions" like providing learning by doing, using local environment , creating an interesting class room, preparation of lesson plans, improvisation of teaching aids.
- The teachers should be given coloured paper, gum, scissors, drawing pins card board geometrical instruments in the form of a kit. Each school should sanction Rs. 500 per annum towards supply of teaching material kit. The teachers should also be supplied with teachers' hand books with instructions in mathematics, environmental studies; containing lesson plans, which is prepared by practising teachers and experts.
- Regular visits to surrounding areas for children enrolled, especially to post office, health centre and neighbouring fields must be encouraged, so that the children become more aware of the environment and community. At times community leaders, policy makers like police officers, doctors etc.; should be called at the NFE centres to have free exchange of views with children.
- Teachers of several NFE centres should meet once in a month to exchange their experiences. The participation in these meetings will enrich their knowledge in the process of instruction. It will help them

to know about different types of individuals and group activities. They can get their doubts cleared with the help of teachers' educators.

- NGO's should ensure that teachers employ joyful, demonstrative and participative methods to inculcate educational skills to the enrolled children. Rigid and traditional teaching methods must give way to child centred approaches of teaching. The teaching methods should include, our-door environmental trips, demonstrative experiments, cultural programmes, sport activities, songs, drama, painting competitions and testing of skills learnt by the children.
- The curriculum adopted and subjects to be taught in the NFE schools must follow either State Board Primary Education levels or Minimum Levels of Learning prepared by NCERT. NGOs must monitor the monthly targets of curriculum to be completed by teachers. State Education Boards should ease procedures for conducting examination of the children from these NFE schools. A set of model question papers should be circulated by NGOs to the teachers, so that students are well prepared to face the examinations.
- NGOs teachers and other workers must evolve efforts to inculcate general awareness related to moral values, public health, preservation of natural environment, cleanliness, civic and sanitary sense among the children. Presentation of awards for best groups of children projecting and implementing these skills should be promoted.
- Data regarding children enrolled, their age, sex, caste, previous work occupation, their attendance rate, drop-out rates must be regularly maintained by NFE staff. The information should be supplied to the funding agencies as and when required.
- Funding agencies should conduct regular performance assessment of NFE programme. The assessment committee should be independent and not associated with funding agency or NGO. The body should have powers to inspect special schools and take follow-up action. The body should assess the competencies of children enrolled in special schools and also evolve a mechanism to deal with children coming out of such schools for further studies. The mechanism evolved should provide education in primary and secondary schools for further education or provide necessary apprenticeship training. The body should suggest methods to deal with special schools not functioning properly. The release of funds should be automatic on receipt of report from the assessment committee.
- The budget estimates stipulated under various heads should include:

one time special grant for building infrastructure, purchase of teaching aids and materials, books for library, sports equipments vocational training equipments and other necessary infrastructure. The grant released must be utilised for the specified purpose only, Per child per annum expenditure should be raised to Rs 25000 minimum.

- Special preference for opening NFE schools in the Peripheral zone and Child Labour Catchment zone should be given.

  Sanction of funding for opening of NFE schools by local NGOs should be guided by
  - Performance of NGO in creating mass awareness and propagating eradication of child labour in carpet weaving.
  - Community rapport created by NGO in the area.
  - Survey and identification of children (details about family's socio-economic position) to be covered by NFE programme.
  - Site selection with identification of building to be used for NFE programme (the building could be either rented/provided by local community or to be constructed)
  - Before final recommendation for sanction of NFE school, a team should visit the site and talk to community leaders. Once satisfied, the project should be recommended for financial support.

AWARENESS GENERATION

The awareness generation strategy should aim at:

- Mobilising public opinion for creating community participation for educational environment for children and elimination of full time child labour.
- Sensitising all sections of society, particularly the literate society.
- Formation of people's committees at various levels.
- Involve various social, political and cultural movements.

The objectives would be achieved by

- Launching a publicity blitz, through electronic and print media, to sensitise society against child labour. Models of awareness could be posters, stickers, slogans including songs, newspapers, bulletins, calendars, wall hangings, hoardings, banners, wall writings, regular advertisements, cultural shows, rallies, music padyatras, street corner meetings, formation of human chain, folk songs and dramas, debates essay competition, quiz competition etc.;

Bibliography

Acchard, David (1993): *Children: Rights and Children,* London: Routledge.

Administrative Staff College of India (ASCI); 1996: *Eliminating Child Labour Through Community Mobilisation,* CLASP, ILO, New Delhi, India.

AICMA (1989): *Proceedings of Annual General Meetings.*

Ankur Foundation (1988): *Report of Workshop and Other Activities on Child Labour,* Allahabad.

Anon (1983): "Child Labour Abolition: Sivakasi Match Units Threaten to Mechanise" *Financial Express,* October, 17.

Anti-Slavery Scoeity (1984): *The Exploitation of Child Labour* (London).

Anti-Slavery Society (1988): *A Pattern of Slavery India's Carpet Boys,* London: Anti-Slavery Scoeity Child Labour series.

Bandhua Mukti Murcha (1995): *Report*

Barse, Sheela (1986): "Glass Factories of Ferozabad", *Indian Express,* April 5, 6 & 7.

Bequela: *Towards a Global Programme of Action of Child Labour.*

Bequela, A., and W.E. Myers (1995): *First Things First in Child Labour: Eliminating Work Detrimental to Children,* UNICEF/ILO, Geneva.

Bequela, Assefa and Jo Boyden (1985): *Combating Child Labour*, ILO, Geneva.

Bhathy, Kiran (1996): "Child Labour: Breaking the Vicious Cycle", *Economic and Political Weekly,* February 17, 1996.

Bordia, A (1986): *Working Paper on Child Labour in India—Implication for Educational Planning,* ILO.

Burra N., (1998): "Health Hazards", *Seminar,* October.

Burra, N. (1986): "Glass Factories of Firozabad", *Economic and Political Weekly* (15 & 22 November, 1986).

Burra, N. (1995): *Born to Work: Child Labour in India, Oxford* University Press, New Delhi.

Cantwell, Nigel (1985): "UN Child Labour Seminar, An Intolerable Evil" in *International Children's Rights. Monitor, 2.*

Carpet-e-World, Annual, 1991.

Carriere, Rolf (1996): *In the Child's best Interest: Planning for and Progressively Eliminating Child Labour',* unpublished presentation.

Census of India 1981: *Bhadohi Woolen Carpet Industry,* U.P. Part—XC, Series 22.

Census of India 1981, *Part–II, Special and Table based on 5 per cent Sample Data* Table C–4.

CEPC (1997): *Experience the Role Luxury of Indian Carpets.*

Chandra, K.S. (1997): "Education is the Key", *Social Welfare,* Vol. 44 *8–9) November December 1997.

Chaudhri, D.P. (1996): *Statistical Profile of Child Labour in India* 1961–91 CLASD, ILO, New Delhi.

Chhabra, R.K. (1996): "Vocational Training & Income Generating Activities" *Shramik Vidyapeeth,* Delhi.

Consumer Unity & Trust Society: *Carpets at what cost!*

CREDA (1996): *Child Labour in Carpet Industry, Mirzapur.*

Dogmaci, Ihsa: "Child Labour: An overview is PM Shah and Nigel Cantwell (eds) *Child Labour: A Threat to Health and Development,* Geneva.

Dube, Leela, (1981): "The Economic Roles of Children in India: Methodological Issue" in Rodgers, A & G Standing (eds) *Child Work Poverty and Underdevelopment,* Geneva, ILO.

Falkens, Mal Colm (1996): *A Survey of Child Labour in South-East Asian Manufacturing Industries: Summary and Reflection* IDEC Asia paper.

Fernandes, Walter, (1987): "New Laws and Human Rights", *Social Action* January-March.

Eyfe, Alec (1989): *Child Labour,* Cambridge: Polity Press

Gramodaya Sansthan (1997): *Rehabilitation & Prevention of Child Labour Project.*

Gupta Manju, (1987): Government Programmes for the Rehabilitation of Working Children", unpublished study for ILO.

Gupta, Manju (1987): "We cut our Fingers but no Blood Falls" in *Young Hands At Work Atma Ram.*

Gupta, Shaibal (1995): "Problems of Literacy Mission in Hindi Heart/and" *Indian Journal of Adult Education,* Vol. 56/4, Oct. 1995.

Human Rights watch/Asia, (1998), *Police* Abuse and killing of street children in India, Human rights watch children's Rights project.

ILO Report, (1995), *Child Labour,* Targeting the intolerable.

Indian Social Institute (1995): *Freedom from Bondage, Citizens Commission and Bonded and Child Labour.*

International Labour Organisation (ILO); (1983): *Report of the Director General ILO* International Labour Conference, Geneva.

Jain, Mahaveer, (1994): "Perspectives on Child Labour" *in Child Labour in India: A Select* Bibliography, NOIDA, National Labour Institute.

Joseph, M.P. (1996): *IPEC in India 1992-95* : Looking Back ILO, New Delhi.
Juyal B.N. et.al. (1980): *Child Labour: The Twice Exploited,* Varanasi, Ghadhian Institute of Studies.
Juyal B.N. (1993): *Child Labour in the Carpet Industry in Mirzapur-Bahadohi,* A situational Analysis & National Child Labour Project, ILO, New Delhi.
Juyal, B.N. (1994): *Evaluation of Ankur Foundation.*
Juyal, B.N.: *Child Labour and Exploitation in the Capret Industry,* Indian Social Institute, Monograph series (29).
Kanbargi, K. (1991): *Child Labour in the Indian Sub Continent—Dimension and Implication,* New Delhi, Sage.
Kanbargi, R. (1998): "Child Labour in India: The Carpet Industry of Varanasi", in Aseefa Beguele, Jo Boy deu, *Combating Child Labour,* Geneva ILO.
Khatu, K.K. (1983): *Working Children in India,* Operation Research Group, Baroda.
Kothari, Simitu (2 July 1983): "There's Blood on Those Match sticks: Child Labour in Sivakasi" *Economic and Political Weekly.*
Krujitbosch, M. (1995): *RUGMARK*; A Brief Resume of concept to Reality for Visual Guarantee of Carpets Made with out Child Labour. SACCS, New Delhi.
Kulshrehtha, J.C. (1978): *Child Labour in India,* Ashish Publishing House, New Delhi.
Kundu, A. (1993): "Child Labour: Trouble Lies Ahead" *The Economic Times,* September 13.
Lorentz, A. and M. Wetzel; (1978): "Health and nutritional Survey of bonded Labourers in Palmau District, Bihar", in *National labour Institute Bulletin,* New Delhi.
Lyakat Ali (1997): *Law Relating Child Labour* Indian Social Institute, New Delhi.
Mahadev, PD. (1997): *Measures for Eradication of Child Labour, Fundamental Right to Primary Education,* Indian Social Institute, New Delhi.
Massey, I.P. (1997): *Conceptual Narratives in Human Rights of the Child Discause in Developing Countries.*
Ministry of Education: *Challenge of Education,* p. 18.
Ministry of Labour (1985): *Annual Report—1983–84,* New Delhi, Govt. of India.
Ministry of Labour (Govt. of India), 1995: *Circular on Identification, Release and Rehabilitation of Child Labour.*
Mishra, G.P. and Pande P.N.; (1996): *Child Labour in Carpet Industry,* A.P.H. Publishing Corporation.
Mishra, L (2000) 'Child Labour in India, Problem, Constraints and Challenges,' paper presented in Trade Union Workshop, July 14–16.
Mittal, Onkar (1997): "Compaign Against Child Labour", *GRAMODAYA SANSTHAN,* Kanpur.

Mode Research Pvt. Ltd. 1996: *"An Evaluation of the Action Programme Implemented by CREDA, As Part of ILO, IDEC".*

Mohsin, N. (1996): *Special School Programme for Child Labour.*

Mohsin, N. (1997): *Social clause and Child Labour,* NRCCL, NOIDA.

Mohsin, N. (1993): "Child Labour: Strategy for Combating Right" In (Eds) Singh, Bhagwan *P.D. Children at Work, Problems and Policy Option.*

Mustafa, N.M., Onkar, Singh (1996): *Child Labour in India. A Bitter Truth,* New Delhi, Deep.

Naik, J.P. (1975): *Elementary Education in India: A Promise to keep* New Delhi: Allied Publisher.

Nandlal, Ji. (1984): *A Study of Labour Problems and Requirements in Carpet Industry,* unpublished Ph.D. Thesis, Varanasi, BHU.

Nangia, Sudesh (1988): *Child Workers in Carpet Weaving Industry* in Jammu & Kashmir (with special emphasis on Girls) UNICEF, Regional office for South Asia (Mimeo).

Narayana, Ashok (1988): "Child Labour Policies and Programmes: The Indian Experience" in Assfa Bequele, Jo Boyda (Eds) *Combating Child Labour,* Geneva, ILO.

NCAER (1994): "Child Labour in Carpet Industry" *Margin.* October-December 1994.

NCERT (1986): *Fourth All-India Educational Survey Some Statistics on School Education.*

NCERT (1991): *Minimum Levels of Learning at Primary Stage.*

Nieuwehuys, Olga (1994): *Children's Life Worlds; Gender, Welfare and Labour in the Developing World* Levels Routledge.

NORAD: *Child Labour Impact Assessment.*

Patil, R.V. and God A Vari, D.P. (1993): "The Role of Motivation in Learning" *Indian Journal of Adult Education,* Vol. 54/4, Oct.-Dec. 1993.

Prem Bhai (1985) *Working Conditions of Child Labour in Carpet Industry in Mirzapur-Bhadohi Belt* Banwasi Sewa Ashram Govindpur, Mirzapur U.P.

Prem Bhai (1985): "Summary of the findings of the Supreme Court Commission on Child Labour in Carpet Industry in Mirzapur-Bhadohi Belt, U.P., India in *Awads Digest, Journal of Labour Legislation* vol. XX. No. 7–12.

Project Mala (1997): *Records of Enrolments* unpublished.

Project Mala (1994a): *Field Directors Report for the year 1993–94,* unpublished.

Project Mala (1994b): *Census for Identification of Enrolment for Academic year 1994–95,* unpublished.

Project Mala (1995): *End Term Reports* unpublished.

Project Mala (1996–97): *Summary of Project Mala* unpublished.

Project Mala (1998): *Proposed New Advanced Weaving Academy,* unpublished.

Rangpal, D. (1996): *The Problem of Education of Working Children—The Challenges and Future Directions,* unpublished paper.

Reddy, A.V.R. (1996): *"Andhra Pradesh Primary Schools Project: An Activity Based International Programme" Perspective in Education,* Vol. 6. No. 3, 201–05.

Remington, Francoise (1993): "The forgotten ones". A story of street Children and Schooling in South Asia", *Indian Journal Of Training & Development, Vol. XXII,* No. 3, July–Sept. 93.

Richard Anker, Sandhya Baege, S. Rajagopal, M.P. Joseph (1998): *Economics of Child Labour in Hazardous Industries of India,* CORT, Baroda.

Roa, Narain, Singh: *Elimination of Child Labour Through Rehabilitation and Education of freed Children from Carpet Belt of U.P.*

Rodgers, G. & G.: Standing (ed.) 1981): *Child Work, Poverty and Under-development* Geneva, ILO.

RUGMARK FOUNDATION 1996 & 1997: *Special Newsletters.*

Rugmark Foundation 1997: *BALASHRYA*

SACCS (1996); *India Core groups at a Glance.*

SACCS (1996); *Mukti Ashram.*

Sahoo, Umesh Ch (1990): "Child Labour and Legistlation". Economic and Political Weekly, November 17, 1990.

Saini, D.C. (_ _ _ _ _ _ _ _) : *Children of Lesser God, Child Labour Law and Compulsory Primary Education.*

Satyarthi, K. (1996): *Break the Chains, Save the Children,* SACCS.

Shah, P.M. (1985): *Edited Children. A Threat to Health and Development.*

Samshad, M. Khan; (1987): "How Child Labour can be Eradicated" in Manju Gupta *Young Hands at Work.*

Singh, A.N. (1990): *Child Labour in India, Socio Economic Perspective,* Shipra Publication.

Singh, Bhagwan P.D.; (1993): *(Eds) Children at Work Problems and Policy option,* D.K. Publishers, New Delhi.

Singh, Surendra & Verma R.B.S. (1994): *Child Labour in India,* D.R. Associates, Lunchnuo.

South Asian Coalition on child Servitude (SACCS) 1997: *Attempting to break the shackles of Servitude since 1980.*

Subrahmanyam, R.K.A. (1987): "Can be Child Labour Act. of 1986 Effectively control Child labour in Manju Gupta, *Young Hands at Work Child labour in India."* Delhi: Atnia Rai 1987.

Supreme Court on Child Labour 1996: *(A Report).*

SVSS (1997): *Progress Report from Jan. 97 to June 97* (REHA Programme).

SVSS (1997): *Transit Rehabilitation of Released Bonded Children from Carpet Industry of Mirzapur.*

Swami Agnivesh (1994): "Child Slavery in India", *The Child and the Law, UNICEF, P. 40.*

Tara, S.N. (1985): *Education in Rural Environment*, New Delhi, Ashish Publishing House p. 58.

Terre Des Hommes: *In Support of Children in Distress.*

Terre Des Hommes; (1996): *Project Policy Meetings.*

Tourinho, Irene (1995): "Music Control and Ritual of Schooling", *Perspectives in Education,* Vol. II nd, Nos. 384.

Trench, Tim; (1996): *"Negotiating Education: Child Labour Childhood and Primary Schooling in the Carpet Weaving Belt of Eastern Uttar Pradesh, India,* unpublished.

Tripathy, M.S., (1989): *Child Labour in India,* Discovery Publishing House, New Delhi.

UNICEF (1986): *"Exploitation of Working Children and Street Children."*

UNICEF (1994): *Convention on the Right of the Child.*

UNICEF (1994): *The Child and the Law* UNICEF, Country office, New Delhi.

UNICEF (1995): *The progress of Indian States.*

UNICEF (1996): *The State of the World's Children 1996, New York.*

UNICEF (1997): *The State of the World's Children,* Oxford University Press.

UNICEF: *UNICEF in India: The Continuing Revolution for Children.*

V.V.G.N.I. (1996): *Child Labour Challenge and Response, NOIDA.*

V.V.N.G.I. (1996): *Child Labour: Report of Workshops for District Collection and Project Directors.*

V.V.N.G.I. (1996): *Child Labour: A Report of Workshops for District Collection and Project Directors.*

V.V.G.N.I. (1996): *Towards Eliminating Child Labour.*

Verghese, J.P. et At (1996); "Summary Report of a Fact Finding Committee appointed by the Supreme Court of India" in Mohd Mustafa, Onkar Sharma, *Child Labour in India: A Bitter Truth,* New Delhi.

Vijaya Gopalan, S et. et (1996): *Project Report on child in Mirzapur,* N.C.A.E.R.

Weiner, Myron (1985): "State Intervention" *Seminar Issue on Child Labour* October.

Weiner, Myron (1944): "India's case Against Compulsory Education", *Seminar,* Jamkary.

Weiner, Myron (1994): *The Child and the State in India,* Princeton University Press; Princeton.

Weiner Myron (19960: "Child Labour in India: Putting compulsory Primary Education on the Political Agenda" *Economic and Political Weekly,* November 9–6, 1996.

Zutshi, B., *et al*; (1997); *Child Labour Issue and Rehabilitation Assessment: A Case Study of Special Schools Sponsored by NGO, Uttar Pradesh.*

Zutshi, B., (2000); *A Situational Analysis of Education for Street and Working Children in India,* Study Supported by UNESCO, New Delhi.

Zutshi, B., (2001); Impact, Community Response and Acceptance of Non-formal Education Under the NCLP- A case study of carpet weaving belt of Mirzapur-Bhadhoi and Glass bangle region of Ferozabad, Study Supported by National Human Rights Commission, New Delhi.

Zutshi, B ad M. Dutta (1998): "Child Labour in Carpet Weaving in India", *IAMR, Manpower Journal',* vol. XXXIV, Number 3.

Annexures

Annexure – I

THE CHILD LABOUR (PROHIBITION AND REGULATION) ACT., 1986

(Act., No. 61 of 1986)

23rd December, 1986

An Act to prohibit the engagement of children in certain employments and to regulate the conditions of work or children in certain other employments.

Be enacted by Parliament in the Thirty-seventh Year of the Republic of India as follows:

Comments

Social beneficial legislation: Social legislation is designed to protect the interest of a class of society who, because of their economic conditions, deserves such protection. With a view to pass the test of reasonable classification there must exist intelligible differentia between persons on things grouped together from those who have been left out and there must be a reasonable nexus with the object to be achieved by the legislation.

The Court must strive to so interpret the statue as to protect and advance the object and purpose of the enactment. Any narrow or technical interpretation of the provisions would defeat the legislative policy. The Court must, therefore, keep the legislative policy in mind in applying the provision of the Act to the facts of the case.

PART—I PRELIMINARY

1. **Short title, extent and commencement:**
   1. This Act may be called the Child Labour (Prohibition and Regulation) Act., 1986.
   2. It extends to the whole of India.
   3. The provisions of this Act., other than Part III, shall come into force at once, and Part III shall come into force on such date as the Central Government may, by notification in the official Gazette, appoint, and different dates may be appointed for different States and for different Class of establishments.

Comment

May and shall: Where the Legislature uses two words "may" and "shall" in two different parts of the same provision prima facie it would appear that the Legislature manifested its intention to make one part directory and another mandatory. But that by itself is not decisive. The power of the Court still to ascertain the real intention of the Legislature by carefully examining the scope of statute to find out whether the provision is directory or mandatory remains unimpaired even where both the words are used in the same provision.

In interpreting the provisions the exercise undertaken by the Court is to make explicit the intention of the legislature which enacted the legislation. It is not for the Court to reframe the legislation for the very good reason that the powers to "legislate" have not been conferred on the Court.

In order to sustain the presumption of constitutionality of a legislative measure, the Court can take into consideration matters of common knowledge, matters of common report, the history of the times and also assume every state of facts which can be conceived existing at the time of the legislation.

2. Definitions: In this Act, unless the context otherwise requires,

(*i*) "appropriate Government" means, in relation to an establishment under the control of the Central Government or a railway administration or a major port or a mine or oilfield, the Central Government, and in all other cases, the State Government;

(*ii*) "child" means a person who has not complete his fourteenth year of age;

(*iii*) "day" means a period of twenty-four hours beginning at midnight;

(*iv*) "establishment" includes a shop, commercial establishment, workshop, farm, residential hotel, restaurant, eating-house, theatre or other place of public amusement or entertainment;

(*v*) "family", in relation to an occupier, means the individual, the wife or husband, as the case may be, of such individual, and their children, brother or sister of such individual;

(*vi*) "occupier", in relation to an establishment or a workshop, means the person who has be ultimate control over the affairs of the establishment or workshop;

(*vii*) "port authority" means any authority administering a port;

(*viii*) "prescribed" means prescribed by the rules made under Sec. 18;

(*ix*) "week" means a period of seven days beginning at midnight on Saturday night or such other night as may be approved in writing for a particular area by the Inspector;

(*x*) "workshop" means any premises (including the precincts there of) wherein any industrial process is carried on, but does not include any premises to which the provisions of Sec. 67 of the Factories Act, 1948 (63 of 1948), for the time being, apply.

Comments: This section defines the various words and expression occurring in the Act.

Interpretation of section: The Court can merely interpret the section; it cannot rewrite, re-cast or re-design the section.

Ambiguous expression: Courts must find out the literal meaning of the expression in the task of construction. In doing so if the expressions are ambiguous then the construction that fulfils the object of the legislation must provide the key to the meaning. Courts must not make mockery of legislation and should take a constructive approach to fulfil the purpose and for that purpose, if necessary, iron out the creases.

PART—II

Prohibition of Employment of Children in certain Occupations and Processes

3. **Prohibition of employment of children in certain occupations and processes:** No Child shall be employed or permitted to work in any of the occupations set forth in Part A of the Schedule or in any workshop wherein any of the processes set forth in Part B of the Schedule is carried on:
   Provided that nothing in this section shall apply to any workshop where in any process is carried on by the occupier with the aid of his family or to any school established by, or receiving assistance or recognition from Government.

Comment: This section imposes prohibition on employment of children in the occupation and processes specified in the Schedule.

Proviso: A proviso is intended to limit the enacted provision so as to except something which would have otherwise been within it or in some measure to modify the enacting clause. Sometimes proviso may be embedded in the main provision and becomes an integral part of it so as to amount to a substantive provision itself.

4. **Power to amend the Schedule:** The Central Government, after giving by notification the official Gazette, not less than three months' notice of its intention so to do, may be like notification, add any occupation or process to the Schedule and thereupon the Schedule shall be deemed to have been amended accordingly.

Comment: This section empowers the Central Government to amend the Schedule so as to include therein any occupation or process considered necessary.

Construction of Section: It is an elementary rule that construction of a section is to be made of all part together. It is not permissible to omit any part of it. For, the principle that the statute must be read as a whole is equally applicable to different part of the same section.

5. **Child Labour Technical Advisory Committee**
    1. The Central Government may, by notification in the official Gazette, constitute an advisory committee to be called the Child Labour Technical Advisory Committee (hereinafter in this section referred to as the Committee) to advise the Central government for the purpose of addition or occupations and processes to the Schedule.
    2. The committee shall consist of a Chairman and such other members not exceeding ten, as may be appointed by the Central Government.
    3. The Committee shall meet as often as it may consider necessary and shall have power to regulate its own procedure.
    4. The Committee may, if it deems it necessary so to do, constitute one or more subcommittees and may appoint to any such sub-committee, whether generally or for the consideration of any particular matter, any person who is not a member of the Committee.
    5. The term of office of, the manner of filing casual vacancies in the office of, and the allowances, if any, payable to, the Chairman and other members of the Committee, and the conditions and restrictions subject to which the Committee may appoint any person who is not a member of the Committee as a member of any of its sub-committees shall be such as may be prescribed.

Comment: This section empowers the Central Government to constitute the Child Labour Technical Advisory Committee for giving advice in the matter of inclusion of any occupation and process in the Schedule.

PART—III

Regulation of Conditions of Work of Children

6. **Application of part** The provisions of this Part shall apply to an establishment or a class of establishments in which none of the occupations or processes referred to in Sec. 3 is carried on.

Comment: This section lays down that provisions of this Part shall apply to an establishment in which none of the prohibited occupations or processes is carried on.

7. **Hours and period of work**
    1. No child shall be required or permitted to work in any establishment in excess of such number of hours as may be prescribed for such establishment or class of establishments.
    2. The period of work on each day shall be so fixed that no period shall exceed three hours and that no child shall work for more than three hours before he has had an interval for rest for at least one hour.
    3. The period of work of a child shall be so arranged that inclusive of his

interval for rest, under sub-section (2), it shall not be spread over more than six hours, including the time spent in waiting for work on any day.

4. No child shall be permitted or required to work between 7 p.m. and 8 a.m.
5. No child shall be required or permitted to work in any establishment on any day on which he has already been working in another establishment.

Comment: This section prescribes working hours for a child labour.

Provision in mandatory or directory: The surest test for determination as to whether the provisions is mandatory or directory is to see as to whether the sanction is provided therein.

8. Weekly holidays Every child employed in an establishment shall be allowed in each week, a holiday or one whole day, which day shall be specified by the occupier in a notice permanently exhibited in a conspicuous place in the establishment and the day so specified shall not be altered by the occupier more than once in three months.

Comment: This section lays down that a weekly holiday should be allowed to every child labour.

9. Notice to inspector

1. Every occupier in relation to an establishment in which a child was employed or permitted to work immediately before the date of commencement of this Act in relation to such establishment shall, within a period of thirty days from such commencement, send to the Inspector within whose local limits the establishment is situated, a written notice containing the following particulars, namely:
   (a) the name and situation of the establishment;
   (b) the name of the person in actual management of the establishment;
   (c) the address to which communications relating to the establishment should be sent;
   (d) The nature of the occupation or process carried on the establishment.
2. Every occupier, in relation to an establishment, who employs, or permits to work, any child after the date of commencement of this Act in relation to such establishment, shall, within a period of thirty days from the date of such employment, send to the Inspector within whose local limits the establishment is situated, a written notice containing the particulars as are mentioned in sub-section (1).

Explanation: For the purposes of sub-sections (1) and (2), "date of commencement of this Act, in relation to an establishment" means the date of bringing into force of this Act in relation to such establishment.

3. Nothing in Secs. 7, 8 and 9 shall apply to any establishment wherein any process is carried on by the occupier with the aid of his family or to any school established by, or receiving assistance or recognition from, Government.

Comment: This section makes provision for furnishing of information regarding employment of a child labour to Inspector.

Explanation: It is now well settled that an explanation added to a statutory provision is not a substantive provision in any sense of the term but as the plain meaning of the word itself shows it is merely meant to explain or clarify certain ambiguities which may have crept in the statutory provision.

10. Disputes as to age: It any question arises between an Inspector and an occupier as to the age of any child who is employed or is permitted to work by him in an establishment, the question shall, in the absence of a certificate as to the age of such child granted by the prescribed medical authority, be referred by the Inspector for decision to the prescribed medical authority.

Comment: This section makes provision for settlement of disputes as to age of any child labour.

11. Maintenance of register There shall be maintained by very occupier in respect of children employed or permitted to work in any establishment showing—

(a) the name and date of birth of every child so employed or permitted to work;

(b) hours and periods of work of any such child and the intervals of rest to which he is entitled;

(c) the nature of work of any such child; and

(d) such other particulars as may be prescribed.

Comment: This section makes provision for maintenance of register in respect of child labour.

12. Display of notice containing abstract of Secs. 3 and 14: Every railway administration, every port authority and every occupier shall cause to be displayed in a conspicuous and accessible place at every station on its railway or within the limits of a port or at the place of work, as the case may be, a notice in the local language and in the English language containing an abstract of Secs. 3 and 14.

Comment: This section makes provision for display of notice in a conspicuous place at every railway station or port or place of work regarding prohibition of employment of child labour, penalties, etc., in the local language and in the English language.

13. Health and safety

1. The appropriate Government may, by notification in the official Gazette, make rules for the health and safety of the children employed or permitted to work in any establishment of class of establishments.
2. Without prejudice to the generality of the foregoing provisions, the said rules may provide for all or any of the following matters, namely:
   (a) cleanliness in the place of work and its freedom from nuisance;
   (b) disposal of wastes and effluents;
   (c) ventilation and temperature;
   (d) dust and fume;
   (e) artificial humidification;
   (f) lighting;
   (g) drinking water;
   (h) latrine and urinals;
   (i) spittoons;
   (j) fencing of machinery;
   (k) work at or near machinery in motion;
   (l) employment of children on dangerous machines;
   (m) instructions, training and supervision in relation to employment of children on dangerous machines;
   (n) device for cutting off power;
   (o) self-acting machines;
   (p) easing of new machinery;
   (q) floor, stairs and means of access;
   (r) pits, sumps, openings in floors, etc.;
   (s) excessive weights;
   (t) protection of eyes;
   (u) explosive or inflammable dust, gas, etc.;
   (v) precautions in case of fire;
   (w) maintenance of buildings; and
   (x) safety of buildings and machinery.

Comments: This section lays down that the Government is required to make rules for the health and safety of the child labour.

PART–IV

Miscellaneous

14. Penalties

1. Whoever employs any child or permits any child to work in contravention of the provisions of Sec. 3 shall be punishable with imprisonment for a term which shall not be less than three months but which may extend to one year or with fine which shall not be less than ten thousand rupees but which may extend to twenty thousand rupees or with both.
2. Whoever, having been convicted of an offence under Sec. 3, commits a like offence afterwards, he shall be punishable with imprisonment for a term which shall not be less than six months but which may extend to two years.
3. Whoever
   (a) fails to give notice as required by Sec. 9, or
   (b) fails to maintain a register as required by Sec. 11 or makes any false entry in any such register; or
   (c) fails to display a notice containing an abstract of Sec. 3 and this section as required by Sec. 12; or
   (d) fails to comply with or contravenes any other provisions of this Act or the rules made thereunder;

   shall be punishable with simple imprisonment which may extend to one month or with fine which may extend to ten thousand rupees or with both.

Comments: This section makes provision for penalty for contravention of the provision of the Act.

Penalty—means rea: Essential penalty proceedings arc quasi criminal proceedings. Before penalty can be imposed it has to be ensured that means rea has been established.

15. Modified application of certain laws in relation to penalties

1. Where any person is found guilty and convicted of contravention of any of the provisions mentioned in sub-section (2), he shall be liable to penalties as provided in sub-sections (1) and (2) of Sec. 14 of this act and not under the acts in which those provisions are contained.
2. The provisions referred to in sub-section (10 are the provisions mentioned below:
   (a) section 67 of the Factories Act, 1948 (63 of 1948);
   (b) section 40 of the Mines Act, 1952 (35 of 1952);
   (c) section 09 of the Merchant Shipping Act, 1958 (44 of 1958); and
   (d) section 21 of the Motor Transport Workers Act, 1961 (27 of 1961).

Comment: This section mak provision of penalties under the Act even when any person is found guilty and convicted of contravention of any of the provisions of Sec. 67 of the Factories Act, 1948, Sec. 40 of the Mines Act, 1952, Section 109 of the Merchant Shipping Act, 1958 and Sec. 21 of the Motor Transport Workers Act, 1961.

16. Procedure relating to offences

1. Any person, police officer or Inspector may file a complaint of the commission of an offence under this Act in any Court of competent jurisdiction.
2. Every certificate as to the age of a child which has been granted by a prescribed medical authority shall, for the purposes of this Act, be conclusive evidence as to the age of the child to whom it relates.
3. No court inferior to that of a Metropolitan Magistrate or a Magistrate of the first class shall try any offence under this Act.

Comment: This section lays down that any person, police office or inspector can make a complaint, regarding commission of offences. It also lays down the procedure for disposal of such a complaint.

Court duty of: The Court should meticulously consider tall facts and circumstances of the case. The Court is not bound to grant specific performance merely because it is lawful to do so. The motive behind the litigation should also enter into the judicial verdict. The Court should take care to see that it is used as an instrument of oppression to have an unfair advantage to the plaintiff.

17. Appointment of inspectors: The appropriate Government may appoint inspectors for the purposes of securing compliance with the provisions of this Act and any inspector so appointed shall be deemed to be a public servant with the meaning of the Indian Penal Code (45 of 1860).

Comments: This section empowers the appropriate Government appoint inspectors for securing compliance of the provisions of the Act. Such inspector is deemed to be a public servant with the meaning of the Indian Panel Code (45 of 1860)

Public servant: Every public officer is a trustee and in respect of the office he holds and the salary and other benefits which he draws, he is obliged to render appropriate service to the State. If an officer does not behave as required of him under the law he is certainly liable to be punished in accordance with law.

18. Power to make rules

1. The appropriate Government may, by notification in the official Gazette and subject to the condition of previous publication, make rules for carrying into effect the provisions of this Act.

2. In particular and without prejudice to the generality of the foregoing power, such rules may provide for all or any of the following matters, namely:
   (a) the term of the office of, the manner of filling casual vacancies of, and the allowances payable to, the Chairman and members of the Child Labour Technical Advisory Committee and the conditions and restriction subject to which a non-member may be appointed to a sub-committee under sub-section (5) of Sec. 5;
   (b) number of hours for which a child may be required or permitted to work under subsection (1) of Sec. 7;
   (c) grant of certificates of age in respect of young persons in employment or seeking employment, the medical authorities which may issue such certificate, the form of such certificate, the changes which may be made thereunder and the manner in which such certificate may be issued:
   Provided that no charge shall be made for the issue of any such certificate if the application is accompanied by evidence of age deemed satisfactory by the authority concerned;
   (d) the other particulars which a register maintained under Sec. 11 should contain.

Comments: This section empowers the appropriate Government to make rule for carrying out the provision of the Act.

Rules for effectuating the purpose of the Act: The general power of framing rules for effectuating the purposes of the Act. would plainly authorize and sanctify the framing of such a rule.

19. Rules and notifications to be laid before Parliament or State Legislature

1. Every rules made under this Act by the Central Government and every notification issued under Sec. 4, shall be laid, as soon as may be after it is made or issued, before each House of Parliament, while it is in session for a total period of thirty days which may be comprised in one session or in two or more successive sessions, and if, before the expiry of the session immediately following the session or the successive sessions aforesaid, both Houses agree in making any modification in the rule or notification or both Houses agree that the rule or notification should not be made or issued, the rule or notification shall thereafter have effect only in such modified form or be of no effect, as the case may be, so however, that any such modification or annulment shall be without prejudice to the validity of anything previously done under that rule or notification.
2. Every rule made by a State Government under this Act shall be laid as soon as may be after it is made, before the Legislature of that State.

Under the section the rules and notifications are to be laid before Parliament or State Legislature for approval.

20. Certain other provisions of law not barred Subject to the provisions contained in Sec. 15, the provisions of this Act and the rules made thereunder shall be in addition to, and not in derogation of, the provisions of the Factories Act, 1948 (63 of 1948), the Plantations Labour Act, 1951 (69 of 1951) and the Mines Act, 1952 (35 of 1952).

Comment: This section lays down that the provisions of this Act shall be in addition to and not in derogation of, the provisions of the Factories Act, 1948, the Plantations Labour Act, 1951 and the Mines Act, 1952.

21. Power to remove difficulties

1. If any difficulty arises in given effect of the provisions of this Act, the Central Government may, by order published in the official Gazette, make such provisions no inconsistent with the provisions of this Act as appear to it to be necessary or expedient for removal of the difficulty: Provided that no such order shall be made after the expiry of a period of there years from the date on which this Act receives the assent of the President.
2. Every order made under this section shall, as soon as may be after it is made, before the Houses of Parliament.

Comment: The Employment of Children Act, 1938 (26 of 1938) has been repealed by this section.

Implied repeal It is well settled that when a competent authority makes a new law which is totally inconsistent with the earlier law and that the two cannot stand together any longer it must be constructed that the earlier law had been repealed by necessary implication by the latter law.

*13. Manufacture of products from agate.

*14. Manufacturing processes using toxic metals and substances such as lead, mercury, manganese, chromium, cadmium, benzene, pesticides and asbestos.

#15. "Hazardous processes" as defined in Sec. 2(cb) and 'dangerous operations' as notified in rules made under Section 87 of the Factories Act, 1948 (63 of 1948).

#16. Printing as defined in Section 2(k) (iv) of the Factories Act, 1948 (63 of 1948).

#17. Cashew and cashewnut descaling and processing.

#18. Soldering processes in electronic industries.

---

* Ins. by Notification No. S.O. 404 (E) dated the 5th June, 1989 published in the Gazette of India, Extraordinary

Ins. by Notification No. S.O. 263 (E) dated 29th Match, 1994 published in the Gazette of India, Extraordinary.

Supplement Child Labour (Prohibition and Regulation) Act, 1986

[1]In exercise of the powers conferred by section 4 of the Child Labour (Prohibition and Regulation) Act, 1986, the Central Government hereby adds the following occupation and processes in the Schedule to the said Act, namely:

In the Schedule to the said Act

1. In Part A, after item (5) and entry relating thereto, the following item and entry shall be inserted, namely:

   "6. Work relating to selling of crackers and fire works in shops with temporary licences";

2. In Part B, after item (II) and the entry relating thereto the following items and entries shall be inserted, namely:

   "12. manufacture of slate pencils (including packing).

   13. manufacture of products from agate.

   14. manufacturing processes using toxic metals and substances such as lead, mercury, manganese, chromium, cadmium, benzene, pesticides and asbestos."

23. Amendment of Act 11 of 1948 In Sec. 2 of the Minimum Wages Act, 1948-

(*i*) for Cl. (a), the following clauses shall be substituted, namely;

"(a) adolescent means a person who has completed his fourteenth year of age but has not completed his eighteenth year;

(*ii*) after cl (b), the following clause shall be inserted, namely: "(bb) 'child' means a person who had not completed his fourteenth year of age;".

Comment: Under the section Sec. 2 of the Minimum Wages Act, 1948 has been amended so as to define the terms "adolescent", "adult" and "child".

24. Amendment of Act 69 of 1951 In the Plantations Labour Act, 1951

(a) in Sec. 2 in Cls. (a) and (c), for the word "fifteenth", the word "fourteenth" shall be substituted;

(b) Sec. 24 shall be omitted;

(c) in Sec. 26, in the opening portion, the words "who has completed his twelfth year" shall be omitted.

Comment: Under this section, Sec. 2 of Plantations Labour Act, 1951, has been amended so far as it relates to the employment of child labour.

25. Amendment of Act 44 of 1958 In the merchant Shipping Act, 1958, in Sec. 109, for the word "fifteen", the word "fourteen" shall be substituted.

Comment: Under this section, Sec. 2 of the Motor Transport Workers Act, 1961, has been amended so far as it relates to the employment of child labour.

26. Amendment of Act 27 of 1961 In the Motor Transport Workers Act, 1961, in Sec. 2, in Cls. (a) and (c), for the word "fifteenth", the word "fourteenth" shall be substituted.

---

1. Vide S.O. 404 (E) dated 5th June, 1989.

Comment: Under this section, Sec. 2 of the Motor Transport Workers Act, 1961, has been amended so far as it relates to the employment of child labour.

THE SCHEDULE
(See Sec. 3)
PART—A OCCUPATIONS

Any occupation connected with

1. Transport of passengers, goods or mails by railway;
2. Cinder picking, clearing of an ash pit or building operation in the railway premises;
3. Work in a catering establishment at a railway station, involving the movement of a vendor or any other employee of the establishment from one platform to another or into or out of a moving train;
4. Work relating to the construction of a railway station or with any other work where such work is done in close proximity to or between the railway lines;
5. A port authority within the limits of any port;

*6. Work relating to selling or crackers and fireworks in shops with temporary licences;

#7. Abattoirs/Slaughter House.

PART—B PROCESSES

1. Beedi-making
2. Carpet-weaving
3. Cement manufacture, including bagging of cement.
4. Cloth printing, dyeing and weaving.
5. Manufacture of matches, explosives and fire-works.
6. Mica-cutting and splitting.
7. Sheelac manufacture.
8. Soap manufacture.
9. Tanning.
10. Wool-cleaning.
11. Building and construction industry.

*12. Manufacture of slate pencils (including packing).

The Child Labour (Prohibition and Regulation) Rules, 1988

G.S.R. 847(E), dated 10th August, 1988: In exercise of the powers conferred by sub-section (1) of Sec. 18 of the said Act, the Central Government, hereby makes the following rules, namely:

Comment

Rule-making power: The general power of framing rules for effectuating the purposes of the Act, would plainly authorize and sanctify the framing of such a rule.

1. Short title and commencement

1. These rules may be called the Child Labour (Prohibition and Regulation) Rules, 1988.
2. They shall come into force on the date of their publication in the official Gazette.

Comment: These rules have been framed by the Central Government in the exercise of the powers conferred by Sec. 18 91) of the Child Labour (Prohibition and Regulation) Act, 1986.

Rules—Whether validly framed: The question whether rules are validly framed to carry out the purposes of the Act can be determined on the analysis of the provisions of the Act.

2. Definitions In these rules, unless the context otherwise requires

(a) "Act" means the Child Labour (Prohibition and Regulation) Act, 1986 (61 of 1986);
(b) "Committee" means the Child Labour Technical Advisory Committee constituted under sub-section (1) of Sec. 5 of the Act;
(c) "Chairman" means the Chairman of the Committee appointed under sub-section (2) of Sec. 5 of the Act;
(d) "Form" means a form appended to these rules;
(e) "register" means the register required to be maintained under Sec. 11 of the Act;
(f) "Schedule" means the schedule appended to the Act;
(g) "section" means a section of the Act.

Comments: This rule defines the various expressions occurring in the Rules.

Interpretation by a Court—The Court can merely interpret the section; it cannot re-write, re-cast or re-design the section.

Otherwise—What amounts to The word "otherwise" is not be construed *ejusdem generis* with the word "circulars, advertisements".

3. Term of office of the members of the Committee

1. The term of office of the members of the Committee shall be one year from the date on which their appointment is notified in the official Gazette:

   Provided that the Central Government may extend the term of office of the member of the committee for a maximum period of two years:

Provided further that the member shall, notwithstanding the expiration of his term, continue to hold office until his successor enters upon his office.

2. The members appointed under sub-rule (1) shall be eligible for re-appointment.

Comment: "Shall" cannot be interpreted as "may".

Proviso: In *Abdul jabar Butt* v. *State of jammu and Kashmir,* it was held that a proviso must be considered with relation to the principal matter to which it stands as a proviso.

4. **Secretary to the Committee** The Central Government may appoint an officer not below the rank of an Under-Secretary to the Government of India as Secretary of the Committee.

Comment: This rule empowers the Central Government to appoint an officer not below the rank of an under secretary to the Government of India as the Secretary to the Child Labour Technical Advisory Committee.

5. **Allowances to non-official members** The non-official members and Chairman of the committee shall be paid such fees and allowances as may be admissible to the officers of the Central Government drawing a pay of rupees four thousand and five hundred or above.

6. **Resignation**
   1. A member may resign his office by writing under his hand addressed to the Chairman.
   2. The Chairman may resign his office by writing under his hand addressed to the Central Government.
   3. The resignation referred to in sub-rule (1) and sub-rule (2) shall take effect from the date of its acceptance or on the expiry of thirty days from the of receipt of such resignation, whichever is earlier, by the Chairman or the Central Government, as the case may be.

7. **Removal of Chairman or member of the Committee** The Central Government may remove the Chairman or any member of the Committee at any time before the expiry of the term of office after giving him a reasonable opportunity of showing cause against the proposed removal.

Comment: This rule lays down procedure for removal of Chairman or member of the Committee by the Central Government.

8. **Cessation of membership** If a member
   (a) is absent without leave of the Chairman for these or more consecutive meetings of the Committee, or

(b) is declared to be of unsound mind by a competent court; or

(c) is or has been convicted of any offence which, in the opinion of the Central Government, involves moral turpitude; or

(d) is, or at any time, has been adjudicated insolvent or has suspended his debts or has compounded with his creditors, shall cease to be a member of the Committee.

Comment: This rule deals with the matter relating to cessation of membership.

9. Filling up of casual vacancies In case a member resigns his office under rule 6 or ceases to be a member under rule 8, the casual vacancy thus caused shall be filled up by the Central government and the member so appointed shall hold office for the unexpired portion of the term of his predecessor.

Comment: This rule empowers the Central Government to fill up casual vacancies and it lays down that the member so appointed shall hold office for the unexpired portion of the term of his predecessor.

10. Time and place of meetings The Committee shall meet at such time and places at the Chairman may fix in this behalf.

11. Notice of meetings The Secretary to the Committee shall give at least seven days notice to every member of the Committee of the time and place fixed for each meeting along with the list of business to be transacted at the said meeting.

12. Presiding at meeting The Chairman shall preside at every meeting of the Committee at which he is present; if; however, the Chairman is unable to attend a meeting, any member elected by the members present among themselves shall preside at the meeting.

Comment: **"Shall"**— It is well-known principle that in the interpretation of statues that where the situation and the context warrant it, the word "shall" used in a section or rule of a statute has to be construed as "may".

13. Quorum No business shall be transacted at a meeting of the Committee unless atleast three members of the Committee other than the Chairman and the Secretary are present:

Provided that any meeting in which less than three of the total members are present, the Chairman may adjourn the meeting to a date as he deems fit and inform the members present and notify other members that the business of the scheduled meeting shall be disposed of at the adjourned meeting irrespective of the quorum and it shall be lawful to dispose of the business at such adjourned meeting irrespective of the number of members attending the meeting.

Scope of proviso The scope of a proviso is well settled. In *Ram narain Sons Ltd. v. Asstt. Commissioner of Sales Tax,* it was held:

"It is a cardinal rule of interpretation that a proviso to a particular provision of statute only embrances the field which is covered by the main provision. It carves out an exception to the main provision to which it has been enacted as a proviso and to no other."

14. Decision by Majority All questions considered at a meeting of the Committee shall be decided by a majority of votes of the members present and voting and in the event of equality of votes, the Chairman, or in the absence of Chairman, the member presiding at the meeting, as the case may be, shall have a second or casting vote.

Comment: This rule lays down that the matters considered by the Committee in its meeting should be decided by a majority votes of the member present. The rule further lays down that the Chairman or in his absence the member presiding at the meeting shall have a casting vote.

15. Sub-committees The Committee may constitute one or more Sub-committees, whether consisting only of members of the Committee or partly of members of the Committee and partly of other persons as it thinks fit, for such purposes, as it may decide and any sub-Committee so constituted shall discharge such function as may be delegated to it by the Committee.

16. Register to be maintained under Sec. 11 of the Act

1. Every occupier of an establishment shall maintain a register in respect of children employed or permitted to work, in Form A.
2. The register shall be maintained on a yearly basis but shall be retained by the employer for a period of three years after the date of the last entry made therein.

Comment: Under this rule every occupier of an establishment is required to maintain an yearly register showing the children employed or permitted to work and to retain such registers for a period of three years.

17. Certificate of age

1. All young persons in employment in any of the occupations set forth in Part A of the Schedule or in any workshop wherein any of the processes set forth in Part B of the Schedule is carried on, shall produce a certificate of age from the appropriate medical authority, whenever required to do so by an Inspector.
2. The certificate of age referred to in sub-rule (1) shall issued in From 'B'.
3. The charges payable to the medical authority for the issue of such certificate shall be the same as prescribed by the State Government or the Central Government, as the case may be for their respective Medical Boards.

4. The charges payable to the medical authority shall be borne by the employer of the young person whose age is under question.

Explanation: For the purposes of such-rule (1), the appropriate "Medical authority" shall be Government medical doctor not below the rank of an Assistant Surgeon of A District or a regular doctor of equivalent rank employed in Employees' State Insurance dispensaries of hospitals.

Comment: *Explanation:* It is not well settle that an explanation added to a statutory provision is not a substantive provision in any sense of the term but as the plain meaning of the word itself shows it is merely meant to explain and clarify certain ambiguities which may have crept in the statutory provision.

FROM—A

[See Rule 16(1)]

Year ....

Name and

address of employer .... Place of Work ....

Nature of work being done by the establishment ....

Sl. No.	Name of Child	Father's Name	Date of Birth	Permanent Address	Date of joining the establishment
1	2	3	4	5	6

Nature of work on which employed	Daily hours of work	Intervals of rest	Wages paid	Remarks
7	8	9	10	11

FROM—B
(*Certificate of Age*)
[See Rule 17(2)]

Certificate No ....

I hereby certify that I have personally examined (name ....
son/daughter of .... residing at ....
and that he/she has completed his/her fourteenth year and his/her age, as nearly as can be ascertained from my examination is .... years (completed).
His/her descriptive marks are ....
....
....
Thumb-impression/signature of child ....

Place ....   Medical Authority

Date ....

Designation

Supplement

The Child Labour (prohibition and Regulation) Act, 1986

[1]**S.O. 333 (E), dated 26th May, 1993** In exercise of the powers conferred by sub-section (3) of Sec. 1 of the Child Labour (Prohibition and Regulation) Act, 1986 (61 of 1986), the Central Government hereby appoints the 26th day of May, 1993 as the date of which the provisions of Part III of the said Act shall come into force in respect of all classes of establishments, throughout the territory of India, in which none of the occupations and processes referred to in Sec. 3 of the said act is carried on.

1. Published in the Gazette of India, Extraordinary, Part II, Sec. 3(ii), No. 303, dated May 26, 1993

ANNEXURE – II

Constitutional Provisions

ARTICLE 24: No child below the age of fourteen years shall be employed to work in any factory or mine or engaged in any other hazardous employment.

ARTICLE 39: The State shall, in particular, direct its policy towards securing:

(e) that the health and strength of workers, men and women, and the tender age of children are not abused and that citizens are not forced by economic necessity to enter avocations unsuited to their age or strength.

(f) that children are given opportunities and facilities to develop in a healthy manner and in conditions of freedom and dignity and that childhood and youth are protected against exploitation and against moral and material abandonment.

ARTICLE 45: *Provisions for free and compulsory education for children*
The State shall endeavour to provide, within a period of ten years from the commencement of this Constitution, for free and compulsory education for all children until they complete the age of fourteen years.

The Rights of the Child the United Nations Convention (Excepts)

ANNEXURE – III

ARTICLE 24: 1. States Parties recognize the right of every child to a standard of living adequate for the child's physical, mental, spiritual, moral and social development.

ARTICLE 28: 1. States Parties recognise the right of the Child to education and with a view to achieving this right progressively and on the basis of equal opportunity they shall, in particular.

(a) make primary education compulsory and available free to all;

(b) encourage the development of different forms of secondary education, including general and vocational education, make them available and accessible to every child, and take appropriate measures such as the introduction of free education and offering financial assistance in case of need;

(c) make higher education accessible to all on the basis of capacity by every appropriate means;

(d) make educational and vocational information and guidance available and accessible to all children;

(e) take measures to encourage regular attendance at schools and the reduction of drop-out rates.

ARTICLE 32: 1. States Parties recognise the right of the child to be protected from economic exploitation and from performing any work that is likely to be hazardous or to interfere with the child's education, or to be harmful to the child's health or physical, mental, spiritual, moral or social development.

2. States Parties shall take legislative administrative, social and educational measures to ensure the implementation of the present Article. To this end, and having regard to the relevant provisions of other international instruments, States Parties shall in particular:

(a) Provide for a minimum age or minimum ages for admission to employment;

(b) provide for appropriate regulation of the hours and conditions of employment;

(c) provide for appropriate penalties or other sanctions to ensure the effective enforcement of the present Article.

ANNEXURE – IV

Evolution of India's Child Labour Policy

1. Ratification of No. 6, Night Work of Young Persons (Industry) Convention 1919 of ILO	July 1921	Night work by young persons in any public or private industrial undertaking prohibited.
2. Ratification of No. 15, Minimum age (of Trimmers and Stokers) Convention, 1921 of ILO	November, 1922	Employment of young persons as trimmers and stokers in vessels or ports prohibited
3. Ratification of No. 16, Medical Examination of Young Persons (C) Convention, 1921 of ILO	November, 1922	Compulsory medical examination of children and young persons employed at sea provided for.
4. Enactment of Children (Pledging of Labour) Act, 1933	February, 1933	Pledging of labour of children Prohibited and penalty for parents/guardians pledging child labour prescribed.
5. Enactment of Employment of Children Act, 1938	1938	Employment of children below 15 years prohibited in certain occupations
6. Adoption and Enactment of Constitution of India Act by the Constituent Assembly	1949	Prohibition of employment of children below 14 years of age in factories, mines and hazardous employments in terms of a fundamental right; and Directive Principles laid down against the abuse of the tender age of the children and for free and compulsory education of children until 14 years of age. Night work by children and young persons abolished.
7. Ratification of No. 90, Night work of Young Persons (Industry) Convention (Revised), 1948 of ILO	February, 1950	Night work by children and young persons abolished.
8. Ratification of No. 5 Minimum Age (Industry Convention 1919 of ILO	September, 1955	Employment of children under 14 years of age in any public or private industrial undertaking prohibited.

9.	Report of the National Labour commission	1969	Recommended combination of work with education and flexible employment hours which would not inhibit education.
10.	Ratification of No. 123, Minimum Age (Underground Work Convention), 1965 of ILO	March, 1975	Employment of persons below 16 years of age for work underground in mines. prohibited.
11.	Report of Gurupadaswamy Committee, 1979	1979	Recommended setting up of Child Labour advisory Boards; fixation of minimum age of entry to any establishment; strengthening of enforcement machinery, formulation of effective educational policy with emphasis on integration of educational requirements with local crafts.
12.	Establishment of the Central Child Labour Advisory Board with Labour Minister as Chairman	March, 1981	To review implementation of existing laws; to suggest legislative and welfare measures for working children; to review progress of welfare measures; and to recommend industries where child labour should be eliminated.
13.	Enactment of Child Labour (Prohibition & Regulation) Act, 1986	December, 1986	Employment of children below 14 years of age prohibited in specific occupations and processes; procedure for modification of schedule of banned occupations or processes laid down, regulation f working conditions of children in non-prohibited employments provided for penalties for violation of the law provided; and uniformity in definition of "child" in related laws provided for.

(Contd.)

14. Adoption of the National Child Labour Policy, 1987	August, 1987	Provided for a legislative action plan; focussing of general development programmes for the benefit of working children as well; and formulation of project based action plan in areas of high concentration of child labour,
15. Report of the task force on child labour set up by the child labour Advisory Board under the Chairmanship of Dr. L.M. Singhvi	December, 1989	Recommended amendments to child labour laws and national policy on Child Labour.
16. Report of the National Commission on Rural Labour	July, 1991	Recommended enactment of compulsory Primary Education Acts by States; creation of non-formal education centres; enhancement of outlays for elementary education, guaranteed wage employment for parents of working children universal prohibition of child labour media publicity against child labour.
17. National Authority of Elimination of Child Labour	1994	To lay down policies and programmes for elimination of Child Labour.
18. Supreme Court Direction on Child Labour	1996	Identification, release and rehabilitation of children working in hazardous occupations.

ANNEXURE – V

CIRCULAR ON IDENTIFICATION, RELEASE AND REHABILITATION OF CHILD LABOUR

1. INTRODUCTION

Child labour is a pernicious practice, a denial of the joy of childhood and access to social opportunities (like education) which eventually impairs the personality and creativity of children, the evolution and growth of a full being. Within the broad ambit of child labour, the plight and predictment of girl children (irrespective of whether they are working at home or outside) is worse. Such a practice which is abhorrent to our social conscience should, therefore, be eradicated from our social economic milieu. It is in this perspective that elimination of child labour and integrated development of children have been important objectives of all our development plans and social sector schemes. Prohibition of employment of children under 14 years of age is the essence of various legislative provisions. This central objective has been reinforced further in the Child Labour (Prohibition & Regulation) Act, 1986 according to which children under 14 years of age are not permitted to work in certain hazardous occupations as also in occupations defined and notified as "Hazardous Process" and "dangerous operation" under the Factories Act, 1948. Inspite of the recognition of the pernicious nature of this practice and the corrective steps initiated through these legislations, the problem has continued to persist in several districts and in remote areas of the country. Recognising the imperative need to eliminate this problem the Prime Minister in his Independence Day Speech on 15 August, 1994 had stated:

"Your know that there are around 20 million children in our country who should be attending schools but not doing so. They are working in factories to increase the income of their parents. Working in the factories means end of their education and the children's development forever ... There are about 20 lakh children engaged in such hazardous vocations, that tell upon their health adversely. We want to withdraw then from such industries and put in schools in the course of the next four-five years. The only way to achieve this aim is to provide the parents of such children full employment to increase their incomes because the parents are so poor that they can not sustain themselves without additional income earned by the children. If such parents are provided full employment and their income is raised there is no reason why they should not be sending their children to school willingly ... A new programme aims at improving the prospects of the children whose life may be ruined because of their early employment in hazardous industries ...

2. IDENTIFICATION OF CHILD LABOUR AND STRICTER ENFORCEMENT OF RELEVANT LEGISLATION

At present, the tasks of identification, release and rehabilitation of child labour is being handled mainly by the Labour Department officials. In order to secure the desired objectives, the following steps are necessary:

(a) In the districts where child labour is prevalent, a survey should be conducted under the overall supervision of the District Magistrate in a time-bound manner, to identify child labour, the nature of vocations and occupations in which they are employed and also the families to which they belong.

(b) In addition to the survey, inspections and investigations must be intensified in order to locate the children and file prosecutions against the employers under the existing laws. Statutory inspections, at present, at present, are carried out only by officials of the Labour Department. They are inhibited in achieving the desired results due to large area, less to the Revenue department and other Executive Magistrates should also be authorised to conduct inspections and empowered to enforce the provisions under various laws. The employment of child labour should be made a cognisable offence under the relevant acts and Executive magistrates should be specially empowered to dispose cases pertaining to employment of child labour in a summary manner under all these Acts [as the practice under section 21 of the bonded Labour System (Abolition) Act]. Launching of Prosecutions employers of child labour should be precondition for taking up of rehabilitation of the concerned children and the economic rehabilitation of their families.

(c) A Standing committee of officers comprising of the following under the Chairmanship of the District Magistrate in districts having child labour problem, shall periodically (atleast once in a quarter review the problem of child labour in the district, organise the survey and fix up responsibility for the supporting officers for effective supervision, inspection and strict enforcement of legislative provisions. The Officers are: (i) Head of the District Revenue Administration; (ii) All Sub-Divisional Magistrates in the district; (iii) District Labour Officer, Chief Executive of the Zila Parishad; District Educational Officer in charge of Primary Education; District Woman

---

* Consequent to this announcement, a "National Authority of Elimination of Child Labour" has been set up on 26.09.94 in the Ministry of Labour, Government of India which had conducted a series of review meetings in order to strengthen the implementation of legilsations pertaining to child labour and also to coordinate and converage several socio-economic developemental programmes under implementation by the Central and State Governments with the objective of elimination of child labour.

& Child Welfare Officer; District Social Welfare Officer; (iv) One or two representatives of voluntary agencies working in the area of child labour; (v) one or two eminent social workers involved in release and rehabilitation of child labour; (vi) Project Director, DRDA; and (vii) Chairman of Zila Parishad Standing Committee dealing with labour welfare. This Committee would be in overall charge of identification, release and rehabilitation of child labour and coordination of all programmes relevant to education, economic rehabilitation and convergence of programmes to families of child labour. It can enlist the support of members of the Vigilance Committees constituted at the district and sub-divisional levels under section 10 of the Bonded Labour System (Abolition) Act, and other institutions and agencies which are engaged in similar mature of activities.

3. REHABILITATION OF CHILD LABOUR

After identification and release of a child labour from employment, suitable rehabilitation of the child and the economic rehabilitation of the family are the two distinct and important issues which should be; simultaneously addressed.

Children have often been completed to work on account of economic necessity or on the priorities of current consumption of families; it is, therefore, essential to ensure that the child isn't an economic burden to the family. For this purpose, there will be a need for schools, hostels and other institutions wherein these children could be admitted and their requirement of food, clothing, books, medical care etc. could be met. It is important to note that primary schools and vocational training centres which cannot take care of these requirements in consolidated manner cannot be effectively used for there habilitation of child labour. Only such schools which can provide the children with boarding and lodging facilities, support for their children and skill development and can provide a measure of care and solicitude should be selected for this purpose. It is important to make arrangements for boarding and lodging in schools where such facilities are not existing in the districts where in the practice of child labour is prevalent. In addition to various Central and State Sector Programmes like the National Child Labour Project, District Primary Education Project, Non-formal Education, Social Welfare hostel, Ashram schools etc. should be geared to meet the requirements of the educational and psychological needs of the child labourers. Special support will be provided by the "Labour Ministry" for this type of educational and psychological rehabilitation of the child labourer in the districts with concentration of child labour, by expanding their activities under the programme of the National Child Labour Project.

4. ECONOMIC REHABILITATION OF THE FAMILY WITH CHILD LABOUR

It is obvious that families to who child labourers belong are the poorer sections of the society. The best method of eliminating child labour is to ensure that these families are enabled to have access to adequate opportunities for livelihood and to improve the quality of their life. In order to provide sustained livelihood to such families, the Ministry of Rural Development have agreed to provide to these families on priority basis the following benefits:

(a) Assured employment for two adult members in the family for 100 days each in a year under the Jawahar Rozgar Yojana (JRY); Intensive Jawahar Rozgar Yojana (I-JRY) of the Employment Assurance Scheme (EAS). It will be incumbent on the Collector of the concerned district to ensure this employment under any of these Rural Employment Programme. The shelf of projects will have to be planned in advance so as to ensure that member of these families seeking employment during any time in the year get assured employment. Accordingly, such priority to these families would be emphasised under the relevant manuals of these programmes;

(b) In the matter of allotment of house sites and allotment of India Awas Yojana (IAY) houses, the child labour's family will be accorded a very high priority along with SCs/STs and families of freed bonded labourers. All such families whose details are available at the district level would be given the highest priority in the allocation of house sites and in the construction of IAY houses.

In addition to the above mentioned benefits, these families will be provided assistance under IRDP as per the provisions of the revised IRDP manual with adequate investment for self-employment ventures in land based or related traditional occupations. The investment under IRDP and selection of occupation should be such as to enable these families to earn a minimum incremental income of Rs. 5,000/- to Rs. 7,000/- per year. Necessary linkages like training for skill improvement, supply of raw material and marketing facilities for products shall be made available to all these beneficiaries under IRDP by DRDA.

5. COORDINATION AND IMPLEMENTATION ARRANGEMENTS

There are several Government Programmes in the social sector Ministries/ Departments of Women and Child Development, Health & Family Welfare; Social Welfare and Education, all of which have relevance to the rehabilitation of child labour and prevention of recurrence of the child labour phenomena. The concerned departmental officials shall inform this Standing Committee of suitable projects and surveys relevant to the elimination of Child Labour. A Special Standing Committee of the Zila Parishad should b entrusted with the responsibility to coordinate all these programmes with the primary objectives of eliminating child labour. In order to ensure that various programmes relating to elimination of child labour are implemented without any delay at the district level, funds from the Government of India and the State Governments concerned with these programmes may be made available directly to the Zila Parishads. The Standing Committee of the Zila Prishad can coordinate and take up the formulation of coordinated plans and the schemes for the benefit of child labourers. The DRDAs on whom the responsibility of economic rehabilitation of the families rests shall make available the funds and programmes as decided by the Standing Committee from time to time. The Standing Committee of officials referred to under Para 2(c) above shall also submit a periodical review of the child labour situation in the district to the Standing Committee of the Zila Prishad.

ANNEXURE – VI

SUPREME COURT DIRECTIONS ON CHILD LABOUR

1. A survey would be made of the aforesaid type of child labour which would be completed within six months from today (10–12–96).
2. To start with, work would be taken up regarding those employment's which have been mentioned in Article 24, which may be regarded as core sector, to determine which of the hazardous aspects of employment would be taken up as criterion. The most hazardous employment may rank first in priority, to be followed by less hazardous and so on. It may be mentioned here that the National Child Labour Policy as announced by the government of India has already identified some industries for priority action.
3. The employment to be given as per the directions could be dovetailed to other assured employment.
4. The employment so given could as well be the industry where the child is employed in a public undertaking and would be manual in nature in as much as the child in question must be engaged in doing manual work. The understanding chosen for employment shall be one which is nearest to the place of residence of the family.
5. In those cases where alternate employment would not be made available as aforesaid, the parent/guardian of the concerned child would be paid the income which would be earned on the corpus, which would be a sum of Rs. 25,000/- for each child, every month. The employment given or payment made would cease to be operative if the child would not sent by the parent/guardian for education.
6. On discontinuation of the employment of the child his educaticn would be assured in suitable institution with a view to make it a better citizen. It may be pointed out that the Article 45 mandates compulsory education for the children, until they complete the age of 14 years, it is also required to be free. It would be the duty of the inspectors to see that this call of the constitution is carried out.
7. A district could be the unit of collection so that an executive head of the district keeps a watchful eye on the work of the inspectors. Further in view of the magnitude of the task, a separate cell in the labour department of the appropriate government would be created. Monitoring of the scheme would also be necessary and the secretary of the department could perhaps do this work. Overall monitoring by the Ministry of Labour, Government of India, would be beneficial and worthwhile.
8. The Secretary to the Ministry of Labour, Government of India would apprise the Court within one year of today about the compliance of aforesaid directions. If the petitioner would need any further or other

order in the light of the compliance report, it would be open to him to do so.

9. On the directions given being carried out , panel provisions contained in the Act of 1986 would be used where employment of a child labour, prohibited by the Act, would be found.
10. Insofar as the non hazardous jobs are concerned, the Inspector shall have to see that the working hours of the child are not more than 4 to 6 hours a day and it receives education at least for two hours each day. It would also be seen that the entire cost of education is borne by the employer.

Final Observations of the Court

- The task is big, but not as to prove either unwieldy or burdensome.
- The financial implications would be such as to prove a damper, because the money after all would be used to build up a better India.
- Poverty as such has not stood in the way of other developing countries from taking care of child labour.
- As expressed by Myron Weiner, India is a significant exception to the global trend towards the removal of children from the labour force and the establishment of compulsory, universal primary school education, as many countries of Africa with income lower than India, have done better in these matters. This shows that what has caused the problem of child labour to persist here is not lack of resource, but lack of real zeal.
- All those who are committed to the well being of children must put their heads together and assist them for their good and greater good of the country.

Concluding Words of this judgement

"We part with the fond hope that the closing years of the twentieth century would see us keeping the promise made to our children by our constitution about a half-century age. Let the child of twenty-first century find himself/herself into that "heaven of freedom" of which our poet laureate Rabindranath Tagore has spoken in Gitanjali".

10